MW01153703

Built to Last

Also From Lexi Blake

ROMANTIC SUSPENSE

Masters and Mercenaries
The Dom Who Loved Me
The Men With The Golden Cuffs
A Dom is Forever
On Her Master's Secret Service
Sanctum: A Masters and Mercenaries Novella
Love and Let Die
Unconditional: A Masters and Mercenaries Novella
Dungeon Royale
Dungeon Games: A Masters and Mercenaries Novella
A View to a Thrill
Cherished: A Masters and Mercenaries Novella
You Only Love Twice
Luscious: Masters and Mercenaries~Topped
Adored: A Masters and Mercenaries Novella
Master No
Just One Taste: Masters and Mercenaries~Topped 2
From Sanctum with Love
Devoted: A Masters and Mercenaries Novella
Dominance Never Dies
Submission is Not Enough
Master Bits and Mercenary Bites~The Secret Recipes of Topped
Perfectly Paired: Masters and Mercenaries~Topped 3
For His Eyes Only
Arranged: A Masters and Mercenaries Novella
Love Another Day
At Your Service: Masters and Mercenaries~Topped 4
Master Bits and Mercenary Bites~Girls Night
Nobody Does It Better
Close Cover
Protected: A Masters and Mercenaries Novella
Enchanted: A Masters and Mercenaries Novella
Charmed: A Masters and Mercenaries Novella
Treasured: A Masters and Mercenaries Novella

Delighted: A Masters and Mercenaries Novella
Tempted: A Masters and Mercenaries Novella

Masters and Mercenaries: The Forgotten

Lost Hearts (Memento Mori)
Lost and Found
Lost in You
Long Lost
No Love Lost

Masters and Mercenaries: Reloaded

Submission Impossible
The Dom Identity
The Man from Sanctum
No Time to Lie
The Dom Who Came in from the Cold

Masters and Mercenaries: New Recruits

Love the Way You Spy
Live, Love, Spy
The Bodyguard and the Bombshell: A Masters and Mercenaries: New Recruits Novella
Sweet Little Spies
No More Spies
Spy With Me, Coming September 16, 2025

Park Avenue Promise

Start Us Up
My Royal Showmance
Built to Last

Butterfly Bayou

Butterfly Bayou
Bayou Baby
Bayou Dreaming
Bayou Beauty
Bayou Sweetheart
Bayou Beloved

Lawless

Ruthless

Built to Last

LEXI BLAKE

Built to Last
A Park Avenue Promise Novel
By Lexi Blake

Copyright 2025 Lexi Blake
ISBN: 978-1-963135-21-3

Published by Blue Box Press, an imprint of Evil Eye Concepts, Incorporated

All rights reserved. No part of this book may be reproduced, scanned, or distributed in any printed or electronic form without permission. Please do not participate in or encourage piracy of copyrighted materials in violation of the author's rights.

This is a work of fiction. Names, places, characters and incidents are the product of the author's imagination and are fictitious. Any resemblance to actual persons, living or dead, events or establishments is solely coincidental.

Author's Acknowledgements

Sometimes as an author you come up with an idea that only seems random. In our minds, the story is completely new and came from that muse living deep inside us. In reality, the muse is our subconscious, and it always processing the information around. The relationships we rely on. The people who lift us up and bring us joy. So when I came up with the idea of three unique women who become friends and decide to love each other and support each other while they build something powerful, I believed it was simply a good idea.

Surprise, surprise. I was always writing a version of the three women I watched build the house that published this very series. I watched it happen, watched my friend go from maybe I can to bring in her friend and launch, to call in another who had never thought she could fly this high, and with pure love and belief in themselves became a force in the industry.

Often the best stories play out right in front of us.

For Liz and Jillian and MJ and these stories we talked about while walking the streets of Manhattan.

This book is for Melisse.

Chapter One

I stand in the middle of what was once a grand ballroom and think about all the work ahead of me. Soft light filters in from the big windows that overlook the garden, and I can't help but wonder what it must have been like to stand on the balcony and watch the stars and the moon.

Not that you can do that today, but I don't think pollution was quite as bad during the Gilded Age when this mansion was built. I could be wrong about that. History isn't my best subject.

But architecture is.

Banover Place. Once this magnificent mansion was owned by a railroad tycoon, and the family also ran bootleg booze during prohibition as evidenced by the tunnels below the house that lead to a hotel two blocks away. So much history in one home.

I can't wait to get to work. This is the job I've been waiting my whole life to do.

"What do you think?" Anika asks. Anika Fox. One of my two best friends since we were kids. Anika, who will soon be known as Her Majesty, Queen Anika of Ralavia. Long live the queen and all that.

She's not wearing her crown today, but there's no doubt my bestie rules her world with a kind smile and a lot of love. She's a very modern monarch, and she's the reason I'm standing in this mansion.

"I think it's going to be beautiful when I'm done with it," I reply with confidence.

I've gotten to know this house. While Anika was a contestant on a reality dating show that took place inside the mansion, I was brought in to ensure production didn't ruin the aesthetics of the place. Or destroy a hundred years' worth of history because they needed better lighting. I've worked here for months, but what Anika is now offering is far more than some handywork.

A complete renovation. I'm going to get to completely renovate this glorious monstrosity of a house. The thought of spending hours and hours bringing this place back to its former beauty excites me in a way I can't explain. I've worked in construction all of my life, but this is different. This isn't building something new, some nondescript office structure in Brooklyn or a high-rise condo. This is delicate. This feels like art to me.

"And you're sure it's not going to hurt the business?" My other best friend, Ivy Jensen, walks back in from the hall.

She's got reason to be worried. She helped me pull my father's construction business out of possible bankruptcy. Ivy is a tech goddess who's working on perfecting the AI software she developed with her fiancé, Heath. Beyond that, she simply knows how to run a business. She quickly identified the problems and restructured how the company handles our finances and voila, we're thriving again. She also found me a tax attorney who managed to get our ass out of the fire because Dad and my uncle had never seen the benefit of paying their taxes. So I understand why Ivy wants to make sure the company I inherited from my father is steady. "I can handle both jobs. It's not like I'm on-site much these days. I can take meetings with clients in the mornings and get here to set before lunch. Paul's going to handle the day-to-day operations while I'm working here. It's an eight-week gig."

"We hope," Ivy points out. She gestures around the grand ballroom. "You never know with these things. I've been watching a lot of real estate and renovation shows, and something always goes wrong. Always. Have we checked the water heater? Does anyone know the difference between black mold and regular, won't-kill-you mold?"

"Well, for one thing, it's black in color." It's fun to have Ivy freaking about things in my world. It's a little payback because I freak out about computer stuff, and I swear the damn things hate me and love her. I lose a spreadsheet and call Ivy because I won't be able to make payroll, and she swoops in and it comes back with the stroke of a key.

So I'll tease her a bit about this. "The only mold I've seen is in the bathroom down the hall," I say, knowing she recently used that sucker. There is no mold in Banover Place. "As long as you don't breathe in there, you'll be fine."

Ivy pales a bit. "I want a hazmat suit."

"There's no black mold," Anika assures her. "We've already done an inspection. We had to in order to get the insurance." Anika frowns my way. "You know she gets nervous about mold."

I'm not sure why since Ivy Jensen fears nothing. I mean nothing. She should totally be more worried about her sketchy dining choices. I've watched her down tacos from some dude selling them out of a cooler off 44th Street right before the cops chased him away.

She'd declared them delicious and protested the police.

"There's no mold," I agree, though Ani's being a party pooper. "You're not going to be taken over by some zombie fungus."

Her fiancé is what I like to call a geek of the highest order. Not that Ivy isn't, too, but Heath likes to take it to new heights. I wish she'd never watched *The Last of Us*.

Ivy's nose wrinkles. "We hope. But it is real, you know. It exists in nature, and we're one scientific experiment away from it becoming sentient and taking over the world."

I feel my eyes widen at the hypocrisy. "Says the woman who works on AI all day."

She waves me off. "Emma isn't going to launch nuclear bombs or anything. Though she could take over dating sites and question some women's choices. I might have fed her a bunch of feminist literature, and she's got strong feelings now."

I'm sure Heath loved that. "So when are we starting? I know you have to get through the royal wedding thing first."

Anika grins. "Yes, I do have that to somehow survive. How did your last dress fitting go?"

I sigh. "Fine. It's all fine. I'll put on a pretty dress and watch you become a queen." I sling an arm around her. "I'm proud of you. You know that, right? I tease you, and I hate the five-inch heels that will absolutely wreck my knees, but I'm so happy for you and Luca. One day Ivy and Heath will get their butts in gear. But I bet she doesn't care if I wear sneakers to her wedding. I'm trying to figure out how you managed to plan a whole-ass royal wedding, get a production company up and running, and Ivy still hasn't had an engagement party."

Ivy groans and joins us. "I've been busy. I tried to get Heath to go to Vegas and get it over with, but his nonna isn't having it. I don't understand. My mom's been seeing Thomas, and I heard her saying if she did ever think about marrying again, she would elope. If it's good enough for my mom, it's good enough for me. But she's on Lydia's side."

Ivy's mom recently turned her whole life around and is seeing an incredibly nice man named Thomas, who works for Ivy's mentor, CeCe Foust. She's incredibly happy to see her mother finally moving on with her life.

I wish mine would.

"She wants to see her baby girl get married in a pretty dress with her family all around her." Ani's eyes light with delight. "Maybe in a stunningly beautiful mansion that's been refurbished by one of her friends."

Ivy stares at Ani for a moment. "You think we should get married here?"

It's a brilliant idea. After all, in so many ways this is where our dreams began. "Why not? Do you remember that field trip?"

We were sixteen, and I was the only one excited about touring an old mansion. We found our way to the servant's quarters on the top floor, away from the mean girls and teachers who were only trying to get through a day. We ate our lunches and talked about the future.

Ivy moves in, wrapping an arm around me so I'm surrounded by the women who saved me time and time again. Who make my life better.

Who are moving on with theirs while I stay trapped in the same place.

I am truly happy for them. I just wish I could move forward, too.

"I remember we promised never to let go," Ivy says quietly as though she can read my mind. "And we never will. So you better make this place spectacular because I intend to be a bridezilla. Also, the reason Ani can put together a wedding so quickly is the network gave her a big old checkbook, and her husband literally owns a country. I bet she's not having to battle for a venue. It's like the *Hunger Games* except with glitter and a Taylor Swift soundtrack."

"If everything goes right with Banover Place, you won't have to Katniss your way to a venue. It's possible we'll have time for a wedding. Unless we sell the place very quickly." Ani seems extremely pleased with herself. "You can relax and plan. Or simply relax and let your mom and Lydia take care of everything. You have a couple of months. I think the perfect way to finish out this project is a wedding."

I step back and stare at Ani for a minute. "You're ambitious. This is your first production. Maybe we should go slow."

When Ani told me about her and Luca's plan to bring money back into their cash-strapped country, I thought she was a little... Well, I thought maybe there were better ways than getting into the reality TV game. But she showed me how it could work, and I'm all in.

Ivy seems to consider it. "I don't know. It could be a big deal. Ani owns this place now. Once it's been restored, it's going to sell for millions and millions of dollars, and it will sell very quickly. Maybe the new owner won't mind, but we have to think of the project first. I do promise, though, that I will start wedding planning the minute you're done here. I think it would be great to have my mom and Lydia and CeCe involved, but I need my bridesmaids."

Ani's hands clap together. "I can live with that. I swear this is going to be our year. It will all come together, and I love that we get to celebrate it here. Where we started."

We started long before that day in high school, but I understand what she means. We made a promise here in this house. "Then I need to get to work. Did you interview that designer I told you about?"

Ani winces, a sure sign I'm not getting the designer I want to work with. Jocelyn Hargrove is also a historian. She'll pay close attention to every detail of Gilded Age. She'll have this place looking like a gorgeous museum. As though any guest will have stepped back in time.

"Uhm, about that," Ani begins. "I did find a designer. Two, in fact. Also, I met with Jocelyn. I don't think our vision for the place is the same. Look, I want to keep as much of the original work as I can, but we do have to sell the place at the end. It's going to be a private residence again, so that means we have to marry the history of the place with a sense of modern design. We already sold the show to a distributor on the basis of the fact that we're bringing in..." She takes a long breath as though announcing something spectacular. "Reid and Jeremiah Dorsey."

"Are you serious?" Ivy asks, a light in her eyes.

They're both looking at me like those names mean something. "Okay."

Ivy's eyes widen. "You know. From *The Dorsey Brothers*? Seriously?

You've never seen that show? It got canceled for some weird reason no one understands."

"Well, I don't think they actually need the cash. They come from old money, and they're the last of the Dorsey line, so I guess they work when they want to," Ani says with a shrug. "But the distributors are super high on them. We got a great deal. This money is going to help Ralavia so much."

Ivy's head is still shaking like she can't believe it. "Harper, you're in construction and you don't watch HGTV?"

Why would I? "I used to, but they end up annoying me. I must have stopped before *The Dorsey Brothers* got big. Like you said, I'm in construction. I tried to watch one of those shows and wanted to tell that damn designer that physics is a thing. She wanted to take out a load-bearing wall because the light wasn't right. She argued for hours. No, I don't go home from fighting about construction work to watch people fight about construction work. So I have no idea who these guys are, but I'll figure it out. As long as they don't want to waltz in and tear the whole thing down."

"They're supposed to be here this afternoon. I'm sure they'll only modernize as much as they have to," Anika replies. She gives me a high-wattage grin. "You'll see. This is going to be so much fun."

"I'm not sure about that since you put Patrick in charge of production," I point out. Patrick Dennings is surly, to say the least. A world-class grump, but even I have to admit he knows what he's doing and he'll keep production tight.

"He's doing great." Ani checks her watch. "And I need to go down and let the HVAC guy in and see if Pat needs any help. They're doing a bunch of before shots. They want to document every room in the house before we get started in a couple of weeks."

"I'm going to try the new street vendor. He's selling corn dogs but with a twist," Ivy announces. "I need to see what the twist is. You coming?"

I hope the twist isn't salmonella. "I'll pass. I'm going to sit up here for a while. I want to soak it all in."

My friends walk away, talking about all the plans. They have so many plans for the future. Anika's already talking about kids. That made Ivy update her birth control, but then Ivy's work has always been her baby. Though she told me one night she was thinking about maybe, someday in the future, perhaps thinking about kids. But no more than two.

I'm going to be the fun aunt, it looks like.

I move to the windows again just in time to see a wretchedly handsome man walking in through the garden entrance. I'm pretty sure my eyes have gone anime wide. He's dressed in a suit and tie. Dark hair and a jawline that looks cut from granite. Probably one of the producers Anika's been working with. He's got that look. Wealth and style. Okay, he's gorgeous. He's mouthwateringly masculine, and I kind of wish I'd worn something other than jeans and a T-shirt and work boots. I spent the morning at a construction site, and it shows. No makeup, hair in a ponytail. I might have some dirt under my nails.

I can glam up. I have some pretty dresses, and though not my favorite, I've been known to wear heels.

I'm not sure what I'm thinking, but I can't take my eyes off him.

He's joined by a slightly shorter man in khakis and a tunic. He's handsome, too, but his vibe is artistic and not Wall Street like the other guy. His hair is lighter than Businessman's, and his smile sunny as he points something out to his friend.

Then Businessman smiles and it changes his face. He goes from wickedly handsome to something softer, kinder. He likes the other man. It does something to me. I suppose I know what it means to be around ruthless. My father was fairly ruthless and didn't find joy in much of anything. The smile on that man's face is joy, and it attracts me like nothing else.

Art Guy laughs at something, and then they disappear under the patio roof.

I should start dating again. The thought makes me cringe since my last relationship ended in flames. Not literal ones, but I felt burned. Still, my visceral reaction to Businessman has me thinking.

Or maybe it's because my two best friends found their guys, and I'm still in the dating pool. Still giving it a go.

I hate the dating pool. Sometimes I'm absolutely certain I'll drown in it.

I'm still for a moment, letting the weight of the day sit on me. Soon, I'll go to Europe to watch Anika become a queen. I'll come back and restore this stunning home and after we'll start planning Ivy's wedding.

Where will I be at this time next year?

Oh, I know physically where I'll be. Right here in good old NYC. I'll be in the apartment I've lived in since I got back from college. I'll be working at the company I've worked for my entire adult life.

But where will I be emotionally?

Maybe I should hit the non-moldy bathroom, straighten my hair, and oops, bump into Businessman. I'm being optimistic. It feels like I'm taking an eight-week vacay from my normal life. Why not try to have a little more fun?

I'm about to do exactly that when I hear two masculine voices talking.

"I don't know. The rooms are small and not well ventilated," one says. "I'm not sure what we're supposed to do with the whole top floor."

"Come on, Reid," the other man replies. "It's stunning. How can you possibly say you're not excited?"

Shit. Reid. That's the name of the designer. Ani mentioned he'd be here, but I was kind of hoping to avoid him until I read up on him. If he's some kind of celebrity designer, I'll have to play to his ego. Because he'll have a big one. I look around to see if there's another way out. It's a large ballroom, but it's been locked up since the TV show ended. Maybe I can sneak out the back.

"I suppose it's a challenge." Reid's got a deep voice. It's silky and smooth. "I like a challenge, and it's good to get back to work."

There's a pause, and then the other man's voice is softer. "Hey, you know how much I appreciate what you did for me."

"You're my brother," Reid says, and I'm almost to the point that I'm willing to give this guy a real chance. I like people who stand up for their loved ones. Even if I don't know why they're being forced to stand up. "Let's not talk about it. Let's talk about how to get this H. R. Ross person to quit. I want Lenny. I don't want to work with some guy who got the job because he knows the producer."

"Hey, we talked about this." Jeremiah. That's the brother's name.

"I know we did, and I haven't done much research, but what I do know is this guy is a typical New York construction boss. He does high-rises and big box stores. He can't possibly understand my work."

Oh, and now I hate the sound of his voice. Asshole. All thoughts of running are gone because I'm a rip-the-bandage-off kind of girl. Can't possibly understand his work? His work is picking colors and fabrics and pretending he's some kind of artist.

I stand in the middle of the ballroom/hill I'm about to die on, and the doors come open.

"Trust me. This is delicate reno work, and we want the best. This guy is not the… Hi." Reid stops and stares for a moment. He's looking me over, and he's not good at hiding what he's feeling or the fact that he's a heterosexual male. His eyes stop at my breasts, and his lips curl up. "You must be one of the production assistants." He moves forward, holding out a hand. "I'm Reid Dorsey. This is my brother, Jerimiah. Whatever you do don't call him Jerry. He hates Jerry."

Oh, he's charming, and I might have fallen for it had I not heard them talking before. This man is polished and poised, and I already hate him. I put my hand in his and shake. "Harper."

"Do I look like a Jerry?" Jeremiah offers his hand next. He's got sandy blond hair to his brother's dark, but up close it's easy to see the similarities. They have the same bluish-green eyes. "Of course, I also don't think I look like a Jeremiah. I should have been a Tristan or an Aidan. Something that ends in -an. Much cooler."

And the brother is charming, too, but I get the distinct feeling he won't be looking at my boobs with anything beyond an aesthetic eye. "Well, I think Jeremiah is a lovely name. How are you finding Banover Place?"

"Is that what they call this building?" Reid asks. "This is my first time walking through it. It's definitely dated. I think we can do some good work here with the right people. Anika is very enthusiastic. Do you work directly for her?"

"Yes," I reply and notice Jeremiah is watching me carefully while his brother is flirting. "We're childhood friends. You know the kind that stick together through thick and thin and royal weddings."

"Yes. One doesn't say no to royalty. I was hesitant to do another show like this, but Anika seems like she knows what she's doing. She speaks so eloquently about her new country. Is she around? I'm supposed to meet with her this afternoon." Reid checks his watch and his grin kicks up. "But I have an hour or so. There's a café around the corner. Maybe you would like to join us for lunch and you can tell us all about the work you do for her?"

Yeah, I'm sure that's what he wants to talk about. "Ani's here. She wanted to run through the house with the renovation specialist."

"Ah, then he's here, too," Reid says with a wince.

Jeremiah's gaze goes between us like he's watching a tennis match.

"I suppose so." I want to see what I can get this guy to say. So I can get my bestie to fire his ass. We need a woman designer. If Ivy had a hint of style, I would tell her to do it. Honestly, I don't understand why we need a designer at all, much less a jerk like this guy.

Reid looks like he's contemplating keeping his mouth shut. And then chooses not to. "Any idea why she chose a firm that does high-rises and grocery stores? Is there some kind of familial connection I'm unaware of?"

Says the man who works with his brother. Hypocrite much. I merely shrug. "Ani's been friends with the CEO of that firm for years. But I also know she's got complete faith in them. Do you have a problem with high-rises and grocery stores?"

"I simply think the ones built by this particular firm lack something. Buildings like the ones Ross Construction builds don't add a lot of value to a community, if you know what I mean. Not like this one," Reid says with a smile as though he didn't insult the hell out of an entire company.

"Reid," Jeremiah begins.

"Really? There's no value in a grocery store?" I ask.

Reid seems to finally understand I'm not hanging on his every word. "I meant to the beauty of the community. Not that grocery stores aren't important. I simply wish we could make them nicer than the big boxes we see so much of today."

"Yeah, well no one cares what the store looks like when they live in a food desert, but I suspect from the thousand-dollar loafers you have on that you wouldn't even know what that phrase means," I shoot back.

"Maybe you can explain it to me." The man is optimistic.

"Reid, she's not coming to lunch with us. I do not know what is up with your radar, but this woman does not like you," Jeremiah says under his breath. "You should probably ask what her last name is."

Reid gives his brother a what-the-hell look. "Why? We're just having a discussion."

"No, you're flirting and she's sending you looks that should have you running for your life, and I wonder why that is. I also wonder why she's wearing steel-toed boots," Jeremiah replies. "It's almost like she works construction and you made an ass of yourself."

I like the brother.

Reid turns back my way and has the grace to wince. "Uhm, Harper. Your last name wouldn't happen to be Ross, would it?"

"Harper Regina Ross, and for your information I've studied renovations like this for years. It's a hobby of mine. I also know the history of this house backward and forward, but I do construct grocery stores on occasion. I'll have to remember to try to make the dairy section as pretty as possible next time. Wouldn't want to outrage the designers, would I?" I start for the door because I know how to make an exit.

"Ms. Ross, maybe we should talk," Reid begins.

"I like grocery stores," Jeremiah calls out.

"Did I mention I would pay for the lunch?" Reid tries again. "Anything you like. It's on me. Punish me with surf and turf?"

I simply keep walking.

I run straight into Ivy, who has two corn dogs in her hands and a smile on her face. "The twist is cheese, but you don't know what kind. Also, some of them have ghost pepper in them but the dude forgot which ones, so it's like corn dog roulette. Want one?"

"Sure, why not?" It can't possibly be worse than learning my peaceful job is going to be ruined by an overly privileged dude in designer wear who I absolutely am not attracted to in any way.

Any way.

I follow Ivy down the hall but when I glance back, Reid's there, his icy eyes watching me. Probably still plotting how to get rid of the construction worker in exchange for his high-minded friends who only work on mansions and museums.

"Hey, have you ever tried crab juice? This guy says he makes the best," Ivy explains.

It's going to be that kind of a day.

Chapter Two

"How is my mouth still on fire?" I ask five hours after the worst corn dog experience of my life, and yes, it is sad that I rate them. Being friends with a woman who loves street food can be an adventure at times.

Not that Ivy is the only reason I often eat like crap. I work in construction. We eat a lot of street food.

I prefer the times when I'm doing a quiet reno. I bring my own lunch and sit in the house I'm working on and think about how I'm making someone's home better.

I don't want to admit it, won't admit it out loud, but Reid is right about the normal construction work I do being different. It's necessary, but I don't love it the way I do renovations. I don't get to do them often. There's a lot of administrative work involved in running a company. Even a family one.

"Your mouth is on fire because you lost the game," Ivy points out.

I wasn't aware lunch was a game. I'm losing at all the games today. We're sitting in my apartment, the whole gang having come over for pizza—that did not include ghost peppers but did have cheese.

"I can't believe you ate it," Heath says with a shake of his head.

"She was pissed off at the time," Ivy explains. She called her fiancé over when we left for the day.

I managed to avoid Reid Dorsey the rest of the afternoon. Mostly because I had to take a couple of hours off to run to a job site and deal with a picky client. And yes, it was a grocery store in Jersey. But a nice one. Still, I didn't say a word to anyone about what a massive ass Reid Dorsey is. I'm waiting for the right time. "Why would you say I was upset? Also, why would that make me try a weird corn dog?"

Anika takes that one. "When you are angry, you tend to say yes to anything that might vaguely be seen as a challenge. And you see everything as a challenge when you get into that head space."

I can be prickly, but they don't know I was angry this afternoon. "I wasn't mad."

"Also, I totally overheard you talking to Reid Dorsey," Ivy admits.

Or they did.

"What happened?" Anika sits up in her chair, eyes on me.

I've been thinking about this all afternoon. How to talk to my bestie gently. Ani has a lot of stress right now. She's starting a brand-new business, planning a royal wedding, and getting ready to lead a country. Hearing that she made a poor choice when hiring Reid Dorsey is probably the last thing she needs. So I have to be gentle. Subtle. "That man is a massive ass."

Maybe not so subtle.

"Ah, so this is what he meant when he said he'd met you and didn't make the best impression." Ani puts down her slice of *quattro formaggi*. "I thought maybe he mistook you for a production assistant and asked you for coffee or something. You wouldn't get upset about that. I should have known. What did he do? Did he hit on you?"

I wanted him to hit on me. At first. Then he opened his gorgeous, stupid mouth. "Yes, but that didn't bug me. The man is hot. But he doesn't think a girl can be a contractor, apparently."

Not fair, but I'm not feeling fair. I'm feeling…restless and a little mean. I can't stop thinking about that man, and not in a good way.

"Uh, seriously?" Ivy's eyes narrow on me.

Shouldn't my friends let me be a heinous bitch when I feel the need? Not mine. They call me out when I'm overstating things. So unfair. "Fine. He didn't know I'm the contractor and all he knew were the initials. He thought HR Ross was a man, and he doesn't like my construction business. He said my grocery stores are blights on the city."

Ani looks back to Ivy for confirmation.

Ivy shrugs and sits back. "He didn't use the word blight, but it was kind of implied. He was a bit on the dickish side. But I think it's mostly because he wants to use this other guy he knows."

"How much eavesdropping did you do today?" Heath asks, though he merely looks curious. I think Heath is endlessly amused by Ivy.

"It's a hobby," Ivy admits. "I definitely did enough to know that Reid was totally into Harper. He talked to his brother later in the day and said how was he supposed to know that someone that hot was a construction worker. He thought she was a model or something. You know, a model working her way into reality TV. I don't think he knows how that industry operates. Also, Jeremiah talked to someone named Lenny. Jeremiah told him he didn't think they would be able to get him on the show because there was already a contractor, but Reid said he would work on it."

That gets my eyebrows rising. "He's going to work on getting rid of me."

"I'm not getting rid of anyone," Anika assures me.

"Maybe we should get rid of Reid," I offer since it seems like the best idea ever. "We can keep the brother. He's at least got a brain."

Anika's head shakes. "There is no Dorsey brothers without Reid. He's kind of the leader. Jeremiah does a lot of the artistic work, but Reid moves them along. At least that's how they describe it. Harper, I can't get rid of him. I signed a contract. If I fire him for anything other than a gross violation, I owe him a lot of money. Money I'm supposed to use to rebuild my new country."

"How much are you paying him?" I probably don't want to know. I know how much I'm getting, and it's not much. But then I'm new, and she's taking a chance with me.

Anika bites her bottom lip.

I'm putting her in a terrible position. "You don't owe me that. I'm sorry I asked. I get it. This guy brings in viewers, and you need viewers." I hate the thought of this. I don't want to say these words because I've dreamed of this house since I was sixteen years old. "Maybe I should step out."

"Absolutely not," Anika replies with a frown. "This doesn't happen without you. I need you to find a way to get along with Reid. It makes me sad. I thought he was nice."

Heath holds up a hand. "I am going to get into serious trouble for saying this."

"Then maybe you shouldn't," Ivy counters. "Unless you're going to say the whole 'maybe Harper's being too sensitive about her grocery stores' thing so I don't have to say it. Because she can be mean."

Heath sighs. "I was going to be nicer about it."

I'm not mean. "He was an asshole."

"He was not perfect," Ivy concedes. "He wants his own guy in. Does that sound like anyone you know?"

Again with the calling me out when she could simply let me have this one. Sometimes I long for those years when Ivy wasn't concerned about anything but her coding. "Fine. I did want my friend in. I learned a lot from her. He was an elitist asshole, but it's not like I've never worked with one of those before."

"He's nervous because it's his first time back in front of the camera in over a year. We all want to bring in our own people," Anika says. "I want to bring in my hairdresser. You know Mandi from that salon over in the Bronx. But there's some kind of royal hairdresser, and I have to hold up tradition and stuff. I've been told no glitter. It makes me sad. I look good with some glitter."

Like I said. Real stress. "I will try hard to get along with him."

"Once he sees the kind of work you can do, he'll be thrilled to have you on the team." Anika pours herself another glass of wine.

I'm not so sure of that, but I put a brave face on. "I'll watch some of his show and try to get a feel for his design work. We'll be fine."

I can lie. I can also work with people I don't necessarily like. I do it all the time. Pretty much every time I go into the office.

Anika breathes an obvious sigh of relief and squeezes my hand. "Thank you. I actually kind of thought the two of you would get along. You would make the cutest couple."

"Absolutely not."

Heath takes a drag off his beer. "Emma thinks you would be good together."

I turn to Ivy and hope that the daggers I am sending her with my eyes get my point across. "What did you do?"

Emma is the artificial intelligence program Ivy and Heath have been working on for the last year. It's what brought them together in the first place. Heath's grandmother was an old-school matchmaker in Little Italy. They trained the AI on her methods of finding compatibility. And one of the things they did to train her was have all of their friends fill out Lydia's forms. For practice, of course.

Ivy doesn't bother to look guilty. "What I always do when we meet a gorgeous guy with his very own three thousand square foot Upper East Side apartment. I convince him it's a good idea to help me with a project and then I run him against you and try to find a way to accidently introduce you."

"How many times have you done this?" I'm utterly horrified, and now I'm wondering about all those times I ran into some guy who also happened to know Ivy. I kind of thought she knew them from her tech guru goddess days. And that is precisely why I turned them down when they asked me out. I avoid tech bros.

"Just a couple," Ivy replies. "It's a surprisingly small pool."

"I told you we should also start looking at guys with a little less cash on hand," Heath argues.

"She has expensive tastes." Anika bites back a laugh. "So how did Reid do on the compatibility scale? Also, how did you get him to fill it out?"

"Oh, I lied and said it was part of the contract. The good news is most people don't actually read their contracts. He thought it was super weird but did it anyway. I also have his brother's file, but he is not of the same persuasion," Ivy explains. "I do have some thoughts about him, but I'm going to hold on to them. I want to see him in action."

"How in the hell are we compatible? Has Emma lost her damn mind?" There is zero way I match with that erudite jerk.

"Emma's mind is excellent, thank you." Heath looks a bit offended.

Ivy seems to study me for a moment. "Do you really want to know? Or do you want to just loathe him? It's a valid choice."

"I think loathe is the way to go." There's a buzz from the intercom, letting me know someone is at the door to the building. Except almost everyone I care about is right here. I get up and answer it.

"Hey, I'm looking for Harper Ross," a masculine voice says.

"Who am I speaking with?" I'm not dating anyone, nor have I ordered anything.

There's a hesitation. "Uhm, it's Jeremiah Dorsey, and I promise you a hot chocolate if you come down and talk to me. I'll make it a good one."

Every eye is suddenly on me. Ani's brows rise as though challenging me to do the right thing.

"You can bring him up here," Ivy offers. "We have plenty of pizza."

Heath frowns her way and grabs another slice. "Speak for yourself."

No. If I bring him up here, he'll chat, and I need to know what he wants. "I'll be down in a minute."

I grab my hoodie.

"He's a nice guy," Anika says, looking almost worried.

"I'm not going to blow anything up," I promise. "He wants to talk, we'll talk. Unless you think they're both down there."

Heath is at the window, staring down. "Looks like there's only one guy. He's got sandy hair. Oh, hey. And he's waving."

Reid Dorsey would never wave at people.

"It'll be fine, Ani." I hope she knows I would rather quit than hurt her project.

I make quick work of the stairs since the elevator only functions about half the time. When I hit the lobby, I'm ready to get this confrontation over with.

I step outside and Jeremiah Dorsey is there wearing a smart-looking jacket and the outfit he had on earlier. He's paired it with a tartan scarf that makes him appear like he's modeling a fall look. "Hey."

He makes me feel like I should dress better.

He gives me a brilliant smile. Like a light up Broadway smile. This man was made for TV. "Harper. It's good to see you again." He points down the street. "The hot chocolate place is right down there. They have peppermint mini marshmallows."

I've had enough of street vendors for the day. "I'll pass. What did you need?"

He winces. "Well, I knew you were pissed. Was it the way he hit on you? Or the whole grocery stores are beneath him thing. They're not, you know. He goes into them often. He doesn't like to admit it but he's human and has the need to cook from time to time. He's quite good at it."

"I'm sure he's a gourmet cook. He probably went to that blue place in Paris."

"*Le Cordon Bleu*?" Naturally his French accent is perfect. "Not at all. He didn't learn to cook in culinary school. He learned it from YouTube because our father liked to screw the nanny and we often went without lunch if Reid didn't make something. His grilled chicken is why I survived middle school."

Oh, now I know why he's here. "I'm not going to like your brother."

"You don't have to. But we are going to be working together."

"Are we? Or are you trying to bring in someone named Lenny?"

Jeremiah snaps his fingers. "I knew Ivy wasn't hanging out for fun. I tried to explain to my brother that she's a ruthless tech queen, but he's not that great with a computer. Reid spends almost all his time reading or working on his projects, none of which involve artificial intelligence."

"I'm sure he reads historical nonfiction and books about art."

"He likes science fiction." Jeremiah is studying me, and he's lost that high-wattage smile of his. "He does love art, though. He spends an awful lot of time at MoMA and the Met. He finds inspiration there. His projects include knitting. I'm trying to convince him it's okay to knit on set. He was in an accident a couple of years ago, and his hands were injured pretty badly. One of the physical therapists told him knitting might help his dexterity. I think he finds it soothing, but he's got that masculine thing going."

I love to knit. I find it infinitely soothing. My grandmother taught me, and she'd said anytime I felt like the world was out of control, I could sit down and find a quiet place in my soul and make something beautiful. "I'm sorry to hear that. The accident, I mean. The knitting, well, I enjoy it, too. I'm not great at it, but I can make a scarf. I do it mostly to calm my brain. I can overthink things. I don't think there's anything inherently unmasculine about enjoying making something. But then I work with a hammer and nails and still think I can be feminine."

He's quiet for a moment. "Lenny's been a friend for years. When we ended our show, he lost his job. My brother is trying to find a way to help him out. Reid can be standoffish at first."

"He didn't seem to be standoffish until he knew he was going to have to work with me."

Jeremiah's eyes narrow. "So it's about him being smarmy."

He hadn't been. "He was… I don't mind that he asked me to lunch. Look, it's been pointed out to me that I might have overreacted. I'll send you some pictures of the renos I've done. I've been in the business since I was a kid. I can fix pretty much anything. My father didn't get the son he wanted so he settled for me. Our fun activities included fixing dishwashers and installing toilets and drywall."

"It sounds like you don't like it."

I shake my head because that's not the case at all. "I do. I like looking at this building people use every day and knowing I made that. But I love the artistic part of renovation and restoration. And I've loved Banover Place since I was a kid. It represents something for me. My hopes. My dreams. Getting to work on it, to bring it back to life so there's a family in it again, it feels like being a part of something special. So I didn't like the idea that I don't belong on the team."

His expression goes soft, and he reaches for my hand, giving it a squeeze. "I am so sorry we made you feel that way, Harper. I don't have any excuses or explanations. The fact that you felt marginalized is the only thing that matters. I sincerely hope you can forgive us."

I hate the whole huggy, emotional thing. He's gotten me to admit what truly bugged me, how vulnerable I felt. Until this moment I thought I was mad.

Mad sometimes is easier than hurt. Mad often masquerades as fear. Fear that I'm not enough. That I'm going to fail.

Maybe I'm getting older and wiser. Maybe Jeremiah is one of those people who brings out the best in the people around him. No matter the reason, saying the truth out loud kind of frees something in me. "Yeah, of course. And I don't have my crew filled out yet. Most of the guys who work for me prefer the big jobs. They make more. I've got a couple of women who know a lot about the time period, but I could use someone with experience."

"Really?" Jeremiah breathes a big sigh. "You would do that? Lenny's great."

This is probably a huge mistake. "He's got to understand that I'm the boss. Reid can't try to use him to get around me."

Jeremiah looks positively giddy. "He won't. He's a genuinely lovely man. He's older and he's having a hard time finding work. Oh, Harper, thank you so much. I'm sorry it went sideways today. Reid's upset about it, too, but he takes some time to process. You should probably expect flowers tomorrow. Gifts are how he apologizes."

I actually feel better. "I prefer cookie bouquets."

"I'll let him know," Jeremiah replies, and there's something infinitely comfortable about him.

I like him. A lot. It makes me want to give his brother another shot. Not in a "date me" way. In a "we can work together without killing each other" way. "I'll send you some examples of the work I've done. The reno and restoration work. I volunteer with a historical society from time to time and learned from some masters. Last year I restored a spiral staircase in a Brooklyn brownstone dating back to the mid-nineteenth century."

"I would love to see that," Jeremiah replies. "I'd send you some of our work, but you've probably seen it."

I wince.

His eyes widen. "Seriously?"

I shrug. "I prefer *Real Housewives*. But I'll look it up and watch a couple of episodes."

"Let me know if you want company for that." He looks up at the building. "I can tell you all the background stories. Well, I know you have friends over. I'll let you get back to them."

For some reason, I get the feeling he's lonely. And I can put Ani's fears to rest with one kind gesture. "How do you feel about pizza? Let me warn you, you might have to fight a hungry coder for the meat lovers."

He offers me his arm like he's an old-school gentleman. "I think I can handle it."

We walk up the stairs, and I think I might have made a friend.

Chapter Three

"Oh, a cookie bouquet. Isn't that cute?" My mom looks down at the recently delivered confection of chocolate chip and sugar and shortbread.

It came with a note.

Apologies.

Nothing more. The man knows how to keep it brief. Anyway, I decided I can ignore him and mostly deal with Jeremiah—who I've come to adore in a short time. He sat with us two nights ago and we watched what he called his greatest hits. Four episodes that let me know that Reid has some deeply minimalist tendencies, and Jeremiah likes to make things pretty.

The houses they design are actually nice. They do a good job of marrying form and function, and it seems like they help a lot of people love their homes. The truth is I'll mostly work with them on camera. It's not like they'll be standing over me watching me restore the hardwoods and making the original marble in the foyer shine.

So I'm cautiously optimistic. At least I was until my mom showed up this morning. I wish she showed up alone.

"Are you dating someone? You know when I dated I tended to send flowers." My cousin Paul. Paul is my father's brother's son. "Cookies might send the wrong message."

I hate Paul. By "send the wrong message" what he means is they could make it sound like the man who sent them to me thinks it's okay for me to get fat. He's always on his poor wife to stay in shape. I've seen her at family functions while she's pregnant telling everyone she's on a diet because she doesn't want to gain too much baby weight or she might not get another baby.

I was actually quite close to Uncle Alan when he was alive. I sometimes preferred him to my father. My cousin, not so much. "He's a guy from work."

Paul's brows raise. "You're dating someone from work? Seriously? Who? Is it the new guy?"

My mom gasps. "You're dating? That is exciting. Do I know him?"

I need to shut this down. If I thought Ivy siccing Emma on me was bad, this would be so much worse. And I never heard why Emma thinks Reid and I might be compatible. We were interrupted by Jeremiah and didn't get back around to the subject. It's been bugging me all morning, but I have things to do. "I'm not dating. I didn't mean from the construction crew. I meant from my side job."

"Oh, from the fancy project of yours," Paul says with a sneer. "You're going to be a TV star."

My new project is something of a controversy at my main job. I have my group of supporters. Paul is not one of them. "I wouldn't say that. I'm helping a friend, and it could help the company."

His eyes roll. "You doing fancy shit with moldy old homes isn't going to bring in any clients. We don't do single-family homes, and we're not going to any time soon."

I have to agree with him there. We need big jobs for the foreseeable future. My father left me with fifty-five percent of the family company and all of its IRS debt. Dad was great at construction, but Uncle Alan handled the money. When he got cancer, my dad didn't pay much attention to anything but making his payroll and getting new jobs. He let things like taxes slide away. Mom wasn't much help. When they asked her to take over for Alan, she shook her head and said she was just a housewife and wouldn't have any idea what to do in an office.

She's still in a house, but she's not a wife anymore since Dad passed. So she moves around helping with everyone else's kids and making comments about how she'll never have grandkids of her own. Always the babysitter but never the nana is her catch phrase. I've thought of getting her a T-shirt.

"Is there a reason you're here, Paul?" I don't waste time on my cousin. He's bitter and angry, and he has reason to be neither from what I can tell. He's married to his high school sweetheart. They have two adorable kids, and my uncle left them a paid off condo in Little Italy.

He still complains constantly.

My mom sets her purse on the bar and turns my way, her expression going concerned. Which has me concerned. I've been hoping this was a friendly visit. "Paul is worried that the company is suffering because you're changing things too quickly."

It takes everything I have to not roll my eyes. "I've been in charge of the company for years. I assure you we're not changing too fast. Some of the men don't appreciate that I've been hiring women on the crews. They complain to Paul."

"Of course they do. Having women on the crew means men have to do more work," Paul replies.

I sigh. "I haven't hired a single woman who can't lift what she needs to. Don't come at me with the heavy stuff. We have machines to do that, and the men use them all the time."

"I don't like working with them. They distract the men." Paul's arms cross over his chest.

My mom sighs. "You know how men are, dear."

I do, and most of them don't blink an eye. The women are their coworkers, and they all get along. However, there is a certain subset of employees—mostly Paul's friends—who think we're still living in the fifties and women should exist to have their babies and bring them coffee. The problem is they're all union, and firing them can be complicated.

Like my life seems right now. "I'm not getting rid of the new hires. The men will get used to them. If they don't, then they can move on."

Paul's eyes narrow. "I told her this would be what you said. You only care about your freaking feminist agenda."

"It's not an agenda. It's about having a good, healthy workforce. Those women you don't like are more productive than the guys. They're better at following safety regulations, and I don't have to worry about them horsing around and wrecking twenty thousand dollars' worth of tile."

True story. It happened on one of Paul's sites. They decided to play forklift chicken and the company lost.

"I told you they didn't mean any harm," Paul argues.

I still ended up paying for it, but there's no point in talking. "I'm not firing them but guess what. A couple of them are coming with me on the shoot, so you'll have at least two months without those women around to offend you. Now do you have anything else because I need to pack."

His eyes roll again. It's his go-to move. "Yeah, because you're taking off for Europe when we have five active projects."

"They're all going well. Is there a problem I don't know about?" It's not like I haven't been working. I haven't even really started on the Banover Place project. I've been in the office or on site every day with the exception of yesterday. I'm getting antsy. I hate this feeling. The truth is I want to be alone with my cookies and packing. I'm looking forward to the royal wedding and being with my friends. Now I'm wondering if I have to give up my entire life because my father left me in charge of the family company.

Paul's head shakes. "Well, if you don't think we have problems, who am I to change your mind? You know things can look fine on the outside and be rotten inside. Just remember we vote on another CEO in a couple of months. Maybe it won't be you this time. Aunt Margie, I'll see you tonight. We need to leave by six if we're going to make the show. Maybe you can talk some sense into your daughter before it's too late."

He storms out, slamming the door behind him.

My mother sighs again. She somehow makes it sound whiny. "You have to learn how to handle him better, sweetheart."

"Why do I have to handle him at all? You know I'm the boss. His boss. He works for me. I was forthright. I answered his questions and told him what was going to happen. Like Dad." He taught me everything I know. He and Paul's dad.

"But you're not your dad," my mom replies. "Your father was a man and you're a woman. The world treats and sees you differently. Oh, you have no idea how often we would fight about this."

"You didn't fight about anything, Mom. You did whatever Dad told you to." I often saw her as Dad's doormat. Our world revolved around what he wanted. She shoved down her entire personality for her marriage.

"I fought about the way he wanted to raise you. He treated you like you're a boy but you're not, and so you never learned how to handle the men around you," she says as though she's making any kind of sense.

"He filled your head with a lot of nonsense."

"I have worked with men all of my life. I don't have trouble dealing with most of them. If you're telling me I need to change my personality so Paul feels more comfortable with me, then we'll have to agree to disagree."

"If you would only listen to him," she says.

"About how women shouldn't be in the workplace? You know he's not merely talking about at the site. He doesn't like the fact that I hired a woman accountant," I point out. "I overheard him complaining that women don't have a head for numbers. Should I placate him by firing all the women and then maybe firing myself and finding a good man and settling down?"

"You don't have to be so harsh. You don't have to make it sound like a terrible thing to do. Like my life was a waste."

"I didn't say that. Not even once. But you've been disappointed in me since the day I took over this company. What do you think Dad spent years training me for? I'm exactly where he wanted me to be." I step back, not saying what I'm really thinking in the moment. That there are days I wish I wasn't. That I didn't have this responsibility on me. My father died young, his illness taking us by complete surprise. He hadn't prepared more than a cursory will leaving all the money and the house to Mom and his stock and place in the company to me. At the time I had fifty-five percent. I had to sell some to cover the enormous tax bill since it was that or let the company that employed my whole family go under. Now I'm down to a still major shareholder share, but if my cousins decide to back Paul, they can take my job.

Would that be such a terrible thing?

Yes, because Paul will run the company into the ground. The few times I've sent Paul to deal with clients, I've had to clean up the fires he lights with his arrogance and attitude. I'll never forget my uncle holding my hand on his deathbed, begging me to take care of things for his grandkids because his son wasn't capable of doing it.

"Are you?" She asks the question with a hint of challenge. "You know I haven't told you this because I wanted to spare your feelings, but maybe it's what you need to find a way to readjust your attitude. Your father never meant for you to take over the company. He knew Paul would struggle so you were his best bet, but he always meant for your husband to be the one to head Ross Construction."

The anger that flares inside me is only matched with the hurt. I know I've disappointed my mother all of my life. From the way I dress to the men I date, she finds fault in all of them. I can't please her but she could have left me with this one thing. "Well, then it wouldn't be Ross Construction, would it? Since I would have to be a good wife and take my husband's name. Now if you're through telling me what a failure I am, I have a wedding to pack for."

She stares at me, tears filling her eyes. "I didn't say you were a failure. You said I was. You think my whole life is meaningless because I didn't work some job."

This is well-worn territory. "Mom, you think everyone who wasn't a stay-at-home mom thinks you're worthless. That's simply not true. Why can't you understand that we have choices and they don't diminish the people who make different ones?"

She wipes at her tears. "Doesn't it bother you that your friends are getting married and you're alone? Ivy is getting married. I still struggle to believe someone wants to marry her. How did she get picked before you did? Anika, I understand. She's a sweet girl and so lovely. But Ivy can be rude."

My mother always hated Ivy. I'm pretty sure she blames Ivy for ruining me since she still believes the combat boots Ivy gave me for my sixteenth birthday turned me into a radical feminist. I can't explain to her that she did that every time she found out my dad cheated with the receptionist and she ignored it, saying at least he would come home to her.

See, I don't say everything that hits my brain. I think I'm a fairly good person because I know what goes through my head, and it's not pretty.

"Ivy isn't rude. She's assertive." I'm fudging here. She can be seriously rude if you screw with her lunch. She gets hangry. Heath carries around mini candy bars for just such an occasion.

When I get hangry, I have to make a sandwich. If I went to the store. I glance over at the cookies. At least I have a snack.

Gosh, I am jealous, but not for the reasons my mom would have me be. I'm jealous because Heath gets Ivy. He knows her. Luca understands Anika, and they're working toward something beautiful. They all have these great dreams and dream them together.

I'm not even sure I like my job anymore. I know that many of the people who work for me don't appreciate me.

But they'll get rid of my cold, dead body before they force me out.

"She's awkward and often unfeminine."

"Only because you have one narrow definition of femininity." I'm getting irritated. She's not usually this bad. Usually she comes over, fusses that the apartment isn't perfect, makes some tea or coffee to go with the muffins she brings, and then tells me how all of my cousins' kids are doing. I can listen to tales of Bobby's T-ball game if it makes her happy, but I'm not going to do this with her. "Sometimes women don't get the option of being sweet and unassuming. We're not a monolith."

"I don't even understand you when you talk like that." She frowns. "I'm sorry you had to find out about your dad."

"It wasn't like I thought he was a great guy." He was complicated. I won't use the word complex. He wasn't. He was simple, but his relationships were complicated. Especially the one he had with me.

You're a good one, Harper. You're almost one of the guys.

She's back to tears. "Well, I can see I'm not wanted here. You have a wonderful time in Europe away from your family."

"You were invited."

"What would I do in Europe?" she asks as she moves to the door. "Besides, I would miss Kelly's dance recital, and her grandmother is awful. Can you believe she's choosing a work conference over her granddaughter's recital?"

I know this story well. "She's getting a lifetime achievement award for her research into cervical cancer. Janie is missing it, too, because she wants to support her mother. Dave will be there, and he can tape it."

She pulls her fussy cardigan around her. "Well, that doesn't make up for having a maternal figure there to watch all of her hard work. Think about what I've said, Harper. I know you love running your father's company. If you don't start listening to your board members, you'll be out of a job. I know I've always advised your cousins to vote for you, but I have to think about the health of the company and quite frankly, your future."

"And Paul will run the company into the ground within five years and then where will the family be?"

"He will not. Some things are more important," she insists. "You think about that while you're with your friends. Who are starting their lives with their husbands. A thing you claim isn't important."

She's out the door before I can argue that I never said that. It doesn't matter. My mom tends to make up her own history. For the longest time after my father died, she simply followed me around and tried to "help." Now she's found a new place in the family as the free babysitter, and she's back to hounding me to give her what she wants— a model daughter who stays home and knows her place.

He didn't want me to run the company.

He thought I would get married and my husband would run it.

I can't help it. The words shake the foundation my life is built on. And it isn't like that ground was solid in the first place. No, I've always known my father wanted a son and I was a disappointment, but at least I thought he came around to the idea that I was competent. When I felt bad that I disappointed my mother, I told myself at least my dad wanted me to work with him. He taught me. I kind of convinced myself it was his love language. My father wasn't a good man, but I thought at least he cared about me enough to give me the one thing he did love. His company.

I sit at the bar when I should be packing, thinking about everything my mother said to me.

And wondering if there's a place for me anywhere.

Chapter Four

I look out over the grand ballroom and breathe a sigh of relief. The wedding went off without a hitch. Well, without any hitches that wouldn't be perfectly normal for a televised ceremony. Luca was resplendent in his military uniform. Anika looked every bit the queen in her custom-made gown. There was a formal coronation right after the wedding ceremony, and now my bestie is on the glittering dance floor with a crown on her head.

The last week has been something of a whirlwind, to say the least.

"You look relieved."

I turn slightly and Reid Dorsey is standing next to one of the pillars that decorate the grand ballroom and give the whole place a Baroque feel. Though I suppose it isn't so much a feel as when the palace was built. He's gorgeous in his obviously tailored tux—no rentals for this guy. He looks perfectly comfortable in a European palace, like a superhot James Bond, except instead of government secrets he's looking for designer ones. I am not so comfortable, but there's a reason for it. "I'm glad I managed to make it through the ceremony without tripping or a wardrobe malfunction."

"Everything went well," he concedes and looks out over the ballroom downstairs where it appears much of Ralavian aristocracy is mingling with a whole bunch of reality TV stars. It's an interesting image. "I will say I had my doubts, but it seems to have worked out."

Naturally he didn't think we could do it. I've been here for a week. I heard the Dorsey brothers were coming, but I managed to avoid them for the most part. Not that I don't stalk the man on his socials. I'll admit that I occasionally look him up because that is what one does. Know thy enemy. It's how I know my enemy spent a couple of days in London with his brother before coming to Ralavia for the ceremony. From what I can tell the Dorsey brothers' socials are all done by Jeremiah, but I was almost to the point of giving this dude another chance. In London they did some charity work, and I know they filmed segments for Anika. But now I know nothing has changed. "Didn't think a girl from Hell's Kitchen could handle a royal wedding, did you?"

He finally looks my way, a confused expression clouding his face. "What? Why would you say that?"

"You said you were surprised."

"I meant by how easy the filming was. The director did an excellent job of getting what he needed while letting the ceremony be the ceremony," Reid corrects me. "I suppose I've done enough television that I think every director is willing to put the project over personal feelings, but this one seems to understand history was made here today. He was more respectful than I imagined a television director would be. I'm glad he's going to be working on our show. Though the head of production is a grumpy man. Extremely competent but grumpy."

Patrick. I kind of like Patrick. He's been through some things, and he doesn't prevaricate. He reminds me of a lot of the people I work with in construction. They mostly tell it like it is, and you don't have to worry about backstabbing.

Except in the boardroom. And from my family. And my mom.

It's been oddly drama free being here at a royal wedding.

"Why do you think I don't admire Anika? Excuse me. Her Majesty, Anika." He says the last with a hint of a smile that draws his sensual lips up and lights his eyes. "I assume you meant her. She's a girl from Hell's Kitchen, too, you know."

I wish the man wasn't so gorgeous. "I guess Ani, Ivy, and I spent most of our lives being lumped together, so when you don't like one of us, we think you don't like any of us."

The hint becomes a full-on sunshine of the world amusement smile. "Oh, I bet that's a lot of fun with Ivy Jensen around. Not that I don't find her charming. I do, but I can see where she would intimidate a lesser man. And her mentor. I was introduced to Ms. Foust and now she calls me Hot Designer and my brother Gay Designer, and she wanted to know what kind of underwear I favor."

"That sounds like CeCe," I agree. "The good news is these days she spends an enormous amount of time with Lydia Marino, and she's a good influence. For the most part. Though I heard they went to Monaco and hit a bunch of casinos last weekend."

"Is she the one with the Lower Manhattan accent who told me I should eat more? Very Italian grandmother?"

I nod. "That is Lydia to a *T*." And he's answered all the questions I didn't even want to ask. "So it's only me then that you don't think is competent."

He winces. "The cookies didn't last long. I told my brother I should send you something more substantial. Like a brisket."

I roll my eyes and turn to go. I don't have to deal with this man yet. I still have a whole day until I have to get on a plane, head back to the city, and start the prep work on Banover Place, including the initial design meeting I was informed happens next week. I don't have to deal with him today.

A big hand cups my elbow. "Hey, I was joking. I seem to screw up with you a lot. Can we talk so we're not at each other's throats when it comes time to get to work? This project is important to me. And by at each other's throats, I mean you at mine since I would like to point out the only real thing I've done is been kind of a dick when I thought you weren't listening about a guy I don't know and certainly didn't know was you, hit on you unabashedly, and sent you cookies."

"And what have I done?" I ask. "I haven't exactly come at you."

"You charmed my brother and now he's one hundred percent Team Harper. He hasn't stopped talking about you. I'm pretty sure he's stalking you on your socials. So I've been told about a hundred times that I'm an idiot and should beg your forgiveness. Which I tried to do via sugar cookie."

He's so much easier to ignore when he's not charming. "Ordering cookies is begging?"

"When you've got the sweet tooth I do it feels like it sometimes." He looms over me, and that's not easy because I'm not exactly a short girl. "Harper, I was irritated that day. I admit I did something foolish. I promised a friend of mine I would hire him the next time I found a show for us. That's entirely my fault, and that particular day I was feeling guilty about it. Lenny has been a friend for a long time. He was something of a mentor growing up."

"You knew a construction guy growing up? I kind of thought you were one of those Upper East Siders who lived in a private school bubble."

"It's good to know I'm not the only one who can stereotype."

I take this with a shrug. He's not wrong. He heard construction and thought big burly man. "So no bubble?"

"On the contrary. There was definitely a bubble, just not the way you think."

"Jeremiah mentioned you learned to cook at a young age." I can't help but think about what his brother told me. He didn't go into details, but I can fill some in. "I was surprised by that."

Reid chuckles, though it's not an entirely amused sound. "My brother's been talking." He looks around and snags two glasses of champagne as one of the servers walks by. "All right, we're doing this, we'll do it right."

I'm surprised when he takes me by the elbow and starts to lead me toward the balcony overlooking the back gardens. I explain because this place has multiple balconies—one of which the wedding party stood on and waved at the crowd that filled the palace grounds mere hours before. But now it's night and the balcony is quiet, silvery moonlight coating the marble and making the whole place feel…romantic.

Danger. There should be a bunch of red flags unfurling right now. "We're doing something?"

He lets the French doors close behind us and we're alone, the glitter and sounds of the band fading into the background. "Yes, I'm going to tell you things about my upbringing that I'm not proud of, and you might find some sympathy for me since the cookies didn't work."

Did he think they were magical cookies? "I forgive you. There. Now we don't have to do whatever this is. We don't have to know each other to work together."

A brow rises over his eyes. "But wouldn't it be more fun? Come on, Harper. Give me a chance. If it helps, you should know I have educated myself on your business, and I even went into one of the apartment buildings your company built. It's solid work that will give families homes for years. It's good work, and I don't mean that in a design fashion. You build places people need."

Yep. I wish he'd stayed elitist. "Fine."

"Excellent. Like I said I looked into you. Your company is family owned? I can't figure out if that's a good or a bad thing. You're awfully young to have a whole family's financial success on your shoulders."

"Well, according to my mother, it was never supposed to happen at all." Bitterness wells inside me. "My father wanted a son. He got me and nothing else. I sometimes think he pretended I was a boy, but then Mom recently pointed out that he intended to train whoever I married to run the company. Unfortunately, he died before I could lure the true heir into matrimony, and he left me the majority of the stock and all the bills. So if you're trying to figure out if it's good or bad, it mostly sucks."

Reid winces. "I'm sorry to hear that. I was considering the fact that it might be nice to be so important to those around you. I'm being naïve, aren't I? In my head, I was viewing it as everyone looks up to you because you run the company."

He does not understand my life. "More like everyone comes to me with their hands out. My cousin thinks he should be the one at the helm, and he's dragged my mother into it. She thinks as long as I'm working I won't ever fulfill my purpose as a woman."

"Let me guess. Grandchildren."

I nod. "Is your mother the same?"

"Oh, my mother left when I was six. I barely remember her as anything more than a walking ball of perfume and anxiety. My brother was an infant. He doesn't remember her at all."

"She just walked away?"

"From what I've heard from aunts and uncles, she got tired of playing mommy." Reid takes a sip of champagne. "She didn't walk away. She took the private jet and her affair partner, who happened to be her personal trainer. One of my core childhood memories is hearing my father tell the lawyer if Jeremiah didn't pass his paternity test, he would be sending my brother to child services."

Yes, I'm feeling sympathy. "Sorry. That's awful."

"Needless to say while my father valued his sons having his DNA, he didn't care about us much past that," Reid continues. "He hired a nanny who took care of us when she wasn't sleeping with my father. When he got tired of her, he hired in a new one."

"It sounds like chaos."

"It was. And then when I was fourteen, Marilyn Jennings became our housekeeper. She took one look around and realized she had to take care of us, too. She was the mother figure we needed. And we got a father figure, too. Her husband. They lived in the servant's quarters, and I started spending a lot of my time there. Jer, too. Her husband taught us so much of what we know. He was a contractor."

And now I know why it's important to him. "Lenny."

He nods. "Lenny. Marilyn died five years ago. Cancer. He was a mess. My brother was something of a mess, though I won't go into that. It's his story. I came up with the idea of the show as a way to give us all purpose. Up until then we'd done design work for fun mostly."

"You were one of the most sought-out designers in all of Manhattan." He's underselling himself. It isn't like I didn't look him up. Know thine enemy and all that. Though right this second he's not feeling like the enemy. He's feeling like someone I might enjoy knowing.

"I graduated from an Ivy League, and the first job I took was with my aunt, who is one of the divas of the Upper East Side." He grimaces slightly. "I think she's thrown down with CeCe once or twice. I'm glad we have different last names. My aunt was a *Housewife* before there was a show. She can bring the drama when she wants to, and she usually wants to. However, she's extremely influential. Jeremiah was already showing great signs of being a truly talented artist. So when we redid her brownstone, naturally a major magazine wanted to do a story on it. It's pretty much the definition of privilege, and I know it."

"Uh, I inherited a whole company. I know it's not the same level, but I do understand." I like to be fair, and it seems like Reid and Jeremiah hadn't had it all golden. "We work with what we're given. I like that you want to help your friend. I hired him, you know."

"For which I am eternally grateful," he says with a gallant bow. "Seriously. Thank you. I am hoping this goes well and we can think about starting something new."

I have some questions. When I researched what happened with the show, I found nothing except speculation. It happened after the accident—which sounded even more serious than Jeremiah told me. Reid spent some time in the hospital and in physical rehab. "What happened with the last show? It seemed to be going so well. I know all my friends loved it."

One of the things that made the show work was the banter between the brothers. Reid was the serious one and Jeremiah the heartfelt artist everyone loved. Sunshine and the grump. The hot grump. The charming-when-he-wanted-to-be grump.

I have to wonder if some of it was for the camera. A way to

highlight their differences and bring some interesting conflict to the show. Reality TV isn't so real, as I learned.

He turns to the gardens, looking out over the night. "Appearances can be deceiving. Again, not my story to tell." He turns my way. "Is there any way at all that you would like to dance with me?"

It's a huge mistake. I don't like this guy. Except I kind of do. If I wanted to keep hating him, I shouldn't have talked to him. "Sure. Why not?"

When we enter the palace again, I give my glass to the waiter picking up empties and let Reid take my hand. I follow him down the grand stairs and into the most romantic setting I've ever seen.

Not that it's going to tempt me. It's just a dance. Nothing more.

Chapter Five

Ivy stares at me for a moment, her eyes wide. "Uh, you do know who that is, right? Like you didn't hit your head and now you have amnesia and forgot you hate him?"

I watch as Reid walks toward the bar at the end of the ballroom. He glances back as though making sure I'm where he left me. "I'm dancing with him. Nothing more."

Anika steps in. She changed from the big, poofy traditional wedding dress she wore for the ceremony. She has a different dress for every event. The wedding and balcony greeting, which took place this afternoon. Then the coronation and luncheon. Now the reception with dinner and drinks and dancing. She wears a white dress with long sleeves and a plunging back, and she's wearing the hell out of the royal jewels. "Did I see what I think I saw?"

Ivy has on a black sheath and some spectacular heels that still don't make her Heath's height. Not that he seems to mind. "You absolutely did. She danced with him and she didn't even use the opportunity to stab him. I checked."

The idea is ridiculous. Well, now it feels ridiculous since I don't think I've ever felt as in synch with a man as I do dancing with Reid. I'm not much of a dancer, but the man knows how to lead. While he whirled me around the ballroom, he told me tidbits about some of the wealthy people in attendance. Like the fact that the Duchess of Claireborn divorced her husband when she found out he was allergic to her Cavalier King Charles Spaniel dog and was given an ultimatum. The dog totally won. Or the fact that two of Luca's cousins once tried to date the same Norwegian prince, and the war that started is now officially called the Scandinavian Social Media Slaughter of '18.

You know what they say. Never start a land war in Russia in winter and never post a bad picture of a royal princess unless you want her to release a TikTok of you eating a whole ham hock when your entire personality is vegan.

I love his stories. He seems to know everyone on the European side, too. They all nod as we dance by.

"We had a talk and realized we have more in common than I would have thought," I allow as I watch him walk up to the bar. There are waiters dispensing champagne and wine, but anything else must be acquired at the bar.

"Uhm, yeah, you both look like you're going to devour the other," Anika says.

I frown her way. "I didn't say that."

Ivy's head shakes. "You don't have to. We have eyes. And I think I can smell the pheromones from here."

"Oh, is that because Harper wants to jump TV guy's bones?" Darnell walks up, a plate in his hand. Darnell is Heath's former roommate, though they're still in the same building. I happen to know he feeds Ivy on a regular basis, and she's his first and best beta reader. He's got a science fiction novel coming out in a few months, and we'll use it as another excuse to party.

Didn't Jeremiah tell me Reid likes science fiction? And does Darnell have to be such a weirdo? "I'm dancing with the man not jumping him."

"You kind of did hump his leg." Heath joins his best friend, and he also has a plate piled high with the treats they're serving. Ivy, of course, immediately grabs one.

"It's called a dip," I counter. "I had to wrap my leg around his so I didn't fall back."

It was super sexy. He looked at me and asked if I trusted him and I said no, and he winked and suddenly I was leaning back and he was holding me. My heart did this weird flip-flop thing. But my leg around his does not constitute humping.

Even if I kind of wanted it to.

"I thought they hated each other." Darnell blatantly ignores me.

This is how we gossip. In front of each other. No keeping the weird, awkward stuff behind the backs. Nope. We put it all out there for all our friends to see.

Ivy's head shakes as she picks up another... It has a fancy name, but it's a pig in a blanket. "No. She hated him because he thought she was hot and therefore couldn't possibly spend her life in a hard hat."

"Uh, not how that went down." I mean a little. But I wasn't upset with him for thinking I'm hot. "He tried to get me fired."

"Are we on this again?" Luca slides in behind his bride. "Darling, did he ever actually talk to you about firing Harper? Or was it something he said to his brother when he didn't realize everyone could hear him? Sorry, I have to be on Reid's side in this. We both know the pain. I once talked to my aunt about not liking the pear tarts a certain German politician served and there was a reporter at the restaurant. It caused an international incident."

Being royal must be hard.

Anika leans back against her husband, a dreamy smile on her face. "He never mentioned it beyond apologizing for causing trouble. And he sent a lovely bouquet to my mom's place."

At least I got cookies. Flowers die. Cookies are forever. That's what my mom says. They'll be on my hips forever, and then how will I get a husband? I might have mommy issues.

"Anyway, we talked and now we're getting to know each other," I explain.

Five pairs of eyes stare at me knowingly.

"Not in a biblical sense," I shoot back. I look to Luca, who said something I have questions about. "Did you know Reid before Ani hired him?"

"Yes. I met him and his brother years ago. He did some work for people I know in London and then helped us out with some projects after the flood," Luca admits. "He moves in some of the same circles. We're not close, but I've met him several times. He's dated a couple of women I know."

Oh, I want that gossip. I know I shouldn't. I know it's a slippery slope, but I can't help myself. I'm right back to where I was the first time I saw him. Well, not exactly, but I'm definitely back to being interested in the man. "Really? What kind of a woman does he like?"

Luca suddenly finds his wife's hair endlessly fascinating. "Very much like uhm...what I mean to say is... His relationships are somewhat complex. At least his last one certainly was. He tends to like..."

"Bitches." Anika nods her head and puts it out there. "He's good at finding the ones who are super sweet to him and mean to everyone else. Or at least that's what Jeremiah told me. We had lunch a couple of days ago and I asked. Because I still think you would be a cute couple."

I groan. This is precisely why I should have kept my curiosity to myself. My friends have spent way too much time with Lydia. They think they're matchmakers. "Guys, it's not happening. Well, the couple thing isn't happening, but I have to admit, I might not mind spending more time with him. But like you said, I'm not his type."

I glance toward the bar, and he's talking to a woman. Or rather she's talking to him. He's holding two glasses of whiskey and obviously trying to get away. The woman is roughly my age and dressed to kill in a slinky black dress and five-inch heels. She's pretty but she's got a definite pick-me vibe going. I know because I recognize her. I heard her talking at lunch about how she couldn't understand why the king would choose an American, and a mouthy one at that. Anika, it seems, isn't demure enough, isn't willing to defer to her husband the way a good woman should. It was obvious she was a much better catch, but Luca got tempted by American television.

The good news is Reid does not seem at all interested. He seems wary, trying to back up though making it look like he's not trying to back up.

"Oh, that one doesn't like you, Ani." Ivy sat by me at the luncheon. She heard it all, too. "I guess she's decided to change directions since Luca actually went through with the wedding."

"Why wouldn't I go through with the wedding?" Luca asks, a confused expression on his face. "I'm surprised at all the press surrounding us. They're very negative."

Ani turns and gives her new husband a grin. "Babe, we met on the set of a reality dating show. They are not known for long-lasting marriages. More than half the couples aren't together by the time the show airs. They have their reasons to be suspicious. Also, it sells papers and brings in viewers. There were definitely rumors out there that we did this all for press and would break up right before the wedding. And then there are the people who think I'm using you. I've been called a gold digger more times than I can count."

Luca huffs. "Oh, well, then they do not know the state of my wealth." He puts a hand on his wife's cheek, cupping it and looking adoringly into her eyes. "They don't know that you're the one who will save an entire country with your brilliance. I'm the gold digger. I'm the one who found the real treasure."

Ivy and I exchange looks. Because…I mean, it's a lot of mushy stuff. In this Ivy and I are in synch. I almost snort though when I see Heath staring at them indulgently.

Darnell shakes his head. "This is a messed-up group. And Harper," he begins, gesturing toward the bar, "the man you are absolutely never going to be a couple with looks like he could use some help. It's hard on some men to deal with aggressive women. Not me. I tell them in a loud voice to *get back, temptress*. Or I yell *she tried to touch my no-no zone*. It makes them think twice."

I glance over and sure enough, that harpy of a Euro minor royal has Reid backed up against the wall where he's trying to keep two glasses of whiskey in his hands while protecting his no-no zone. He's not doing a good job of it. She's got one hand on his chest and is way too close. I'm not sure what she thinks she's doing. If the genders were reversed, every woman in the place would be stepping in to help, but as a society we tend to think men want all sexual attention all the time.

"I have to save him, don't I?" I kind of want to save him. I'll admit I don't like seeing that woman put her hands on him, and it's not merely about social justice.

"If you don't, I will," Ivy promises. I'm pretty sure her willingness *is* about social justice. She worked in tech for like a thousand years and understands what it means to be vulnerable. "It's been a while since I put someone in their place. Or I could send CeCe after her. But then I would have to save him from CeCe. She calls them Hot Designer and Gay Designer. The fact that they both get an adjective means she's practically in love."

The last thing this wedding needs is CeCe in a fight. Especially since Lydia and Diane are here, and they've started acting like CeCe's backup. Heath's grandmother and Ivy's mom once told me they didn't like to fight, but you have to back up your friends.

And that was when we had to bail them out of jail in Atlantic City.

"I've got this." I start toward the impending assault. It's not like I haven't had to deal with this before. Some people don't understand that *no* is a complete sentence and one we should honor. It's just usually dudes I've got to deal with. Dudes can mostly be handled with threats and me pointing out that the cops won't look at it kindly if they get physical with me. Chicks can oddly be more difficult.

"Why don't you come to my hotel? I can show you some lovely designs."

Okay, eww. She needs some better pick up lines. "Hey, we need to talk."

Reid's head turns my way, and there's a flush to his face that lets me know he's either embarrassed by the situation he's in or worried I'm about to misinterpret something. "Of course, Harper. We should go somewhere and continue our discussion. Sonja, this is the woman I was telling you about. I'm working with her on the Banover Place project."

He was telling her about me? I'm not going to read anything into that.

I'm totally reading too much into that.

"You can talk to her later. This is not the time or place for work," Sonja says with a confidence she does not deserve. Look, the woman's pretty, but she's got a perpetual sneer on her face. "It's a wedding, and a royal one at that. It's romantic. Despite the fact that the royals are... What you Americans call it? Bargain basement."

Oh, we're having a chat.

"I didn't mean you, Reid," I correct. "I'm going to have a talk with Sonja here. So first off, don't talk about my friends that way. They have more class than you can imagine, and that's worth far more than money. Second, you need to up your game, lady. You asked him to come to your room to look at your designs? Everyone knows that means your vagina. Everyone."

Her face goes red, and she glances around to see if anyone is watching. "How dare you."

Pretty much the entire bar is watching.

I stop the nearest waiter because I have a point to prove, and I actually don't want her to come around Reid anymore. I get the feeling this one could be tenacious if I don't settle this here and now. "Sir."

The waiter stops, offering me a lovely bacon-wrapped appetizer. Like all of the waitstaff, he's in a formal uniform wearing the traditional colors of the St. Marten crest. Red and gold.

I take it because it would be rude not to. "Did you hear the offer this woman made to my friend here? The one about seeing her designs? In her private hotel room, because she apparently forgot to bring her portfolio? Unless she's not talking about art."

The waiter's lips purse as though holding in a chuckle. He manages a professional, "Yes, ma'am. I did overhear that exchange."

"Do you think she's talking about architectural designs? Or perhaps she works in fashion?"

Reid takes the chance to move, claiming a place right behind me. Like I'm a wall between him and all that sexual harassment.

"That was not the impression I was under," the waiter says with a nod.

"Oh, she wants him to look at her female parts." An elderly woman sitting at the table beside the bar looks down her patrician nose at Sonja. She's obviously some kind of Ralavian royalty because she has Luca's accent and a thin tiara around her well-done updo of perfectly silver hair. She might be one of his aunts. "I don't think he wants to. Young man, I believe that woman wants to take advantage of you."

Sonja goes a brilliant shade of pink, says something under her breath in a language I don't understand, and huffs away. If I wasn't leaving tomorrow, I would worry about revenge, but she can find me in Manhattan if she wants to.

I down that app in one bite.

"You have to look after the men," the woman with the tiara says, lifting her glass of champagne my way in an obvious salute. "They are impressionable at this age. Very tender hearted. They can find themselves in trouble with predatory females."

The waiter simply grins and walks on.

I nod the woman's way. She's obviously wise. "They are our greatest gift, and we must protect them."

Reid's laugh booms through the room.

So the guy can take a joke.

He's smiling when I turn his way. He bows slightly and offers me the glass in his left hand. "For my knight in shining armor."

I take it and gesture the way Sonja exited stage left. "Was she an old friend?"

Reid winks back, likely at the woman with the tiara before putting a hand on the small of my back and leading me toward my friends again. "Not exactly. She's the wife of a wealthy former client of mine."

I feel my brows rise. "She's married?"

"You say that like it's shocking," he says under his breath. He smiles at the people we pass, but it feels like a professional expression. Not the smile he's given to me more than once tonight.

"It is. She was practically humping you in public." I say it through my own professional smile. I've probably made enough scenes for the day.

"She's had a bit to drink, and I heard her husband has a new mistress," Reid offers. "So I'm certain she's emotional. This is kind of the way at this level of society. Not for everyone, of course. I suspect Luca is going to be happy with Anika, but there are still a lot of marriages that are somewhat arranged. Luca, in many ways, was lucky." He winces. "I shouldn't use that word because I know how the flooding damaged this country."

I get what he's saying. "But if he hadn't been forced to use a good deal of his personal wealth to save his people, there would have been pressure on him to find the right wife, a woman of a royal line. Because he had no money, no one expected a royal to marry him."

"Oddly, yes. Not many of the women who will hit on him for the rest of his life would have walked into the situation Anika finds herself in now. Sometimes we lose everything and find someplace completely new. I know it seems like tragedy, but it can also take the blinders off our eyes so we value what truly matters."

I stop and stare at him for a moment. "Do you believe that?"

"I do. I know it's true." He's close, our bodies nearly brushing together. "There will always be bad things that happen in our lives. How we deal with them is what makes us who we are. Sometimes in order to change and grow, we have to let go. Even when it feels like the worst mistake we could make."

He's talking about the show. I don't know why or what made him leave, but he walked away for a reason, and not because he got bored. Not because he didn't want to do it anymore. "You're serious about Banover Place."

"I am very serious about Banover Place." He steps back and takes a short sip of the whiskey. "I'm serious about finding something new for me and Jeremiah and some of the crew we worked with. This isn't some vanity project for me. How about you? Are you simply doing it to help your friend?"

I'm not. There are many reasons this job Ani offered me feels like a lifeboat. I've been mired in the daily act of running a company for so long. "In college I studied business. My father pretty much made me. They wouldn't pay for it otherwise. But I minored in architectural design. I took a ton of woodworking classes and specialized courses in restoration. All on my own dime, of course, because my parents didn't think those things would help me build apartments."

"But you love the work."

I love the silence sometimes, the almost communion-like feeling I get when everyone else has gone home and I'm still working in a house. It's not the same in a big, new building. I don't feel the history. "Oh, I fell madly in love with it. Even in high school I loved it. My shop teacher was Mr. Hubbard, and he spent his weekends working on this old farmhouse outside the city. Sometimes a couple of students would go out, and his wife would make these big lunches and he would teach us how we could take something old and make it new again."

"I don't do many new home designs. They don't make me feel the way redesigning older homes does. There's something about the history, the knowledge that one family has already lived there."

I nod because he understands. "I was away from it for a long time after my dad died. I had to concentrate on the company, and the company makes way more by tearing stuff down and starting over than carefully bringing back something worn and used but with great bones. And then one of my best friends ended up on a reality TV show about a king who needed a wife, and she found herself staying at Banover Place. I managed to talk my way into a job there as a kind of handy Girl Friday. I was there so Ani had someone to talk to, but I fell in love all over again. I feel centered and happy when I'm working like I am on Banover."

He holds up his glass. "Then we can do some good together."

I touch my glass to his. "We can."

When we turn and join my friends, I feel more hopeful than I have in a long time.

Chapter Six

The door slams behind me but I don't care because the only thing that matters is getting my hands on this man. "Are you going to kiss me?"

His lips kick up as he pulls his bowtie off. "I'm going to do more than kiss you, baby. Do you have any idea how much I've thought about this? Since the moment I saw you and made a complete idiot of myself." He frowns suddenly. "How much did you drink?"

I set my tiny purse on the foyer table. It's a whole big, gorgeous suite. It looks a lot like the one I'm sharing with Ivy and Heath, so I would bet there are two bedrooms in this sucker. I don't see Jeremiah, so I have to think he's either getting lucky himself or still enjoying the party. "Two glasses of champagne and that whiskey you brought me. I also ate way too much, and that's a much better reason to not do this."

There are so many reasons to not do this. So many.

I can't think of any of them right now. If I'm drunk off anything, it's lust. And maybe longing.

The last two hours have been a whirlwind of dancing and toasting my friends and sitting with Reid and talking about pretty much everything. We had a spirited debate about restoration methods that made all my friends leave the table. Jeremiah sat there watching us argue with wide eyes, as though it was the best tennis match ever.

It was fun to argue with Reid. Fun to dance with him. Fun to try

Ralavian pastries with him. Especially since he apparently can't stand lingonberries, and it was the national fruit. I had to eat his because Luca was walking up and he didn't want to admit he hated it.

It was adorable.

I don't think I've had a boyfriend before who I felt was a teammate. Like we're truly in it together. Not that Reid is my boyfriend. He's not, and I need to remember that.

"What are we doing?" He seems to slow down.

I don't want to. "Having a brief fling at the most elegant and romantic event either of us will ever attend." Now I do kind of wish I had some more of that whiskey he'd given me. It might give me some more courage. I'm wondering if he's come to his senses. I can probably handle it if it's about work. "But if you've changed your mind…"

He reaches for my hand and then drags me close. "No. I'm a careful man. I make very few mistakes, and I've started to wonder if that isn't the problem."

I raise a brow. "I'm a mistake?"

"Probably, since we're about to work together and I think we're going to butt heads a lot. This is your dream project, but I'm the designer. I'm in charge, and you're going to hate me at times. Yes, this is a mistake, but I want to make it. One selfish decision. Something only for me." His hands find my waist and pull me close, our bodies nestling together like puzzle pieces. "Harper, have I told you how fucking gorgeous you are?"

A couple of times. When we danced, he made me feel like I was the princess and he the handsome prince. He was so attentive, making sure I had anything I wanted.

I know it won't last, but for a couple of hours I want to pretend I have the kind of life my friends have.

He even fit in with them. He and his brother had laughed and joked around with Heath and Luca and tried to hide when CeCe came around.

It felt like I fit in that moment. Like I fit in the new paradigm I find myself in.

I know it's not real, but for one night it can be. "You look good, too. That tux suits you. We both know this is a one-night thing."

He's looking into my eyes like he can find something important there. "Why? Why do we have to put a time limit on it? What if it turns out we can handle butting heads at work and still feel comfortable outside of it? Are you a delicate flower who can't handle a little conflict?"

Oh, he's throwing down a challenge that I can't help but pick up. "I've worked with construction crews my whole life. I eat conflict for breakfast."

I had to develop a thick skin to survive. Even as a kid, my dad didn't hold back on the criticism, and I get a ton of it now. Honestly, the idea of working with this man, of sparring with him, kind of excites me. I've been the boss for a long time, and that means pushing back when the men around me think they know better. This will be something different.

"Then why does this have to be a one-night thing?" He strokes a hand over my hair, looking into my eyes like I'm something precious. "Stop thinking, Harper. We both think too much. Let's go with it for once in our lives."

It's the exact right thing to say because he's correct. My life feels like it was planned from the beginning. Like I was set on a path and I never thought to wander off it. I followed my father, listened to my mother. I love the work I do, but what would I do if I didn't have the responsibility the company gave me? What would I have done in college if I wasn't expected to get a business degree?

If my father lived, would he have introduced me to some nice guy he picked out and I would be home having his babies while he ran the company that was supposed to be mine?

Do I even want it?

I toss all the questions aside as Reid's head lowers and his lips brush over mine for the first time.

I definitely wouldn't be here, and here suddenly seems like a brilliant place to be.

He kisses me, his lips exploring while his big, strong hands move over my hips and one trails upward, tracing the line of my spine until he cups the nape of my neck. His fingers sink into my hair, pulling it from the carefully constructed bun I wore all day. I feel it spill out, brushing the tops of my shoulders.

"So soft," he murmurs before lowering his mouth to mine again. This time his kiss moves from gentle into dominating. He holds me still while he explores my mouth, our tongues sliding against one another in a silky dance. He seems...hungry, and having all that sexy energy pointed my direction does something for me.

I tug at the buttons of his shirt. He took the jacket off in the elevator. Yep, my bestie has an elevator, though Luca calls it the lift. So that shirt is the only thing standing between me and warm skin.

My toes threaten to curl as he pulls me against his body and I feel the evidence of his desire for the first time. I press against that hard part of him, warmth flaring through every inch of my body.

It's been so long. My last boyfriend and I broke up over two years ago, and I haven't dated since. Work got busy, and it was easier to simply go home and stare at a TV rather than take care of yet another person. I have to make every decision at work, have to fight over all of them, and then Lewis wanted me to make all the decisions in our relationship. He wanted a mom, not a girlfriend.

Which is likely why this feels so damn different.

Reid takes charge, holding me in place while he devours my mouth. It makes me wonder where else he might want to put it to good use.

I have a sudden vision of Reid between my legs, his mouth hovering over my core before he makes a meal out of me.

He starts to move us toward the back of the suite.

Behind us there's the sound of a door opening, and Reid quickly steps back. Before I can say anything, he's buttoning his shirt and turning to the front of the suite. "Jeremiah? Is everything okay?"

"Well, hello, tiny bag," I hear Jeremiah say from the living area. "I wasn't expecting you here. Hey, brother, you might stash Harper for a minute. We have a problem."

Reid stares at his brother for a moment like they're having an intense silent conversation.

I get the feeling our evening is over, but I'm not sure why. Jeremiah pointedly glances at his watch.

Reid turns my way, and I don't have to have feelings. I know he's about to ask me to leave. I take a long breath before he can talk. "I'll get back to my room."

Reid's expression falls. "I just need to handle one thing."

I was starting to worry about what thing needs handling. Do they have designer emergencies? Does he need to pick up his book of swatches and fly across the country like a superhero because some rich chick needs a bathroom redo at one in the morning? "It's okay. I'll see you when we get back to the States."

"Harper," he begins.

I'm not sure what to say to him. Without his hands on me, all of my doubts start to creep back in. We do have to work together. We spark off each other, and that's not always a good thing. This is Ani's big project, and I don't want my libido to screw it up. I straighten my dress and wish he hadn't taken my hair down. I probably look like we got much further than we did. "It's only a week or so and we'll start filming."

"Or I could come to your room when I'm done," he offers.

But there's something about Jeremiah's expression. He won't quite look me in the eyes. "I'm so tired. I swear I'll be asleep in no time. Also, I'm sharing with Ivy and Heath, and they would never let me hear the end of it."

He sighs. "Okay, but I'll call you. And we have an initial design meeting in a week. I'd like to see you before then."

I give him my brightest smile. If he does call, maybe we can try it again. Maybe this is some weird family thing. Maybe he'll tell me what happened and I'll laugh and we can move on. "Call me. I had a good time."

"I did, too." There's a wistful expression on his face.

And a somewhat sympathetic look on Jeremiah's as he waves my way.

I'm halfway out the door when I hear them talking.

"What do you mean she's…"

The door closes, and I'm alone in the hallway.

So it *is* a she. Well, everyone told me he was something of a playboy. My heart hurts a little. Maybe I don't understand the situation. I walk down the hall. The party is still going on below us. I could go down and talk to Ivy, but the last thing I want is to be the girl crying in the bathroom at the homecoming dance. That had actually been Anika, but I'm not looking to pay her back or anything. It wasn't like I'd had anything better to do junior year.

"Either he was faster than all reports would have him be or his brother cockblocked you," a feminine voice says. I turn and Sonja, the sexually aggressive royal, is standing at the top of the staircase, a glass of champagne in her hands. Her brow cocks as she looks me over. "Which one?"

"Lady, it's none of your business."

Sonja sighs. "It's everyone's business if you get involved with that one. Haven't you figured it out? He's American royalty. You people don't value history, but you do love money. It's the only real god in American society. His family is old-school money, and that means everyone wants something from him."

I should walk on. "You sure did."

She shrugs. "I'm bored and my husband is fucking some twenty-year-old. He looked like a good distraction, but then she showed up and I remembered why I stay away from that train wreck."

"She?"

Sonja frowns. "Are you really so out of the loop?"

"Yes."

A huff comes from the woman's mouth. "Her name is Britta Olensoff. She's a model. I think the term is supermodel."

Nothing rings a bell, and I'm suddenly grateful I don't follow celebrity news. "I'm not big into fashion."

She looks me up and down. "Yes, I can see that."

I'm about to walk off and hide in my room when a gloriously tall woman begins her ascent up the stairs. She's stunning. A Nordic goddess of a woman, and she does not have my problems with fashion. She's in a sheath dress that shows off her slender figure, and her icy blond hair is swept back in a perfect ponytail that sways as she walks in impossibly high heels. She's followed by two men in suits. Bodyguards.

"Britta," Sonja says with obvious disdain. "I suppose I know where you're going. He kicked this one out when he found out you were here."

Shit. I feel my whole body flush as I realize what happened. Well, it wasn't like I asked if he had a girlfriend. I would think he might mention it, but I also hadn't questioned him and neither had he.

The supermodel stares down at me as though contemplating a bug she's thinking about squishing. "Well, I shouldn't be so surprised. We fought when I couldn't come with him. This is how he gets his petty revenge. I'm sorry, miss. He likely didn't mention he has a fiancée."

I feel my jaw threaten to drop. And my heart clench. It isn't like I thought we had a future or anything, but he...he isn't who I thought he was. His brother isn't either since he's covering for Reid. I'm not going to cry. At least not until I make it to my room. "We work together. That's all. I'm managing the crew on his latest renovation project."

Britta's head tilts like she's considering something. And then she smiles. "Oh, you're one of the construction people. Well, I was about to tell you to stay away from my fiancé, but I guess he's not your type."

Ah, yeah. Like I haven't gotten that before. The tomboy probably doesn't like men. Well, I don't right now, and it's a low-key heartache that my sexuality is so hardwired. Reid wants to play games? Well, I can win by refusing to take the bait. I gesture down the hallway I came from. "He's the third door on the left. You kids have a great time."

I hurry down the stairs before Sonja can make another nasty remark.

When I get to my room, I close the door. And do what I promised not to do.

I cry and vow it's the last time I give that man an inch.

Chapter Seven

"Okay, now I've got you trapped in a small tin can flying thirty thousand feet above the ocean," Ivy says as she settles in across from me, "we're going to talk."

Damn. I was hoping to avoid this but then I should have flown commercial and not taken CeCe up on her offer to fly us all back to New York. But at the time I didn't realize I would want to avoid my best friend so I didn't have to talk about how spectacularly I made a fool of myself the night before. I even took the seat next to Darnell, who will not care about my awful taste in men in any way. Unfortunately, he and Heath are now sitting together arguing about hobbits or something.

Flight Attendant came by to take our lunch orders. Ugh. I have to stop thinking like that. "What's her name?"

Ivy's lips curl up like she knows exactly what I'm thinking. "Jane. I know. I make sure to ask because it's way too easy to fall into the whole CeCe, call-everyone-by-their-place-in-your-life thing. She can get away with it."

That's what happens when you're an outrageously wealthy older woman. Which I'm not. "Thanks, Jane," I call out as she goes to get our lunch. "She seems nice. I hope Anika's flight is even better."

"Well, it's CeCe's smaller jet." Ivy frowns. "Does she need two? How many private jets can one person own?"

"Three, darling." CeCe turns in her chair. This particular jet's cabin is something of an elegant living room, complete with chairs that swivel so the occupants can configure the space into conversational settings. She's sitting with Heath's grandmother, Lydia, and Ivy's mom, Diane. We call them the moms, though CeCe's only child is a series of overly privileged Maltese dogs she always names Lady something. "I have them for different occasions, of course. This is the large jet. I call her Big Bertha. She gets the job done when I have to fly a group of obnoxious hedge fund managers places. I like to leave out a single parachute to let them know I can eject them at any time."

"I prefer Jackie," Lydia offers. "That's the small jet we use when we go on our adventures."

"It's got a big screen we watch movies on, and I even managed to talk Stick Up Her Ass to put in a microwave so we can make popcorn." Diane looks so different than she did when we were growing up. She's...smiling. Joking. I suppose I never saw her before she'd gotten lost in grief and depression. She is in therapy now and has a much better relationship with, well, everyone.

"I do not look this good by eating carbs," CeCe shoots back.

"No, she does it by drinking the blood of the innocent," Lydia says with a grin.

CeCe waves them off with an indulgent shake of her head as she pets the dog in her lap. "Angelica is my love jet. I purchased it when I thought I should join the mile high club." She wrinkles her nose. "It turns out I prefer my physical relationships without the turbulence. But I'm glad I kept her because I think Anika and the king are going to have a lovely time."

Ivy's grin lights up the room. "I'm glad she kept it because it's, like, tricked out. I still don't know what half those things are for, but Heath and I tried them all."

Diane's hands cover her ears and she hums.

"I'm the one with a stick up my butt." CeCe's eyes roll but then they're laser focused on me. "I'm not the only one today, Harper."

Shit. She used my name. Like my actual, real name. I'm usually something like Girl with the Tool Kit or Ivy's Friend who Needs a Manicure. She's serious if she's using my name.

Up until now I wasn't sure she knew my name.

They're all looking at me. All the moms and Ivy.

"Hey, do we have some Sprite hidden..." Darnell begins, and then all eyes turn his way. His hands come up like he knows he's walked into a potential danger zone. "I'm good. I'll just…" He backs up. "Return to my assigned seat. I didn't realize this was a meeting of the moms. Good luck, Harper."

Crap. There's an actual name for it? "I can go grab that Sprite for him."

"Sit down, Harper," CeCe commands.

And I do. Which is proof the woman has some witchy talents because I don't tend to blindly obey.

"What happened last night?" Ivy asks. "I would have had this conversation in private and kept the moms off your back, but you skipped on breakfast this morning and then ignored me when I tried to talk to you after Ani's send-off. You ignored my texts."

"I did not. I answered them."

She frowns my way. "You replied to *hey, are you okay* with a thumbs-up emoji. And to *what happened with Reid last night* with a pukey face. That is not an answer, Harper."

I sigh. There's probably no getting out of this. I would argue if I thought they were simply trying to get gossip, but these women are my family. Even more than my own mom who I would never go to for advice because somehow it would get turned around on me and whatever I was worrying about would be my fault. Still, I can try. "We were both tired and decided to go to bed."

The moms all lean in, anticipation clear.

"Not together," I clarify.

They all sit back, obviously disappointed.

This is where my own mother would give me advice about cows and free milk and how she made my father wait, and look how that turned out. Unhappy. Unfulfilled. Constantly disappointed in everything around them, including their only child.

"He seemed so into you," Ivy muses. "I was even taking bets with his brother about who had to make sure the two of you ate breakfast this morning."

"Well, no one won that bet since we made the decision to be adults and not let sexual attraction ruin what might be an excellent working relationship," I reply.

Ivy's eyes narrow. "Really? You're going to be friends and have a great working relationship? That's what you were doing last night when you were dancing with him and looking at him like he was the last man in the world?"

"Like you were a kid who found the world's biggest candy store," Lydia adds.

"Or a very horny young woman who hasn't gotten any in a long, long time." CeCe isn't good with metaphors. She just puts it out there.

I force a smile on my face. They're not getting to me so easily. "I had a lovely time with him. He's a handsome man, but we decided to be mature adults and not complicate the relationship."

"Mature adults who are planning to be friends reply to each other's text messages and calls," Ivy says.

How does she... "Did you look at my phone?"

"I didn't have to. Reid texted me to see if he had the right number," Ivy explains. "He didn't understand why you wouldn't reply, and he worried he'd gotten the wrong number since it appears the one he's been calling has blocked him."

I probably shouldn't have done that. "I'll talk to him when we get home." Why am I holding back? These women aren't looking to make fun of me, but I'm protecting myself like they're the mean girls from high school. Maybe talking about it will give me perspective and I'll be able to do what I vowed to do—take the high road. "I went back to his room and things got hot and heavy, and then his brother rushed in and I was hustled out because his fiancée showed up."

"I'm going to need that popcorn," Diane says, leaning in. "He has a fiancée?"

Lydia huffs and holds on to the tea she ordered. "He never once mentioned that in his questionnaires."

"He *had* a fiancée. Some Swedish stick figure," CeCe says. "But according to the European gossip rags, they broke up."

CeCe knows something? "Anika didn't mention it. Neither did Luca."

"Why would Luca tell you Reid had a girlfriend? He broke up with her before you met him," CeCe replies. "Although they do have a history of breaking up and making up. It's all on the report I did on him and his brother before Anika hired him."

"You had him investigated?" It's a bit shocking to me.

CeCe waves me off. "Of course. What do you think Private Detective does?"

Well, he's six foot two inches of pure muscle with a movie-star-like smile, so I kind of thought he did CeCe. She's a mystery. "Why would you look into him?"

"Because Ani is in a position where people can and will try to take advantage of her. I would allow her mother to handle things, but she's not exactly the ruthless kind," CeCe points out.

Lydia nods. "Yeah, we need someone without any ruth to watch out for our girls."

"I helped Paul," Diane admits. "He's the investigator. Thomas and I did some of the legwork ourselves. He seems to be a fairly solid guy, though I question the talk about his wealth. I think his father left them with less than society thinks."

I'm super confused. "Okay, so *we*, and by *we* I mean the moms, have made it a habit of playing *Law and Order* with anyone who comes into Anika's life?"

"Yes," Ivy says with an annoyed sigh. "And they left us out. I would say it's all terrible and invasive, but I kind of wish they were around when I was living with my ex."

"I was around, love," CeCe says with annoyance of her own. "I did send you a report. You were somewhat stubborn."

"I think we should all take a moment." Lydia is always the voice of reason. "I have also done a bit of a study into Mr. Dorsey."

"You had him fill out forms," Diane points out. "He can lie on forms. I'm fairly certain he did."

"What do you mean he lied?" I trust Diane's instincts. She's worked with lawyers for a very long time.

Diane looks uncomfortable with all the attention on her, but she soldiers on—something she wouldn't have done before a shit ton of therapy and antidepressants to help her handle her grief. If I didn't believe meds could help mental disorders before, she's walking proof that they can help a person get their life back. "I read Lydia's questionnaires, and I've spent some time with the young man. He claims to have no problems with his brother, but I would say there's quite a bit of tension between the two. I don't know why. It could be a childhood thing, but something's going on between them. Didn't you see him watching Jeremiah like a hawk when we were at the bar the other night?"

"I did," CeCe notes. "It seemed like he was worried about Jeremiah for some reason. Have we considered that the tension has to do with the car accident and the subsequent loss of their TV show? Perhaps Jeremiah distracted Reid, and that's what he's still angry about."

I never saw him angry with his brother. "The accident was Reid's fault. I doubt he would take it out on his brother. And wasn't there someone else in the car?"

"Yes, her name was Britta something," Diane confirms.

Ah, the supermodel. "That's his fiancée."

"They broke up," Ivy insists.

CeCe sends me a sympathetic look. "They do that quite often, from what I can tell. Their history goes back a few years. They have what can only be described as a tempestuous relationship."

Passion. He was passionate about Britta Olensoff.

I was probably a way to make the woman he did care about jealous. Or they were on a break and he thought he could play around before they got serious again.

"I don't think he's lying about his relationship with another woman," Lydia says thoughtfully. "I know it's a bunch of questionnaires, but you can tell a lot from the answers. If anything, I would say he's lonely and overwhelmed with responsibility. He's the type of man who takes the weight of the world on his shoulders. I think he pretty much raised his younger brother. We're reading too much into it. He's used to watching out for Jeremiah."

"His father was a terrible human being," CeCe admitted. "Dorian Dorsey—such a terrible name. It brings to mind casual sexism—slept with any woman he could. We were in different circles, but I certainly had my run-ins with him. I remember when his wife walked out and everyone worried about the children being left with him."

"Did anyone check?" I ask, and even as the question comes out of my mouth I know it's naïve.

"Of course not," CeCe admits. "Everyone thought at least they'd be raised by the nanny. Look, I don't say any of this to get sympathy for Reid. I barely know him. But I did know something of his father, and oftentimes the apple doesn't fall far from the tree. He's got a bit of a reputation when it comes to women. Normally I would say go and have fun, but our Harper isn't a fun girl. More's the shame."

See, I don't know if that's a good thing or a bad thing in her head. "I wasn't trying to have a relationship with him."

They all stare at me like I said something ridiculous.

"I wasn't."

Ivy's head shakes. "But you would. Harper, you have never once in your life just had a fling. Jon Keller junior year. You made out with him at the homecoming game and told us it was a one and done thing, and he was still hanging around when we went to prom."

"Okay. I had issues breaking things off," I begin.

"The wrestler freshman year of college," Ivy continues. "You hooked up at a party and then you suddenly knew things about takedowns and falls and something called a Wheeler Whip."

It was a weird time. When Ivy starts to talk about the dude I met backstage at a community theater show, I know she'll end up telling the story of how I played a witch on one episode of a local children's TV show, and I would like to avoid that. "Okay, I get it. Maybe you're right."

"I was all for it because at least this time you're on the same page," Ivy concedes. "You both like all the home stuff. He can pick out wallpaper and you can install it. It's kind of perfect."

"That's what I'm saying," Lydia insists. "They're a great match. I don't think Reid is a player. If anything, I suspect he could get caught in a relationship he can't get out of. He doesn't necessarily think about himself. He needs someone who can have his best interests at heart and be strong enough to make the point that he should do what's right for him. And by him, I mean for them. He'll be better at making decisions that forward himself if he truly believes he's making the decision for his partner."

That doesn't sound like the playboy CeCe described. Nor does it make me think of the arrogant ass I first met. I was caught up in the romance of the wedding. That's what I decided around two a.m. the night before. It wasn't Reid himself. Any gorgeous, charming guy would have done the same thing for me.

He got rid of me mighty fast the minute Britta showed up.

"It doesn't matter," I tell this found family of mine. "I'm not interested in a relationship with him."

Ivy shifts, leaning toward me. "Are you sure you're not interested in him? You laughed more last night than you have in forever."

I don't have a choice. Beyond my own self-respect, there are other things to consider. "He's got a fiancée, and I don't need to bring a bunch of drama to the set. This is Ani's first big project, and she's taking a chance on me."

I don't like the thought that Ivy's right and last night was the first time in forever that I relaxed and enjoyed myself. Right up until the moment I realized he was keeping things from me. Important things.

Ivy nods and sits back. "All right, then. I'll handle the moms. You concentrate on making Banover Place pretty. I wonder what it'll sell for when you're done?"

Millions. Millions that will help Ani's new country.

I try to relax and think about the good I'll be doing. Whatever it takes to get my mind off that man.

Chapter Eight

I sit at the desk I keep in the small office where we handle all the administrative things that come with running a construction company. There's a larger warehouse outside the city where we keep equipment, but this space is where we do things like payroll and meeting with potential clients.

And worrying about the fact that I have a board meeting coming up in a few months and half the family is irritated with me because I won't give them money we don't have.

Like my cousin, Claire, who sits across from me wearing more designer wear than a single person should own. It's a mishmash of brands. Chanel bag. Prada shoes. A Dolce and Gabbana jacket. Dior sunglasses. I don't even want to think about the jewelry. "But the sorority fees are due. What am I supposed to do?"

She's a college student. I think she's studying fashion, but what she mostly does is whine.

"You can't allow Claire to be out on the streets." Unfortunately, she knows how to get under my skin since she brought my mother along.

"She won't," I point out. "She'll be in a dorm, or better yet, she can live at home and commute to school. Her mom lives across the river. It's literally three subway stops away."

This brings out a gasp in both my cousin and my mother. Like I've asked her to battle her way through a pack of werewolves to get her higher education.

"I stayed in a dorm last semester," Claire says. "I'm not doing it again. I need to be in Tau Alpha Kai. It's for my career."

"It's for her career," my mother parrots.

Where was she when I wanted to study architecture? She hadn't cared about the career path I wanted to take. She told me my father didn't work all his life to have me turn my back on him. "She can be in the sorority and not live in the house. Look, I know our dads used company funds for things like this."

"It's called dividends," Claire protests. "Daddy used to say it was all our money."

"Yeah, well all our money is now going to the IRS." I'm tired. The last eight days have weighed on me. I tried to get to Banover Place to do some prep, but I've been forced to put out fire after fire here at work.

And I got a peek at a European gossip sheet. It had a picture of Reid and Britta in a café in Ralavia. I think it was taken the next day. The paper's headline said it all. *It's Back On.*

I have to see him soon, and I am not looking forward to it.

"I don't understand," my mother says. "This didn't happen when your father was in charge. When he was in charge everyone got what they needed."

"Yes, he did it by not paying taxes," I reply, though I explained this a million times. "I had to sell equipment to keep us from getting taken over by the government. I had to sell stock. My personal stock. Our aunt now has it. I'm sorry, Claire. I don't know what to tell you."

"I'll handle this for you, sis." Paul stands in the doorway, wearing a button-down and slacks. He's in for a client meeting, or at least that's what he told me. I suspect he's here to make me look as bad as possible in front of his overly privileged sister. Who has a fifteen percent stake in the company as one of her father's heirs. Paul had been given more, but they don't have enough between them to challenge me alone. I'm the majority holder, but there are some other relatives who hold small shares. Luckily most of them understand business. He tried to wrestle control away before, but I held him off.

Still, I'm not fighting this battle today. "Good for you. See, Claire, Paul is going to pay for you to stay in a way overpriced apartment so you can make contacts with the people you drink too much with. All's well that ends well."

My mother huffs. "It shouldn't be like this. Harper, both you and Paul's educations were paid for by the company disbursements."

"Would you like to check the accounts, Mom? I can show you where we're running light on cash. We've been undercut by some of the bigger companies recently, and I'm still digging out of the IRS debacle Dad left behind."

She stands, her shoulders going back. "You should have respect for the dead. Your father ran this company the best way he knew how. So did your uncle."

"Our parents made sure we always had what we needed." Paul has to chime in. "And I wonder if we're getting undercut or if we're not making the right impression with new clients."

"What is that supposed to mean?" I have to ask since he's obviously talking about me. I'm the forward face of the company.

He shrugs. "It means we've lost bids, and I don't think it's all about money. Make of that what you will. Come on, Claire. Let's go back to my office and we can talk. I'm not going to make you drop out of school."

Claire shoots me the nastiest look as she joins her brother. I do not feel bad in any way.

Unfortunately, my mother is still here, and I do feel bad about that. "You are going to break this family if you keep this up. Harper, I didn't raise you to be unkind."

"How is it unkind?" This isn't an argument I can win since logic means nothing, but I feel compelled to try. "I know you don't understand, but a lot of what Dad and Uncle Alan did was illegal."

"How is it illegal to help family?" my mother asks, all self-righteousness.

"Because it's company funds and there are rules about it."

She shakes her head, obviously dismissing me. "We're a privately held firm. That's how your father explained it. As long as we made our payroll, the rest of the funds were ours to do what we wanted with. Your father never missed paying his people."

"No, just the government." I don't understand how she can ignore this point.

My mother waves that away. "Like they deserve anything."

I'm tired of arguing. "It doesn't matter. We're governed by laws, and if we don't follow them, they can seize everything. The money is not there to keep up the lifestyle Claire has obviously become accustomed to. You love her so much, why aren't you offering to pay for it yourself?"

My mother frowns. "That's not my place. I can see you're going to be unreasonable about this, so I'll drop it. But you should understand you're not making friends here. There's talk about replacing you."

"If you do that, Paul will have this place in federal hands within two years." I need her to understand the ramifications of backing Paul. "If you get the aunts and cousins together and oust me, you might have a year of the old days, but then the company will go under."

"Well, I suppose I don't understand business the way you do, but this isn't how your father did things." She appears on the verge of tears. "I don't understand why things have to change. This is not the life I wanted at all."

I sigh and sit back, feeling sympathy for her. She hadn't wanted my father to die and leave her a widow. In her mind, she'd done everything she could to have a comfortable life, including putting up with a philandering husband. "I'm sorry. I wish Dad hadn't died, but we're here and I'm doing the best I can."

"Are you?" My mother's anger seems to be bubbling up to the surface. She pretends like everything is fine. Always. It has to boil over at some point, and it looks like it's headed my way. Naturally. "What I see is you prioritizing those friends of yours. You spent two weeks in Europe."

"One of my best friends was getting married," I point out, knowing it won't do me any good.

"You didn't have to be gone for two weeks. You missed so many family events. You made me go alone."

"Mom, I don't know if you've noticed, but I'm not well-liked by these people. And I scarcely think my cousins care whether I show up to their kids T-ball games," I explain.

My mother's head shakes. "Well, I care. I care that you don't seem to want to be a member of this family at all."

I feel my eyes narrow in anger. "I've spent every day of the last two years trying to save this company. I used a good portion of my inheritance to do it. I put myself on the line. Don't tell me I don't care about this family because I don't want to spend every second with a bunch of people who will do nothing but hold their hands out for cash. That's your thing, Mom. You let them walk all over you."

"Well, what am I supposed to do when I have a daughter who

refuses to do the right thing?"

"Just so we're clear, what is the right thing?" I'm pretty sure I know, but I like to give people enough rope.

"You should worry about finding a husband and giving me grandchildren. Have you even thought about what this is like for me? Everyone else has grandbabies. I have to go to every party and coo over their babies and know that I have none. What am I supposed to do with my life, Harper?"

Yup. Exactly what I thought she would say. "Personally, I think you should find a hobby. Or, I don't know, get a job. Find some meaning that isn't wrapped up in my vacant womb."

She stands there for a moment, tears in her eyes. "You don't care."

I don't even know what to say. I'm tired. "I'm not going to live your life, Mom. Serving a man to your own detriment was your thing, not mine."

She turns and strides out, not bothering to look behind.

"Damn, that was a scene. Is that what it's like to have a mom? Maybe it was best mine took off for Southern France when I was a baby," a familiar voice says. Jeremiah turns, watching my mother walk away.

My day is getting better. "I suppose my admin is taking a break."

He shrugs as he walks into the office. "Nah. I explained the situation to her and she told me to go on back. I'm charming. I make all the straight girls comfortable. Oddly, the lesbians tend to see through my bullshit."

I know who I should hire next. "What can I do for you, Jeremiah? Also, what is the situation?"

He walks around, looking at the pictures on the walls. "The sitch is that you and my brother had a moment, and I wanted to find out why you've now blocked him. He tried to call you."

It was an impulse. "Sorry. I'll reverse that. He needs to be able to get in touch with me. I gave him my personal cell. I only use that for friends. I'll give him my business number."

He glances back, giving me a frown. "You're not friends now? You looked like friends a couple of days ago. Who is this?"

He points to one of the pictures on the wall.

"My father and uncle. Way back when they first started the company. They're standing in front of the first building they ever broke ground on," I explain. "It was built in the seventies. It was an apartment building. They tore it down two years ago for a new high-rise."

Nothing is permanent. I've learned that over the years. That lesson is why Banover Place feels so sacred to me. There's history. A small part of it mine.

"That's sad." He gestures toward the door. "I'm right? That was your mother?"

"I don't know anyone else who would yell at me for not pumping out kids."

He chuckles a bit and takes the seat in front of mine before leaning forward and getting serious. "Was it Britta?"

Well, he gets right to the point. "Are you talking about Reid's fiancée?"

He groans. "I knew it. I knew she would wreck everything. Harper, they are not engaged and haven't been in a long time. Over a year."

"It's not my business."

He stares for a moment. "It seemed like it was about to be your business. I can see things. You didn't go back to our room to talk about design plans." His expression softens. "I haven't seen my brother react like this to a woman in…ever. He is not involved with Britta. Not anymore. Not the way you think he is."

"Again, it's not my business." I've come to the conclusion that I'm happy things went down the way they did. I made a fool of myself, but it wasn't anything lasting. We didn't go so far that I feel any real shame. I almost feel like I avoided a massive mistake. "We were high off romance and champagne that night. It's a good thing she showed up because I think there would have been a whole lot of regret in the morning."

"Not on my brother's end."

"Jeremiah, I'm not willing to discuss this with him. Why do you think I would discuss it with you?"

He gives a glowy smile. "Because I'm sweet and sunshiney? Come on, Harper. I'm the guy all the girls talk to. You know I spent most of my high school and college days as someone's gay bestie. I find myself shockingly alone right now. All my girls have betrayed me by marrying boys and suddenly they move to…I can barely say it…Jersey. They know I can't walk into Jersey."

He's cute, but I have to keep my distance. Although there's a part of me that wants to connect with him. The truth is I'm the third wheel most of the time. My girls "betrayed" me by finding themselves amazing men, and now all I have is this job I'm holding on to by a thread, an extended family that thinks I'm an ATM, and a mom who wants to get my baby factory operating so she can pass her delusional love for the patriarchy down to another generation. Maybe I should get a dog. "I'm sorry. I don't think getting involved with your brother is a good idea. I mean, he's in European tabloids. I'm not the kind of woman who gets into tabloids."

"Which is exactly why I like you," he mutters under his breath and then sits up straight, obviously deciding on a different tactic. "Can we at least agree that he didn't lie to you?"

"I never said he did." We didn't talk about whether or not we had partners. I assumed, and we all know where that gets you.

"Can we agree he didn't lie by omission? He hasn't seen Britta in months. They broke it off last year, and he had no intention of getting back with her. She showed up at the reception with an old friend who was invited to the wedding. She wasn't. Apparently the security at the reception wasn't as tight as the ceremony."

He's forgetting the important part. "But she was looking for him."

Jeremiah sighs and sits back. "She does this to him. She throws some massive fit, breaks things off, and then comes back months later. I've often wondered if she does it because she wants to see someone else for a while."

"So *she* broke off the engagement."

He winces like he wishes he hadn't said something. "He would have broken it off this time. He was planning to. He hadn't found the right way to do it."

This is not my fight, and yet I find myself still asking questions. Likely because I can't stop thinking about the way the man kissed me. Like I was the sweetest thing he'd ever put in his mouth. Like he could do it forever and still want me.

I read too many romance novels.

"How long were they together?"

He stares for a moment like he knows he's in a mine field and isn't sure he wants to take that tentative first step. "A few years, and that should tell you something. It's always been off and on. They had a major fight and he was done, though technically she said the words before he did. I know my brother. He's not going back."

I don't know his brother at all. "Well, he certainly shoved me out fast enough when he knew she was on her way up."

"He did that to spare you," Jeremiah says. "Britta can be...mean is too small a word. Apocalyptic when she wants to be. He didn't want you in the middle of that fight."

"Did he think I was too fragile to handle one supermodel? I assure you I had already handled one obnoxious woman for him that night. I could have done it again." And honestly, the sex when I was filled with that kind of adrenaline would have been spectacular. I enjoy taking down assholes. It's a good triumphing over evil thing. Again with the romance novels. I should switch to mysteries or something. At least they would teach me valuable, usable information. Like how to murder my enemies and get away with it.

"I didn't handle it right. I saw her and I kind of freaked out," he admits. "I thought it was over. I know how bad it can get and how Reid can get. Dark. He's been so much happier lately. I didn't want him to go back. She can talk him into things."

Most stunningly gorgeous blondes can do that. It's good to remember that Reid Dorsey is a man like all the rest. He talks a good game, but in the end he'll want the sexiest woman he can find. And that is not the woman who walks around with a tool belt on most of the time. I need to get out of this conversation. I need to hold myself apart from Reid, and that means being professional. Maybe this was why their show shut down. Maybe he was so distracted by Britta, he forgot to do his job. Yes, this is what I should actually be worried about. After all, he didn't exactly send her away. There was a picture of them sitting in a sundrenched café looking awfully comfy the next day.

Did she spend the night with him?

Suspicion is rattling around in my head. Is Jeremiah telling me what he thinks I want to hear so filming goes smoothly? How often does he have to smooth over things for his brother? An unwilling sympathy hits me. I can understand what that means. I watched my uncle walk around after my dad, making sure he didn't do any permanent damage. It's hard to be the one who cleans up all the messes. I had to do a bit of that as well. "It's all okay. I'm not mad. I think it's good that we didn't do something we couldn't take back. We have to work together. It's always a bad idea to mix business and pleasure."

His expression falls and he sighs. "I'm not going to get through to you, am I?"

"There's nothing to get through to." I'm not sure exactly what he wants. I've told him we'll work fine together. "It's all going to be okay. We've got a great job coming up, and we'll have fun. Should we expect

Britta to show up on set? If so, we should inform Patrick. He's going to be running production. Grumpy guy, but good at his job. However, he doesn't like surprises."

"Well, I'll do my level best to ensure there are no surprises." Jeremiah stands and straightens his jacket. I can't help but notice the deep disappointment in his expression. "We're having a dinner party to welcome Anika and Luca back home. I don't suppose you want to come? It's on Friday."

We start filming Monday. I have a lot of preparations to make. We're all having dinner at Lydia's Saturday night, so skipping the Dorsey brothers' party won't keep me from seeing my bestie. "Thank you, but I have a lot to do before Monday. Do you know when you're going to give me the initial designs on the ballroom?"

We're working our way through the house. I've already done some of the more non-interesting work like ensuring the plumbing in the powder room makes it into this century's standards. The ballroom is our first big project, and Anika wants us to be as organic about the process as we can. So I'm basically walking in Monday and hopefully not discovering anything tragic. But I would like to know what the brothers are thinking.

"I'll send over the files as soon as they're ready. He's working on it right now. He's kind of burying himself in work. Well, I'll see you on Monday then." He gives me a nod and starts for the door. He's almost out when he turns and looks my way. "Your mother is wrong, of course."

"Always." But I have questions. "But what specifically are you talking about?"

"Your friends are your family," he says quietly. "Those women she thinks you're wasting your time on when you could be hanging with Cousin Susie or whatever, they're your sisters. They're the people you live your life with. They don't have to share some magical amount of DNA."

"I find that interesting coming from a man whose best friend is his brother."

His lips turn up in a rueful grin. "Well, part of it comes from trauma bonding. You survive some of the stuff we have and you kind of cling to the life raft that got you through. I just thought it was interesting that you're going through something similar to me and Reid. You have parents who didn't treat you as well as they should have."

"They weren't like your father. There wasn't neglect. Sometimes I wished they weren't all up in my business." At least my mom and dad had been there. Mostly.

And yet when I need advice now and I want some wisdom, I find myself on Lydia Marino's doorstep. When I need someone to tell me I can do it, Diane has become my go to since therapy taught her all the right words to say.

When I need some cash or a backhanded compliment, I go to CeCe.

"I know. Our parents damage us even when they don't mean to. It's inevitable, but you found a family, Harper. You're a good sister," he says. "I enjoyed spending time with your friends, but that's what I got out of it. You function like a family, and it's a beautiful thing to be with the people you pick. So when your mother complains you're not spending time with family, you are. With her behavior, she's chosen not to be a part of it." He sighs. "See you Monday."

He walks away and I'm left with the desire to ask him to stay, to explain it all to me better because he's right about one thing. He and Reid felt like they fit with us.

And my mother is choosing to not be a part of my life because she doesn't understand what it means to be me. I'd kind of like to talk to him about that, too. The last person I talked to about my parents was his brother, and for that moment, I felt like one person in the world truly understood. Naturally it was Reid and it was all a lie.

But I sit and get back to work because I have to deal with my blood family and this business they entrusted me with.

Reid Dorsey will have to wait.

Chapter Nine

Four days later I stand outside the gorgeous, high-tech building where Reid Dorsey lives and makes his plans to ruin the world and all of the beautiful things in it. And history. This is where the fucker plots and plans to shove all history aside in exchange for turning Banover Place into some kind of spa. I don't even understand half of what this man is expecting me to do to that poor multimillion-dollar work of art and history.

I only know I can't let him do it.

This is not what Anika signed him up for. I have to stop this crap before we start work on Monday.

"You're one of Mr. Dorsey's guests?" Naturally this isn't the kind of building where one simply buzzes in or waits until someone else does and slips inside. Nope. There's real security and everything. An older man in a crisp blue suit stands behind the security desk, bringing his glasses up and staring at the screen. He frowns. "I show them all checked in."

The words don't mean anything to me. If he's got Britta up there or is having a party with all his uber-rich friends, then they can get an earful, too. It will serve him right. "I'm a coworker of his. It's an emergency."

Yep. It's a design emergency because this project is about to fall apart.

The security guy raises a bushy brow as though proving to me that he knows what the Dorsey brothers do for a living. Well, for work at least. I think the billion-dollar trust fund fixes the whole living thing. "I'll call up. What was your name, dear? I'm sorry for all the trouble but we're worried about reporters. The press is coming around again."

"Yes, so I've heard." Even one of the New York rags picked up on Reid's epic love story. There have been days the last week or so that I wish I could go back to the bubble where I had no idea who this man is. Now I know and he's everywhere. He's invading my life, and it's only going to get worse because the man annoys me and we're not even working twelve-hour days together yet.

I hate the fact that at some point my phone heard me say his name enough that now my socials all offer me information about Reid Dorsey and his fabulous brother and his stunning fiancée/ex-fiancée, depending on who you ask.

I now know that he was voted one of New York's most eligible bachelors five times since he turned twenty-one. *People* magazine put him in their sexiest issue. I've read all kinds of rumors about why their popular show stopped filming, and they are mostly about how arrogant and controlling Reid Dorsey is.

He's about to find out I can't be controlled. Well, if I get past his security.

"Yes, I need to speak to Mr. Dorsey," the security guard says. "He has another guest. She says her name is Harper Ross and she works with him." He nods my way. "The housekeeper is going to ask him."

Of course there's a housekeeper. I'm sure she's imported from France or something and makes him croissants every day. Except there's no way that man eats carbs. None. I got my hands briefly on his abs and there was not a single pastry detected.

And honestly, that's a strike against him, too, because pastries are delicious, and it's men like Reid who make other guys feel bad about eating them. Men might be way easier to deal with if they weren't hungry all the time.

"He's such a nice man." The guard gestures around. "You know he designed the lobby and a couple of the common spaces. And he didn't charge at all. Just said we deserved updated spaces."

Sure. The wealthiest of the wealthy for his pro bono work, and he charged the rest. Asshole. I want to point this truth out to my new friend, but I simply nod and give him a "sure."

He puts the phone back to his ear. "Well, yes, thank you. I'll send her up. And if there's any of your delicious food left over that those boys can't finish, you know where to send it." He giggles like a schoolgirl. "Damn straight, Aggie. See you soon."

See, normally I would be deeply interested in this man's love life and his obvious flirtation with the Dorsey brothers' housekeeper. I live for that kind of thing. But all I can see right now is beautiful period-appropriate wallpaper and sconces being ripped out so Reid can turn half the ballroom into a stone wall complete with creeping ivy and night-blooming plants. Because that's how people live. They grow walls of plants in their mansions. Nothing bad could ever come from that.

The guard is still smiling when he directs me to the last of the bank of elevators. "It's a private elevator for the upper floors, so I will program it to take you straight to Mr. Dorsey's penthouse."

Excellent. Everything is state of the art. I tromp over to the elevator, well aware that I do not look like I belong here. I got Reid's plans about an hour ago, and I was on a job site. The plans came in late, of course. Likely because he knew damn well I would be angry. He knew how I would react and so he sent me the plans on the Friday before we start shooting. He's already put in purchase orders. He'll use that against me. So that's why I'm wearing jeans and steel-toed boots and look like I'm cosplaying a lumberjack. I watch a woman in a cocktail dress shake her head as I walk by.

The doors to the elevator open as if they know I'm there. Which apparently they do. This whole building is sleek and futuristic and devoid of any warmth and humanity. And the elevator walls are all mirrored, so some poor schmo has to come in and Windex the whole thing seven times a day. There's a keypad but it only goes to the three highest floors, and the highest one is lit up because this elevator is now my AI overlord. I'm having such a talk with Ivy. Her baby seems like a good idea. I mean what bad could happen by letting an artificial intelligence take over your dating life? Nothing. Not a thing. Except she thinks I'm a near perfect match with a man who wants to gut history. Also, I gendered the AI. What the hell?

Needless to say, I'm a whirling ball of rage by the time those doors slide open, and I find myself in the most elegant foyer ever. It's like I stepped into *Fifty Shades* and I'm asking for Mr. Grey to see me now.

Except I'm going to punch Mr. Grey in the balls, and we'll see who ends up getting a spanking.

"Ms. Harper," a woman who has to be Aggie says in a perfectly posh British accent. She's dressed in a sturdy pantsuit, an apron around her like she just walked out of the kitchen. "I've informed Mr. Dorsey of your change in plans." She looks me up and down. "You seem far…angrier than was described."

"Someone described me?"

"Oh, yes. Jeremiah is excellent at descriptions. He said you were lovely and had a pleasant energy. Where did that go?" Aggie asks with a frown. "Also, you are not up to dress code for this evening's event."

"Somehow I don't think she's here for this evening's event," a deep voice says. Reid steps out looking so deliciously masculine in a three-piece suit he's taken the jacket off of. It makes him look elegant and lean and predatory, and I wish this man didn't get my motor running.

I wish he didn't make me feel the way he does. If this was anyone else, I would sit down and have a long discussion. I wouldn't stand here feeling my adrenaline shoot sky high. "I'm here because the plans you sent me aren't happening."

A brow rises as he looks me over and then turns to Aggie. "Thank you, Aggie. I'll deal with her from here."

"Are you sure?" Aggie doesn't look sure. "She seems to be in a state."

"I'm not in a state. Unless the state is righteousness because that man is not going to turn my mansion into some cheapo massage parlor."

Now those blue-green eyes widen. "Excuse me. I think we should take this to my office."

I'm not going to be further drawn in. We can do this right here. Especially when I have examples of what I'm about to protest. Reid's foyer looks an awful lot like what he's proposed for the ballroom. Dark wood floors and a whole wall dominated by a waterfall feature and a bunch of plants that make me think I've walked into one of those James Bond sets. You know the ones where the over-the-top bad guy lives and interrogates Bond and the floor opens up to a shark tank below? I could buy that coming from him. "No. What I have to say won't take long. I need you to understand that you are not turning Banover Place into…" I gesture around. "Whatever this is."

"Oh, I think you called it a cheap massage parlor," he replies.

That might have been a tad over the line, but I can't exactly take it back now. "I thought we discussed the fact that this whole project is about restoring Banover Place to its former glory."

Reid's eyes narrow. "No, this project is about getting Anika and Luca enough money to get their projects off the ground."

"Yes, by restoring Banover Place to its former glory." He's forgetting a few important points.

"You know if we were going to do that, it should have been purchased by a historical society." He seems to think. "Wait. It was. They sold it to Anika's production company. So guess what—we get to do whatever we like with it."

"The only reason they sold it to us was we promised to keep everything as period appropriate as possible," I point out. "I sent you all of my historical research."

"First of all, there's nothing in the contract that says we have to decorate or renovate in any particular way. That doesn't exist, Harper, and you're naïve to think it does. The society we bought the house from wanted to get rid of it."

I shake my head. "No, they couldn't afford the taxes."

"They couldn't afford anything because for years it's been held up by tourist dollars, and they don't care anymore. I know this is some kind of magical place for you, and that's precisely why I told Anika we should consider another contractor. You're far too close to the project to be able to see things clearly. You're too emotional."

Oh, that is the last thing he should say to me. "Am I?"

"Yes," he says with a shrug.

"What should I do about that?"

"You should probably calm down and listen to reason."

A hiss comes from behind Reid as Jeremiah rounds the corner. "Damn, brother. You are supposed to know better than to tell a woman to calm down. She set a trap and you fell right into it. What is it with hetero men? Do you never think maybe you should sit down and figure out the female psyche? Do you enjoy getting your balls busted again and again. See, we do not have this problem. Harper, is there any way I could talk you into maybe castrating my brother in his office?"

The Dorsey men want to get me somewhere private. So I'm not going. "No. I'm not staying, and you can't talk me into seeing logic. I know women with our tiny brains can't possibly understand logic. Isn't that what you think, Reid?"

He huffs and his hands shoot to the air. "Sure. I'm a misogynist douchebag, and you are named properly because you're a harpy. Tell me something—how many men do you run off with that attitude? Is there some reason you're the last of your friends without a date?"

"Reid," Jeremiah says, obviously shocked.

Reid's head shakes. "No, if she's going to stereotype me with no real reason, I can do the same."

"Or you could be the bigger person and maybe figure out what's behind all of this?" Jeremiah offers.

"What's behind it is not wanting your brother to ruin a very important job by throwing up shitty shiplap everywhere or deciding that we join the farmhouse revolution."

Jeremiah put a hand to his chest, his eyes wide. "We never do farmhouse. Ever. We are not monsters."

Oh, I disagree. "But you happily take out a mural that's been in the ballroom for a hundred years to put up cheap plants and make someone feel like they're on the set of the revival of *Little Shop of Horrors*."

Reid's spine seems to stretch, and he feels impossibly tall as he snarls my way. "It is called biophilic design, you plebian. Do I need to get you a dictionary so you can figure out how I insulted you?"

I get right in his face. I have to go up on my toes, but I do it. "Oh, I know exactly what you think of me, you elitist asshole."

"I actually don't think it was an insult. The show reference, not the plebian thing. That was absolutely an insult, but I don't see why we're hating on *Little Shop*. I love that show," Jeremiah adds. "I do a great rendition of 'Suddenly Seymour.' My high school was progressive. I doubt in the current political climate that I would have been allowed to play Audrey, and that would be a shame. I was very good."

We're not paying attention to Jeremiah anymore.

"I assure you my designs are not some shoddy, off-Broadway play," Reid replies, his face taking on some pink as he points my way. "And I don't think I have to take this from a woman whose highest heights of taste is an apartment building that looks like it's probably built on cinder blocks. I wouldn't let you build a bodega much less an actual home someone is going to live in. Do you think I haven't seen the lawsuits you've dealt with?"

"Every builder deals with suits." My rage is reaching a pulse point. I can feel my blood pressure rising. How dare this man who has never actually run a business question me? "Would you like to mansplain the US legal system for me?"

"We could have a lawyer do that," Jeremiah offers. "I think there's one inside. Though the scary lady just called him Lawyer. Do you think that's his name?"

Reid never takes his eyes off me. "I wouldn't dare. As often as you've been sued, you should know it backward and forward. And yet you still don't understand the concept of taxes since your company was in arrears for years. I like that. We could make you a T-shirt."

I hate this man and yet I can't miss the fact that he seems to find this argument exciting. "If you designed it, it would be the most boring shirt in the history of time. Are you going to staple some greenery and stones on it so it can be biophallic?"

"It's biophilic," he corrects.

I give him a smirk of my own. "I was talking about your pants, Dorsey, since they seem to be tighter on you than they were before. Is that a swatch or are you happy to see me?"

His jaw tightens. "Well, I could say the same damn thing about your nipples, Harper. Because those headlights are on, baby, and they definitely seem happy to see me."

Damn, my overly sensitive nipples. It's the cold. Except I'm not feeling cold. I'm actually feeling weirdly alive for the first time in forever.

"I don't know whether to cry or start live streaming this," Jeremiah says under his breath.

Reid isn't through. "And if you think I'm going to spend the next several weeks of my life fighting you, you're wrong. I'm not listening to this. I do not need a contractor complaining constantly."

Oh, we're back to me being a harpy. "I'm just some nagging woman out to ruin your life, is that it, Reid? Is that what that night in Ralavia was about? You thought maybe since you couldn't get my friend to fire me, you could control the pathetic wallflower with sex?"

The smirk on his face is pure arrogance. "I thought maybe I would see if the room got warmer if you lost some of that ice, Princess."

"Oh, for fuck's sake," Jeremiah says under his breath as his head shakes. "We should have invited a therapist to dinner. Always. Anytime we have a party, there should be a therapist on call. I would have invited my friend but he's a vegan, and I really wanted some red meat."

"I'm an ice princess?" It's nothing I haven't heard before, but it hurts. And when I'm hurt I tend to…well, hurt right back.

He gets in my space, looking like a gorgeous, angry bull about to charge. "If the frost fits…"

"You are a lying cheater," I shoot back. He wants to do it this way, he'll find out I can throw it right back in his face.

His head shakes. "Oh, am I? Who exactly am I cheating on?"

"History for one, and that blonde idiot for another." I don't care what Jeremiah told me. He's looking out for his brother.

"First off, I can't cheat history. I simply choose not to worship a time when they didn't even have running toilets. I also think we're not talking about the same history. You don't care about Banover Place because it was once a smuggler's home or because some famous author once lived there. This is about you. You want to take this place back to some sad-sack moment in time when you and your friends thought you could take on the world or something. It's the sad dream of a pathetic teenager, and I'm not going to wreck this project so you can feel like you're seventeen again."

The words split something inside me. Is that really what I'm doing? Am I causing all this trouble because I'm desperate to hold on to some moment in the past when the world seemed softer and warmer than it does today? When life held promise?

Reid's expression falls and he runs a hand over his hair. "Harper, I'm sorry. I didn't mean that. You came at me with claws flying and I...I wasn't ready for a fight tonight."

"Harper, I would like to speak with you privately," a deep voice says, and I look up to see Luca St. Marten standing there looking especially regal in a button-down and perfectly pressed slacks. And he is pissed. His eyes are narrowed, and every muscle seems rigid with irritation.

I started this fight and I'm about to get fired.

Chapter Ten

"Luca, we were having a minor difference of opinion," Reid says, stepping back. "Nothing to be worried about."

"Oh, that was more than minor." The king of Ralavia, and more importantly my bestie's husband, shakes his head. "Is there a place we can go to talk?"

"Maybe you should talk to me first." For some reason Reid seems nervous about letting Luca talk to me.

"I can handle myself," I assure him even when my gut is in turmoil. Maybe it's for the best. Maybe a clean break is better. Not that we'll call it a break. We'll get busy in our lives, and time and distance will do their work on our friendship.

"I said some things I shouldn't have." Reid moves to my side. As though if I'm being called into the principal's office, he'll go along for the ride.

"Yes, we've had a lot of that tonight," Jeremiah agrees. He looks to Luca. "Your Majesty, they have serious problems with sexual tension. I know. It's weird because grumpy and even grumpier shouldn't, like, go together, but here we are."

Reid frowns at his brother. "You do not have to help."

Jeremiah's voice goes low. "Well, if I didn't, she might have taken your balls, brother."

Luca's gaze goes between me and Reid, and then his lips curl up the slightest bit and he loses some of his obvious irritation. "Which one is grumpier?"

Jeremiah takes a long breath as though realizing the danger passed. "I think it depends on the day. They pass the crown between the two of them."

"We are not attract…" I begin.

"Really?" Reid shrugs. "I mean we can at least be honest about that part. I find you very attractive."

And he has a fiancée. Such a lucky woman. "And I find you annoying."

"Yes, your office will do." Luca's back to being irritated, and now it's all turned my way because I don't have a charming wingman who softens me. Nope. I'm alone and I'm going to be more alone soon when I don't even have this project to work on.

Reid nods and steps into the hallway. "Fine, but you should understand she's not the only one who said things she shouldn't. It was mutual. Mutual… I don't know… Should we call it hate? That seems a bit dramatic."

"Hate works for me." I can't stop. Now that I'm walking into my worst nightmare, there's a part of me that wants to get it over with. I've been moving toward this ever since Ivy came back and found her guy. I knew Anika would find her Prince Charming, but I guess I always thought Ivy and I would end up as bog crones somewhere cursing men who wander into our territory.

Now I'll have to do it alone, and that sucks.

I should have done what I was taught to do—put all of my complaints in a well-worded email. But no, I had to rush right over, and I totally forgot I'd actually been invited to this party. I hadn't even thought about the fact that Ani would be here.

She'd even texted me yesterday to let me know she and Luca were in town and would see me on Saturday since I was skipping this party.

Did I rush over here because subconsciously I want her to pick me? To prove to me that I'm more important than some country she's trying to pull out of tragedy?

I suck.

Luca closes the door to Reid's sleek office, shutting the Dorsey brothers out of their own space. He does it without a blink and then walks to the big floor-to-ceiling windows like he owns the place.

It's good to be king.

"Has he done something he shouldn't?" Luca asks.

He takes me off guard. But the answer is obviously yes. "He wants to take out a wall, Luca. A whole wall. Not take it out, exactly, but take this beautifully crafted architecture and turn it into a houseplant."

"Harper, has he harassed you?" Luca carefully enunciates each word as though he needs to ensure he's got the English right. His first language is German, though he speaks with only a hint of an accent.

I stare for a moment, the lights of the city illuminating this man my best friend married. I thought he was going to fire me. He's worried about me? This is the perfect opportunity to take out my enemy. I can't help it. There's a ruthless asshole inside me. I think about it for half a second and then do what I always do, what I hope I will always do, shove the asshole down and do what's right. "No. He's hit on me, but I'm going to admit that was a mutual thing."

A long sigh of relief goes through Luca. "Thank you. I was worried. I've never heard him talk to a woman that way. I brought him on this project because he's always been so easy to work with."

I hadn't. "Well, rest assured he hasn't done anything I would call harassment. I kind of came on strong tonight. He was giving me back what I put out. But I stand by my criticism. He is going to ruin the history of the house and turn it into some bland, resort-looking thing."

"He's going to turn it into a property someone has already paid eighty-two million dollars for," Luca admits.

I feel my jaw drop. "What? I thought it wasn't going on the market until the show was done. It's kind of the point of the show. We're supposed to rehab the place and then hope we can sell it."

"And if I've learned anything in my time working in reality television, it is that reality is a word we play with," Luca admits. "Banover Place has already been sold. At least in theory, though Anika trusts the buyer. This is the show that will hopefully fund the rest of our company. We're new. We don't have the capital to buy the building, pay for everything, and hope we can get the price we need. So this is how we're working."

My gut sinks. "And Reid is working with the buyer, isn't he?"

Luca nods. "Not on everything. Just on the basics of design. We want it to be a surprise. The buyer won't be visiting, but they will be making decisions on certain aspects of the design."

"Then I'm not needed, am I? I was supposed to come in because preservation is my specialty." I'm not sure why I'm here if they're going to gut the place and turn it into…well, this. The apartment I'm standing in is gorgeous by modern standards, but there's such beauty in the past, too. Do we have to change everything?

"Harper, do you have to have everything your way in order to work on this project?" Luca asks the question with a surprising lack of judgment. "This is likely my fault. I told Anika I wanted to film your real reactions and negotiations. Perhaps we should have brought you in on the entire process."

But that isn't how a contractor works. The truth is I'm here to work with the designers. I'm not supposed to argue whether the design is good, only to tell them if it can work and how much time and money it will take to see the thing through. I feel guilty because I'm turning this into something it's not about. Me. "I'm sorry. Banover Place is special to me, and I might be doing exactly what Reid accused me of. I'm trying to control something that isn't mine to control. If this was any other job, I would simply tell you whether I can make it happen. I certainly don't argue with the dude who owns the big box store about where to put his aisles."

"It's special to Anika, too," Luca replies softly. "This isn't some retail store. We're talking about a home. We're talking about history. Do you think it's not important to me? I fell in love with Anika in that house. I want it to shine. But I have to balance what I want with what the person paying us millions wants as well. We believe after all is said and done and we sell the house and the show, we could bring in over a hundred million. Do you know how many homes can be fixed in my country for that money? We can attract some contractors and get real work done. We're a small country. We don't have the professionals needed to deal with the overwhelming destruction we suffered. We still have people living in tents."

Tears well. Yep. I suck. "I think it might be best if you got someone else."

"And break my wife's heart?" He's right back to looking like a king. "Do you think she doesn't feel the distance? She's living in a foreign country, away from the women she views as sisters. She's been looking forward to this for a long time. She's worried you'll drift apart, and working on this with you is one of her ways of keeping the connection."

"But I don't know that working with Reid is going to be a good thing for the project in the long run, and I am starting to suspect whoever bought the place wants him on board."

He gives me a curt nod before leaning forward, placing his hands on the desk and staring at me like I suspect he would stare at one of the members of his cabinet who upset him. "Reid isn't going anywhere. He's doing the job we need him to do."

"Then I understand."

"No, you don't. You're not going anywhere either. Do you remember that contract I had you sign? The one you were so sure you didn't need to read? Because you thought Anika had control. She did not. I did."

Oh, I'm not sure I like this side of Luca. Except I kind of do. He's always a gentleman. Like I've watched the man pick Ani up so her feet don't get wet when it rains. I kind of thought he was a little soft. I worried he wouldn't protect her if he had to choose between his office and his wife. I'm starting to understand the man won't allow anything or anyone to harm Ani.

Even the woman she sees as a sister.

"What's in my contract, Your Majesty?"

"A clause. It's the fine print. I knew Ani wouldn't read it either. She was only concerned about you getting a good salary and promised screen time," Luca admits. "I believe she would tell me contracts are boring. They don't even have murders in them, so she won't read them. In this case my wife's need for interesting reading means she missed the part where you have to buy your way out of the contract."

My jaw nearly hits the floor. "What?"

"Yes, we've already bought the supplies you requested. You filled out all the forms for tools and equipment you'll need, and we even designed a room for you when you're not filming. I kept all the receipts. Would you like to know how much?"

Oh, I know. Thousands and thousands. He's an evil shit. I kind of like him. He's forgotten one thing though. "I can just go to Anika."

"Ah, you could," he allows. "But honestly, the contract is there so you can have a decent excuse for staying. I rather thought you and Reid would spark off each other. I worried when we began that you would have some dramatic chemistry. Good for a dating show. Perhaps not so good for a show about home renovations."

He's making my point. "Which is why you should let Reid bring in his own contractor."

"Reid's contractor isn't my wife's best friend," Luca argues. "You were right about one thing. This isn't merely about you, Harper. Are you willing to let this chance go? I'm not talking about working on Banover Place. I'm talking about working with your friend. When she got stuck in Banover Place while filming our show and production wouldn't allow anyone in to see her, what did you do?"

He knows exactly what I did. "I lied my way into a job that gave me access to Banover Place and therefore to Anika. I made sure she was okay and was there when it all went to hell."

When Luca cut Ani from the show and sent her away. At the time we didn't know he was doing it for the right reasons. Ani thought he dumped her.

"Yes, and I was happy you were there," Luca admits. "So is the woman who did all of that for her friend going to walk away from helping her through her first big production because her feelings are hurt? Because she doesn't like how a coworker makes her feel? If you truly don't want to work on this project because you don't like the direction it's going in, I'll release you. I don't want you miserable. But if you're leaving so you don't have to deal with Reid, I'm going to ask you to reconsider."

I'm back to not liking this side of the man. But he's right about a couple of things. I'm letting Reid Dorsey run me off a project I'm passionate about. I understand the financial implications of the job, and I can handle compromising on some of it. "The foyer is the most Gilded Age specific room in the house along with the front sitting area."

A brow rises over his aristocratic eyes. "Are we negotiating?"

"Yes."

His lips curl up in a smile. "There's the woman my wife loves. The one I admire. Fine, then. Let's negotiate. I think I can convince the buyer to allow you to keep many aspects of the original home. I want a list of your recommendations. But you should know Reid will likely fight you on it."

I want to say the idea disgusts me, but the truth of the matter is fighting with Reid actually sounds like fun. In an "I hate him and want to best his arrogant ass" way. Not in a "this is going to lead to righteously nasty, shameful and invigorating sex" way. Because it's not. "Bring it on."

"As long as you don't bring Anika into the middle," Luca advises. "I need you to understand I want her to enjoy this. To do her job, but I don't want her in the middle of some war between the two of you."

"It won't only be the two of us, will it? He's got a brother. I assure you Jeremiah will stand with him."

"Did you not hear? We have a new executive producer. Ivy decided she doesn't enjoy being left out." Luca gestures to the door. "She and Heath are enjoying an excellent roast right now. You are only hurting yourself with this isolation. I'm asking you not to push your family away because Reid Dorsey hurt your feelings."

I went through this with my mother days ago and yet Luca's request hits so much more softly. Jeremiah's words have haunted me for days. This is my family. Ivy and Ani and now Heath and Luca. They support and love me. I do owe these people. "All right. I won't let Reid take anything else from me. He did kind of take my dignity, but I can get that back."

Luca chuckles. "If it helps in any way, he's not engaged to Britta anymore. It was a mistake he made when he was young, and he's had trouble correcting it. I sometimes worry that woman is holding something over his head."

I ignore that part. The other thing he said is much more important. Ivy is here? "So you're telling me I can drag Ivy into what will likely be my multitudinous battles with Reid? And it doesn't matter. I'm not getting involved with him, but it is good to know he wasn't cheating, and I will apologize for the remark."

"Drag Ivy in as much as you like. She'll enjoy the fight. Simply keep Ani out of it. She'll be torn, and she has other things to worry about. This project is everything to her," Luca says softly.

"I'll talk to him," I promise. "We'll find a way to make this work. And honestly, even a show about renovations can use some drama. At least I think it can."

Before he can answer there's a knock on the door and then Anika is walking in, followed by Ivy. My besties are dressed in cocktail gowns, looking all gorgeous and glowy.

"I heard you were here." Anika's expression goes tight as she looks from me to Luca. "Is everything okay?"

This is why Luca brought me in here. She's already nervous, already anxious about the project. She's gone through so much change in a short time. I'm not going to make this harder for her. She could easily have found someone with more experience. If my friend wants me here, I'm going to do the best job I can. I'm going to enjoy being here for her first big project.

Isn't this what we asked for when we sat in Banover Place? To be together while we built something for ourselves? I'm not sure I'm really building anything, but I can get into togetherness.

Damn. I am not going to cry. I notice Reid and Jeremiah hovering outside the door. Reid stares in like he's surprised I'm still here.

"No problem at all. I came by because I realized I didn't have to work as late as I thought." There's no time like the present to start this war of ours. "Reid protested my clothing."

He snorts and then sighs as though he knows this is inevitable. "Sure. Well, Harper, the invitation clearly stated no steel-toed boots."

I give my besties a shrug. "I came straight from a site. I had to go out to Jersey and check on the new build because I'm pretty sure my cousin is trying to see if sabotage can help his case. I thought I would miss…" I have no idea what is being served for dinner except what I picked up from Luca. I have no idea what kind of roast they're enjoying. "…all the meat. You know how much I love meat. So I didn't stop to change, and I offended Reid with my impoverished state of dress. His words, not mine."

Reid groans. "Yes, I called you impoverished. I now know that I must accept all forms of dress so I'm not an elitist douchebag. Can we have dinner now?"

"You *can* be fussy about clothes," Jeremiah begins.

His brother sends him a look that has him backing down.

"We're sure everything's okay?" Anika looks from me to Luca like she senses something went down.

I give her my brightest smile and walk right up to Reid, threading my arm through his. Like we don't hate each other. Like we can totally get along and not dream at night of killing the other. Like those dreams don't include other things that I will never admit, maybe even to myself. "We're good. We have some differing opinions, but that's the nature of collaboration." I look up at Reid, who hasn't tried to move away from me. His arm tightens around mine. "Thanks for the invite, coworker."

"You're welcome," he says as everyone starts to move out of the office, "pain in my ass."

I let him lead me out.

The name fits, so I don't argue with him. I'm about to be a massive pain in his ass, and I feel pretty good about it.

Chapter Eleven

"Do you want a drink?" Reid asks as he returns from closing the door behind Ivy and Heath. Anika and Luca left an hour before since they were still dealing with jet lag, but Ivy stuck around as though she wanted to watch over me. Or was waiting for the façade of politeness to crack and the real fight to begin.

She finally gave up and I agreed with Reid earlier in the evening that we should talk when everyone left, so here I am in his Upper East Side palace of an apartment at midnight and I'm oddly anxious about the potential of being alone with him since I heard Jeremiah say something about going out.

Anxious in a weird, almost anticipatory way.

"Sure. I'll take a little of whatever you're having." I'd been surprised at the lack of wine at dinner. I suspected he was like a lot of Manhattan hosts, completely free with the booze and light on the actual food. Instead, we'd gotten some excellent tea and a truly lovely roast and potatoes and green beans almondine, complete with a delicious cheesecake I was assured is an Aggie special.

"I'm going to run Aggie home and stop by Harry's." Jeremiah stands in the foyer, wrapping a scarf around his neck. He put on a jacket and is helping Aggie into her light coat.

"I told him I can take the subway," Aggie protests.

"Absolutely not," Reid insists. He moves toward the older woman. "Since you're too stubborn to take one of the bedrooms here, you must allow Jer to take you home. You're precious cargo. Thank you for everything this evening."

I was surprised at how tender he was with the older woman. He checked on her several times this evening and helped her bring out the food, asking her to sit and eat with us when everything was served. I'd expected a host of servers, but it had been just us and Aggie.

She turns her head slightly, welcoming a light kiss on the cheek. "Well, it was fun to meet royalty. They were far more normal than I expected. Far kinder and more personable than many of your clients. You behave yourself, Reid Dorsey."

Jeremiah frowns and glances back at me. "Yes, behave. I'm not sure I should leave the two of you alone."

Aggie pats his shoulder. "They'll be fine. Ms. Ross, it was lovely to meet you. He doesn't mean half of what he says, but when he's backed into a corner, he's not sure how to get out."

"I'm not in a corner," Reid grumbles.

I smile Aggie's way. "It was nice to meet you. Dinner was excellent. Really, the best I've had in a long time."

I missed a couple of Sunday dinners at Lydia's because I was working, so I've been subsisting on ramen and takeout. Between preparing for the Banover Place job, fighting with my cousin over all things construction, and catching back up after the wedding, I haven't spent much time doing anything but working, and I think that might have made me a wee bit cranky.

"Just remember what's at stake," Jeremiah says cryptically as the elevator doors open.

"You do the same, brother," Reid replies as Jeremiah leads Aggie onto the elevator and we're left alone. He turns my way. "Seriously? I shamed you for your boots? You couldn't come up with anything else?"

I knew he wanted to call me out for that all night. It was kind of fun to pick at him.

"Probably, but why bother when it was right there?" I ask. I'm surprisingly chipper after the talk with Luca, and honestly, the food worked wonders for me. "What were those things? The delicious things that were like bread but also not?"

Reid sighs and crosses over to the bar, pulling out two rocks glasses. "Are you talking about the Yorkshire pudding? It's a common

English comfort food. Luckily for us, Luca spent a lot of time in the UK, so he enjoys English food. Aggie is a very proper Brit."

"She seems nice." I watch as he puts in a code to open the liquor cabinet. Odd. I guess he's got the good stuff under lock and key so the servants don't take a nip.

He pulls out what looks like old Scotch and pours a couple of fingers into each glass. "She is. She's a lovely woman. She was our nanny's sister. She came over to the States when Marilyn got sick and my father kicked her out. At the time Jer and I were at boarding school. We came home that summer to find my father had installed a new bang maid, and we were told we didn't need a mother figure anymore. I had to enroll us both for fall semester and go to his accountant for the tuition."

I hate when I feel for him. And I feel for him all the time. I take the glass when he passes it to me. "How old were you?"

"Seventeen," he replies, taking a sip. "Younger than this Scotch."

"And what did you do?" Somehow I don't think he simply allowed it to pass.

"I found her. My father fired her without severance. He tossed her out like she never meant a thing, which I suppose she didn't to him." Reid walks over to the windows that offer a spectacular view of Central Park. It's dark now, illuminated by the moon and stars and the buildings around it. Reid stands in shadows as he speaks, his eyes on the park below. "The worst part was I contacted her often. We had a standing phone call. Once a week. The week before I was coming home, she confessed what happened. She only told me because she knew I was about to find out. Even when she was making not a dime from my family, she treated me like a son. I used the trust fund my grandfather left me to make her comfortable. She was in a filthy nursing home in hospice care because the cancer was too far gone. Sometimes I wish I'd been the one to take my father out, not some random heart attack."

I have to check the instinct to move into his space and offer him comfort. The funny thing is I'm not naturally affectionate. That's Ani's job. She's the most open and loving of us. Ivy and I can be standoffish, but I'm struggling with him. "I'm sorry but I'm glad she had you. I'm glad you had a trust fund you could help her with. At least you used your money for some good. I get requests for company cash all the time, but it's about buying a new car or funding my cousin's sorority life."

He turns, frowning my way. "Company cash? Are you telling me your father wrote checks from the company to pay for personal business?"

I nod, glad at least someone understands the implications. "Yep. My father and uncle treated the business like their personal banking system and taught the family to do the same, and let me tell you, there are tax implications."

"Damn straight there are." He moves back toward me, sinking down onto the sleek modern couch that dominates the room. "Are you seriously telling me your father used company funds to buy things for family members?"

"Oh yes." It's good to know I can shock him. "You should understand that my father's accountant at the time was one of his second cousins. I believe he called it dividends."

"That's not how it works," Reid says with a shake of his head. "A licensed accountant would know that."

"I think they just call Carl an accountant," I admit. "He didn't go to school or anything. You would not believe the uproar when I fired him and hired an actual accountant. You would have thought I burned the whole place down."

"I suspect that's when you had to deal with the aforementioned implications."

"Oh, yes." I sit across from him, one big cushion between us. The light is low and it feels far too intimate, but I'm sure that's only me. Or it's how he wants it because he's right back in control-the-rogue-girl mode. "I had to deal with the IRS. Naturally they didn't audit the company until a year after my father passed. I had barely gotten my feet wet, and I had to deal with nearly losing everything. And my mother told me it was all my fault. I remember it vividly. She cried that they were going to take her house and all because I didn't let Carl work his magic. His magic was to be incompetent at best, illegal at worst. But I got through it. Now I'm the mean lady who won't pay their bills. It's not easy being the villain in the family."

"Don't I know it," he says with a sigh. "Your company is still family held? You didn't open it up to investors? I would think that would be a way to get out of having to foot the tax bill on your own."

"Don't think I didn't float that idea around. I thought we should sell thirty percent of our shares to an outside investor. It would have given us an influx of cash and perhaps inroads to new business. That was the first time they threatened to put Paul in my seat. He turned them down because he knew what I was facing."

"He knew he could potentially be in trouble," Reid replies with a shake of his patrician head. "He knew that whoever was in the CEO seat had a hard road ahead. So how did you manage it?"

"I sold some assets and some of my stock," I admit.

"You took care of it personally, didn't you?"

I shake my head. "Not all of it, of course, but some of it. My father left me a couple of properties. I had to sell them."

"And what did the rest of the family pony up?"

I huff, a cynical sound. "Not a dime. They didn't see the purpose. I was told I should fight the IRS. Like that wouldn't have cost even more money, and we would be accruing interest the whole time."

"Sounds like a pain in the ass. It makes me happy we never went past an LLC," he says, clearing his throat. "It seems like you have your hands full. How much stock did you have to give up? And I assume you had to sell it to a family member. So let me see if I understand. They bought your stock knowing you would have to use the money to get the company—that they also own—out of trouble? That sounds like family to me. I didn't realize the Upper East Side rules were in play in Hell's Kitchen."

"Your father wasn't the only ruthless bastard out there," I reply. "Sometimes I think it would be a relief to let the whole thing go. Right now I still have the majority behind me, but my cousin is working on the rest of them," I admit. "I wasn't lying about why I was in Jersey this afternoon. I can't prove it, but I think Paul is sabotaging some of our jobs to make me look bad."

"What's the worst that can happen?"

"I lose control of the company and it goes under in three years," I reply. "My family depends on the company. Most of them are employed by the company, and even those who aren't depend on the cash that comes from actual legal dividends. Losing the company would devastate my family."

"That would not be your fault." Reid studies me for a moment. "And the real question is would it devastate you?"

He's wrong about the fault because my father told me everything was my fault. If only he'd had a son… I shove the remembrance aside. I don't need to have a therapy session with this man. Though it does seem he understands what it means to have a complex relationship with family. "I assure you everyone would blame me in the end. They always do. And the other part doesn't matter. Now let's stop procrastinating. How are we going to do this thing without making Anika's life miserable?"

I need to think of the part of my family that actually brings me joy—the one I picked. I owe Anika.

"It's simple," he replies. "We try to communicate like adults. We don't maybe go straight to calling the other person a cheater."

I wince. I was wrong about a lot of things today. "Sorry. I guess I misinterpreted the situation that night, but you can't blame me."

A brow rises. "I don't see why not."

"Because you were engaged to her," I point out. There are reasons I made that call, and a whole lot of it was about the choices Reid made. "Because the press all seems to think you're on again. Because you dropped me like a hot potato the minute you had a hint that she wanted to see you. It's okay. I get it. She's a supermodel."

His eyes roll. "She's a mistake I made when I was at a low point in my life, and I'm still paying for it. I didn't ask you to leave because I wanted to see her. She wasn't supposed to be invited. I specifically asked the palace if she was. If I'd known she would show up, I would have sent my regrets."

Somehow I can't see this man missing the social event of a lifetime. "She came as someone's plus one, from what I understand. And only to the reception. I think I would have noticed her."

"She knew I would leave if she showed up at the ceremony. The reception wasn't as formal, and she could slip in without immediately warning me of her presence. I'm lucky Jeremiah saw her or she would have caught me off guard. As it was, she still fucked everything up. I didn't want to put you in the line of her fire. I told you I wanted to come back to your room after I dealt with her."

"I would have been waiting a long time since you went to breakfast with her the next morning." I said no. She said yes. It was as simple as that.

He stares for a moment and then sits back and huffs. "If I told you I didn't spend the night with her, would you believe me?"

"No." Why would I? I can't imagine anyone saying no to that woman.

"Then I suppose you won't believe me when I tell you that she comes back into my life when she feels the need to get some tabloid attention and I…" He sits back. "Well, we both have family obligations and responsibilities, and it's good to remember that. It doesn't matter. What does matter is finding a way to work together because I have no intention of pissing off Luca St. Marten. So you've told me why it matters so much to you."

"And you used it against me." I tip my glass his way in honor of his villainy. It had been a good play. Threw me right off my game.

He has the grace to flush. "Yeah, that wasn't well done of me but you…you know how to push my every button. I know it will come as a shock to you, but I'm actually known for being something of a gentleman."

"I thought you were known for being difficult to work with." I can throw things back at him, too.

His lips curl up in a smirk that holds not an ounce of humor. "I suppose so. Maybe you bring out the real me. The rat bastard selfish asshole."

I'm screwing this up because talking about Britta unsettles me. The truth is I don't know what to believe since I don't think Luca would lie to me. He told me they weren't together and hadn't been. There's a lot I don't understand, and I shouldn't. And yet I was there. I saw how fast he got rid of me. I saw the pictures of them having breakfast. So I'm antsy and I shouldn't be because it doesn't matter if he has a girlfriend. What does matter is finding a way to work with him. For Anika's sake. For Banover Place. "I'm sorry. Luca told me about the sale, and I'm afraid it bothers me that I didn't know. I thought I had a shot at talking you into sparing the place."

Like I'm going to tell him the real reason. *Hey, you kind of broke my heart and the fact that I still want you to kiss me makes me wonder who the hell I am.* But also history.

"Sparing it." He sighs like I'm the worst. And I probably am in his head. "Spare it from what, Harper? From joining the modern age? Look, I am sorry I said those things to you earlier. I didn't truly mean them. You made me feel small, and I did the same to you. I do understand what Banover means to you, but we don't get to choose."

"You mean I don't get to choose." I can't help the bitterness in my tone. "Whoever is laying out the cash definitely gets to choose. I'm sure you get to choose all the time." I'm the one who's stuck in a corner, not Reid. I'm the one with no way to fight my way out.

"Far less than you would think," he replies. "Is there anything I can say that will make this easier on you? I've been tasked with turning

Banover Place into a home where someone who is alive in this century can reside. I was given specific, if odd, instructions, and they change every day."

"Can I meet with the buyer? Maybe I can explain why it would be best to keep the place as original as possible."

"She's in Europe. I think the owner is a she," he confesses. "I don't know. We communicate through email. I sent her my presentation and she rejected it. Three times. I think we should be ready for her to decide she doesn't need a ballroom."

I sit up. "She wants to what? Get rid of the ballroom? Turn it into a mancave or maybe a bowling alley?"

"She wants to live at Banover Place with her family," Reid points out. "That means turning it into a functional space. I know you think it's sacred, but it was only sacred to the people who lived there. Now it will be sacred to someone else, and that almost always means change. I'm sorry. Luca told me we should discuss what parts of the house you think we should try to preserve."

That's an easy answer. "All of it. If she doesn't want a Gilded Age mansion, I could show her fifty contemporary brownstones that would suit her."

He huffs, a deeply frustrated sound. "Harper, that's what I'm trying so desperately to tell you. No one wants to live in a Gilded Age mansion today. They don't need servant's quarters and parlors. No one throws balls anymore. It needs to be functional. Have you thought about working on historical homes? I know some people who would love to consult with a woman of your skills. There are places right here in the city that are museums, and they need restoration. I can even likely find someone to fund it."

It's a nice offer and one that I'll think about for a long time, but it's a pipe dream. I build grocery stores and parking garages. "I have a job. I'm risking it by taking this much time off. The truth is this is a moment in time for me. I'll never get the chance to do something like this again, and the idea that it's turned into tearing down everything beautiful about the home makes me sad."

He's still, as though trying to decide if he wants to continue. "Do you really think it's ugly? My designs? I'm genuinely asking. I have a thick skin. I'd like your opinion. If this was any other home, what would you think?"

I sit for a moment, formulating a response because this is an important moment. He's been honest with me. He's working for someone. I've made him out to be the all-powerful wizard, but there's someone tugging on his strings, too. I sigh and decide to be utterly honest with the man. "I think the designs are beautiful. The funny thing is that whole bringing nature inside is something Ivy and I have talked about forever. When we discussed building our dream homes, she wanted a courtyard. I think it's mostly because she wanted to be outside in a place where she didn't have to deal with people. Anyway, that's what the sketch reminded me of. But not in a ballroom. I don't want to know what the owner is going to eventually do with it, do I?"

"I'm not sure they know yet," Reid replies, taking another sip. "And the great news is we have to pretend like it's all my idea on camera. Like we're coming up with it organically. I'm sure the last episode will be a bunch of people walking through the mansion like they're thinking about buying it. And I'll have to be there to show them through even though it's already purchased."

"It's such a weird business." I'd been surprised at how they filmed *The King Takes a Bride*, the reality show that brought Luca and Ani together. If he hadn't snuck into her room at night, they wouldn't have had much time alone. But the man knew what he wanted. "I still don't understand half of it. Some of the selection ceremonies took eight hours to film. And the dates were weird, too. It would look like they were alone, having a normal date, and yet they would stop every couple of minutes and adjust the lights. I have no idea how people fall in love like that."

"I don't think they normally do. I don't actually watch those shows. My brother loves them, but I can't see the appeal. I don't believe many of the couples survive, though I think Ani and Luca are solid. Likely for the very reason you said. But it's often that way with shows like this. Did you know on those house hunter shows the buyer has almost always already selected the home they want and they build the episode around it? It's something like that. Television is too delicate an industry for the instability of actual reality."

I suppose it's about knowing the outcome and building toward it. It still feels wrong to me. "Was it like that on your show?"

"A bit," he admits. "Though most of our renovations were subsidized. There was a lot of work we didn't show."

I'm not sure I understand. "Like what? What do you mean by subsidized?"

He sets his Scotch down. "There were times in the second season when we worked in some rougher neighborhoods for people who couldn't afford the basic stuff. Like the house we redid in Pittsburg for the firefighter and his family. We got in and realized he had a slab leak that was going to eat up his reno budget. So we handled that part for him along with replacing his HVAC. But those are not sexy things, so they don't show up on air. Now if the client had the money to add to the budget, they certainly would have enjoyed filming the messy and complicated conversation that always happens when you tell a homeowner their house is sinking. It's a lot of drama. However, in that case it would have ended the reno entirely, so they left it out."

"But those repairs are necessary." Again, I'm seeing a man I like. Unfortunately, he shares a body and soul with one I don't like. "It's wonderful that you did that."

"These shows run on the idea that anyone can do it. We had forty thousand for that reno. We're selling the illusion that for forty K, you can transform your home. In some ways you can. Especially if you have the know-how and can do it yourself. There are ways to find what you need for far less than most have to spend. In others it's pure fantasy. Most people don't know how to install their own plumbing."

I stare at him for a moment. "Are you trying to tell me you know how to install plumbing?"

His lips curl up in the sexiest grin. "Absolutely not. That's why we have a contractor. My job is to design as beautiful a space as I can." He takes a long breath. "So I know why you do what you do and why Banover Place is important to you. Would you like to know my reasons?"

I try to think of something pithy to say, but the truth of the matter is I do want to know. "Hit me."

"I got into design because I've always cared about the space around me. Even at a young age. I thought about things like curtains and carpet versus tile or hardwood. My grandmother was the only person in my family I was close to. She had the loveliest apartment on the west side. I felt comfortable there in a way I didn't in this one. My mother had it done in all white at one point. When she left, my father didn't care to change things, and none of his women lasted long enough to redo the place, so Jeremiah and I grew up worried constantly we would ruin the expensive pieces that made up our home. It was more like a museum."

"That's funny. I kind of thought this place looked like a museum."

His brow arches again, and I'm coming to understand this is his *I'm offended* face. "It certainly does not. I admit to having a high level of aesthetic, but everything is comfortable. Everything in this place was selected with comfort and durability in mind. When designing for myself I tend to go with what makes me feel good. I would never put tile or hardwood in my own bedroom because I like the feel of plush carpet under my feet when I wake up in the morning. I like to sit for a moment and wriggle my toes in it. I like this couch because when I fall asleep on it, my legs don't hang off. I like knowing my brother and I took this place and made it ours after years and years of feeling like we didn't belong here."

"It is comfy." I don't like how the idea of Reid working late and falling asleep on the couch makes me warm. I don't like how soft I get when I think about Reid as a child trying so desperately to not make a mess. Kids should be allowed to be messy. "And I love the dining room. The table has a mid-century feel."

"Because my grandmother bought it in 1956," he admits. "She died fifteen years ago. This was before our father passed away, and Jeremiah was living with her since dear old dad made it clear we were on our own after we turned eighteen. Luckily, we both had trust funds, and I used part of mine to go to Parson's. Jer moved in with Grandma halfway through his last year of high school, and he lived in that apartment for several years after she died. Then we inherited this place, and it made more sense for us both to live here than it did to sell it or buy the other out, and when we moved, Jer brought the table with him. Says it makes him feel likes she's still there, still sitting beside him telling him he needs to eat more."

I sit up because if I don't get out of here soon, I'm going to repeat the mistakes of Ralavia. I toss back the rest of my drink and stand. "Okay, we will be civil and make this work. I promise not to get in your way. I'll cry silently at the atrocities I'll be forced to commit in the name of design."

He stands as well, setting his glass down on the table. I'm surprised he doesn't have coasters. I would have thought he was a coaster man, but now that I've heard his story, I guess he's not as uptight as he seems. "And I will ignore your silent crying like the asshole I'm known to be." He sighs. "I don't suppose we should talk about the whole wild-chemistry thing we have going."

"Absolutely not." If there's one thing I want to avoid, it's making a fool of myself over this man, and opening the door even a crack will lead to destruction. "We are going to utterly ignore it. It's a flash fire, and the only thing it could lead to is both of us getting burned."

"Or if we found a way to tame it, it might keep us warm for a long time," he says quietly, and then seems to shake off some unnamed feeling. He holds out a hand. "But you're right. Ignoring it is the best path forward. So we have a deal?"

I nod and reach for his hand. "We do. For Ani's sake."

I try not to think about the wave of warmth I feel the minute my skin touches his.

Chapter Twelve

I stare at the camera and wonder how the hell Anika did this.

It's only a camera. I tell myself that. I've done some establishing shots, but those were mostly of me walking into the place and setting up for the demo we're doing this afternoon. I wasn't forced to talk, and suddenly talking seems to be a hard thing to do.

"Harper, you're supposed to look relaxed and ready to get started." Patrick Dennings stares at me like he can force me to do his will. He's the head of production and the man knows his stuff, but I don't think he's had to deal with someone like me in a long time. He's worked mostly on reality dating shows and some competition shows where everyone is comfortable with the camera because they're mostly looking to get into the industry.

I am not.

I'm used to walking into work and getting to the job at hand. Instead I spent an hour in a makeup chair because apparently my complexion is ghost-like, and it's not that kind of show. I'm not sure why the lead contractor needs glued-on eyelashes that I swear I can see whenever I blink, but I have them. There was also a lot of talk about flyaways. I have those too. Or I had them until someone superglued my hair.

"I am relaxed." Not true, but I'm pretty much as relaxed as I'm going to get.

"Girl, you look like someone is about to throw you into *Squid Games*, not hand you a multimillion-dollar mansion to play in." Patrick has his clipboard in hand and shakes his head the director's way. "Maybe we should do this as an exterior shot. The fresh air might wake her up."

"She's fine," Anika assures them. "It's the first day of shooting. You know how hard it is to get into a groove. I nearly faceplanted my first day."

She had, and worse, it was a live shot. Her near miss with the concrete was broadcast to anyone with an Internet connection. I suppose I'm lucky they're not doing that here.

"Harper will be awesome." Jeremiah strides in, setting down a leather portfolio on the chair with his name on the back. "She needs time to adjust. We can start with me if you like. I'm ready to go. Or I can do the shot with her."

"It's her establishing shot," the director says from behind the camera. "All she has to do is tell us a bit about herself, but when we try she locks down and goes monotone."

"Which is why we should make this conversational," Jeremiah offers. His eyes trail over to Patrick. "Hello, Patrick. How are you today?"

Patrick kind of grumbles and won't look Jeremiah in the eyes, and now I'd like to know what's going on with them. "I'll be better once I get the shots we need. Is your brother here? He's up next."

"I'm here." Reid has obviously been through the makeup and hair department. And maybe the wardrobe since he looks practically perfect in his three-piece suit with his hair slicked back and those blue eyes piercing through me. He's looking like a million bucks, and I'm in jeans and a T-shirt, and despite all the work they did in the makeup chair, I still pretty much look like a woman who spends a lot of time with a hammer in her hand.

It's been a couple of days since we made our deal, and everything is going well. We've had two meetings and nothing exploded, and we didn't throw down on the conference table. We've been nice and polite, even when he used the word *shiplap* in connection to the foyer. I was polite and calm, and I did not take his head off and bathe in his blood.

"Let's try it with Jeremiah introducing her." Anika is wearing what I like to think of as her work clothes. Well, her old work clothes since her new job requires a tiara. She's in black jeans and a black T, her hair in a high ponytail. Ivy sits behind her. She's been excellent at providing sarcastic remarks.

Jeremiah steps into the shot. We're standing in the parlor where my crew is about to tear down a wall because this particular parlor is small, probably used for the immediate family. There's another more formal parlor that would be used to greet guests down the hall. We're going to connect the two to create a great room.

"All right, do you need some lines?" Patrick steps close to us while one of the other assistants does the whole lighting check on Jeremiah.

Jeremiah waves off the suggestion. "She'll be better natural. We need to show off her sweet, authentic self."

Patrick's eyes finally come up and he frowns. "Authentic. Sure. We'll go that way. Tom, are you ready?"

The director nods and the clappy guy comes in even though it's not like we're filming scenes or anything. And we're rolling.

Somehow when that camera is on, I freeze up. I can't even explain it. I can talk in front of people. Not like to give a speech or anything, but I can certainly introduce myself.

Except I can't now.

"So this is Harper and she's going to be in charge of making all of our dreams for Banover Place come true. She's our construction fairy." Jeremiah sounds chipper. And like he's done this about five thousand times, which he has.

I have not. I try to smile and wave at the camera. "Hi."

Patrick's eyes roll when I say nothing else. "We're going to need more than that, Harper."

Ivy moves in beside Anika. "Just tell them about yourself. I know it feels weird, but it gets easier."

"In a couple of days you won't even notice the cameras," Anika assures me.

Ivy nods. "Remember all the times Ani ripped one on camera because she forgot she was being filmed?" Ivy gasps when Ani slaps at her arm. "Well, they gave you too many protein bars. You get gassy."

Anika gives Ivy a growl and turns back my way. "The point is this is the hardest day. All we need is for you to give us a bit about yourself and then we'll let you actually get to work. You get to sledgehammer a wall. Fun."

It actually does sound like fun. I understand that work. It will be soothing. But I have to get through this first. I nod. "Let's go again."

"We're rolling," Patrick says with a sigh. I'm pretty sure he already told me this information. Something about they'll edit it later and this isn't like acting. They roll until they get what they need.

I stare at the camera and give what I hope is a bright smile. "I'm Harper."

That's good, right? Simple. No nonsense.

"We need more," Patrick says with a huff.

Anika gives me an encouraging nod, her hands gesturing for more.

"I'm Harper and I build things."

When I stop a groan goes through the place.

Jeremiah keeps on smiling. "What my friend here is trying to say…"

Patrick waves a hand after listening to whatever the director said to him. "Nope. We need her to stop trying to say and just say. We've got a woman contractor. We're not going to have a man speak for her."

Well, I don't like the sound of that. Before I can protest, Reid is getting into my space. He turns to the still-running camera, and a slick smile crosses his lips.

"I'm Reid Dorsey and this is my brother, Jeremiah. We're known as the Dorsey brothers, and we're here to take this Gilded Age mansion and make it shine again," he says in a soothing tone. "In order to do that, we've put together a team of professionals, with a trusted friend leading them. Unfortunately, we weren't allowed to hire on our own, so we ended up with this one. I think this might be her first job. I'm not sure. What was her name again?"

I hate him. "I'm Harper Ross, and I've been working construction longer than Reid Dorsey has been playing with swatches and arguing about the many shades of black. I started out in my family company when I was a teen, though there are lots of pics of toddler me in a custom-made hard hat. Ross Construction has contributed over two hundred buildings to the tri-state area." I turn his way. "How many curtains have you made?"

"Absolutely none. I just design, Harper. I don't actually do the work myself. As you are about to learn. It's precisely why we hired you. Well, why Her Majesty hired you. Aren't you two friends?"

I nod, sinking my teeth into this fight. "The way you are with His Majesty?"

"Yes, we're practically all family, and that's what it's going to take to give this place a real makeover and drag her into this century." He looks to his brother. "But don't you think we need someone with a background in historical architecture and maybe some knowledge of restoration?"

I can't smack him because the camera is still running.

"I think that's why we brought in Harper." Jeremiah frowns like he's not sure where we're going with this.

Well, I'm not going to be Reid Dorsey's doormat. That's where we're going. "In addition to working in construction all of my life, I graduated from college with a degree in business and a minor in architecture. I've spent whole summers of my life interning with some of the best restoration professionals in the business. I know the history of Banover Place and respect it as a piece of New York's remarkable past."

"Perfect," the director calls out. "I love the stuff about her child labor past. Can we get some pictures for the editors? We'll add those in and humanize her."

Why do I have to be humanized? I thought I was already a human.

"You're welcome," Reid says with a nod. "The trick to getting Harper to do something is to give her an enemy to rail against. It's mostly me."

"It's entirely you," I mutter between clenched teeth.

"Name one thing I said that wasn't true." He turns to me, a wholly self-satisfied look on his face.

"My first job?"

His lips curl ever so slightly. "It is your first television job. Little virgin."

I'm fairly certain if my eyes could become lasers, I would cut this man in half. "Virgin?"

"It's what we call the newbies." Patrick's head shakes as he moves in closer. "It's not sexist. Men can be virgins, too. So that was not in any way a comment on the state of your femininity."

Jeremiah waves him off. "It's a thing they do. Trust me. She'll give it all back to him and then they will stew in their own sexual frustration. It's playing into the grumpy/grumpier romance they're having. See, the better way to do it is grumpy meets sunshine. I'm sunshine, by the way."

I ignore their obvious sexual tension because I am a focused individual. "I promise I haven't been a virgin for many years, Reid, and you should remember that."

"Well, you're not now since you got that first shot out of the way. I hope I made it as comfortable for you as possible. That first time can be hard."

"Okay, now, see, that does feel like he's talking about something other than the job." Ivy is standing right next to Anika.

"I probably should have hired an HR firm," Anika admits. "I kind of thought I wouldn't need one."

I stare up at Reid, getting into his space. I wish he wasn't so tall. And broad. "Like my other experience, you made it awkward and weird, and I'm going to try to forget it ever happened. Which will probably be easy because I'll get more enjoyment out of using my sledgehammer than I'll ever get from you."

The man lights up. Like he is loving this. "Oh, then I'll have to try harder."

"Yep, definitely needed a human resources department." Anika nods. "Now I'll end up with lawyers when someone sues about the very uncomfortable workplace this set is becoming. I'm talking to you, Reid."

"I don't know. Harper just talked about taking pleasure from a sledgehammer," Ivy points out. "We might have to send her there, too."

My friends are not helping. "I did not say that."

"You kind of did," Reid offers.

"I thought the sledgehammer was a metaphor for Reid's dick." Jeremiah joins Ivy and Ani. "I can't figure out if she's saying his dick can ruin walls or his dick is smaller than a sledgehammer." He looks to me. "Harper, I'm going to need you to be way clearer with your metaphors."

"It was not a metaphor, and I was not talking about anyone's penis," I announce.

The director puts his fingers in his ears and starts to hum.

Patrick frowns my way. "Now you've broken Tom. That man had to survive filming three seasons of *House of Skanks*. Do you know how much he's been through?"

"A whole lot of lawyers, probably," Jeremiah quips. "You know because of all the harassment claims."

Reid sighs. "There's no harassment. I apologize, Harper. I thought maybe some sparring would bring you out of your shell."

I don't want to be an adult, but it does seem like we've sent the poor director into a PTSD episode. "I apologize for making people think I was referring to your penis as a sledgehammer."

"I think we should bar the word *penis*," Ani says with an overly bright smile. "And *virgin*. All those words. We don't need them here. Tom, are you okay? I'm going to check on him. He really did have a hard time."

"Well, it was called *House of Skanks*. Of course it was hard. I bet many of them were hard," Ivy replies as she starts to follow Ani. "I saw that show. He's lucky he didn't get a contact STI."

"You are not helping," Ani hisses.

"Are they going to stop staring at each other?" Patrick asks, leaning Jeremiah's way.

"Eventually," Jeremiah replies. "But that can take a while. They do this thing where they stare and neither one wants to break away, and I can't figure out if it's because they're trying to establish dominance or they really like the way the other one looks. It could go either way. We should grab a coffee."

I am staring at him. And I'm fairly certain I'm trying to establish dominance and not the other thing. I break eye contact and take a step back. I don't need dominance over this man. I simply need to do my job.

"I have some stuff to get done. But everyone else take a ten-minute break and we'll get back to Reid soon," Patrick announces. "After we talk Tom down. Thanks, people."

I didn't mean to send the director into some sort of shame spiral. I don't know what to call it. "Well, I have a wall to remove. Excuse me."

"Have fun with your…sledgehammer." Reid gives me a jaunty salute. "I'll be somewhere planning color schemes that didn't exist in the Gilded Age."

"I'm sure you will," I reply.

"I will," he says back.

"And it will be terrible."

He stares at me with intense eyes. "It will."

I am so annoyed. And a bit aroused. "You have to have the last word, don't you?"

"I don't know, Harper. Do I?"

"Yes, you do."

He's silent for a moment. He waits until I'm about to walk into the hallway. "I do, and I always get my way."

I turn, ready to flay the man, but he's gone.

Jeremiah points to the door. "He fled. That was…shockingly childish of him."

Coward. "And this surprises you?"

"Yes," Jeremiah admits. "Reid is the most mature person I know.

He's kind of known for being a stickler for rules and behaving professionally. Many people we've worked with comment on the stick up his backside."

"Well, he must have changed then because that man is quite an asshole."

"Yeah, I wonder what happened to make him change," Jeremiah murmurs, glancing back to where Patrick is standing, checking over some equipment. "What's his story?"

I should walk away. Jeremiah belongs to Reid, and I am attempting to stay away from all things Reid adjacent. I can tell the man I have work to do. Which is the truth. I still have to stop by the office at some point in time today to make sure everything is running smoothly. But do I use that valid excuse? No. Because despite everything, I'm curious. There's a weird vibe around those two. "You don't know? He's pretty much the reason Ani and Luca got married. I mean, they would have anyway, but what happened with the director sped things along. Now, there was a man who didn't faint when he heard the word *penis*."

Jeremiah's eyes go wide. "Patrick was the production assistant the director was harassing? The one Luca caught on tape admitting to it? They kept his name out of the press pretty well."

"That's him. He and Ani became friends, and she offered him this job," I explain with a long sigh as I think about what I should have been thinking about a few minutes before. "So he's got his reasons for being uncomfortable about what happened. I need to go apologize."

"What did happen?" Jeremiah asks.

I don't even know. "He pushes my buttons. He claims I push his."

"My brother is always calm. He's a freaking oasis of calm. I've seen him face tragedies and accidents and not once lose his cool, but you walk in a room and he loses his damn mind." Jeremiah looks me up and down. "I'm not sure if this is a good development or a bad one."

"It's no development at all. We don't mix well. It's like that with some people." I start moving toward Patrick.

"Not with my brother," Jeremiah calls out. "He gets along with everyone. Everyone except you. I wonder why."

"Just lucky I guess," I retort and move to stand in front of Patrick. "I am very sorry."

He glances up from his clipboard. "For?"

"That whole scene back there. I'm sorry. It was juvenile of us, and it won't happen again."

"Hopefully the you talking like an actual person on camera will happen again." Patrick checks something off, proving he can multitask. He can work and make me feel like crap at the same time.

"Okay. I'll figure it out." I'm about to turn around and do what I should have done the first time. Get to work.

"Harper," Patrick calls out with a long-suffering sigh. He's good at those. "He was doing it to help you."

"Doing what? Insulting me?"

"He was trying to turn it into a challenge. You can't resist those, and the man knows it. I don't care about the inappropriate remarks. Trust me. I know when someone is being inappropriate. You two are fighting a big attraction, and I salute you for it. I mean it. Keep it up. Do not fall into bed with that man."

"I have no intention of sleeping with him."

"Good." Patrick gets back to work. "Because the last thing we need is big drama on set. But he wasn't trying to be an asshole. I watched him watching you, and he was worried. He didn't jump in to harass you. He thought he could help, and he did. You'll be better next time because you got through this time."

Because Reid pushed me, and when he walks into my space, nothing matters except him. "I should get going on the demo. Is the other unit thingee ready?"

"The other unit thingee is Bill with a handheld. So yes, he's probably ready," Patrick agrees. "Think about what I said and maybe go easier on Reid."

"I'm not the only one with a Dorsey brother problem," I point out. "You and Jeremiah seem to be hitting it off."

Now the clipboard lowers. "Oh, that's not happening. That man is hiding something. I'm not sure what it is, but he's wound tight. We went to dinner a couple of times, but I can't shake the feeling that something's off in his life. I'll admit he's exactly my type, but I'm going to keep it professional."

I was unaware they went out. "He asked me about you. I was surprised he didn't know how you and Anika met."

"I don't talk about that time in my life often, and I certainly don't lead with the fact that I put a Hollywood director in jail with help from a European king."

"Okay, then I have something else to apologize for," I admit.

He waves me off. "It's not a problem. We're a crew. I assure you he would have found out sooner or later. It's hard to hide when you're working together twelve hours a day. Like I know your mother is giving you hell for not using your ovaries properly."

"Jeremiah," I huff. "Now I wish I knew something about him."

Patrick smiles for the first time. "If you figure out what he's hiding, give me a heads-up. And again, think about not loathing Reid for what happened today. What I saw was a man who was trying to help someone out the only way he could think of."

"He should have thought of another way."

Patrick shrugs. "It worked. You looked good on camera. You were energetic and gave us some good stuff. And you didn't do it until he pulled it out of you. Think about that. Now go and take it out on that wall. And don't sleep with Reid Dorsey."

That is a promise I am happy to make.

Chapter Thirteen

I manage to avoid Reid for almost a week. Not entirely, of course. I see him coming and going. I see him sitting in the space they've turned into something of a Green Room. He's got a chair like the rest of us, and he sits and knits. I'm oddly fascinated with him when he's got his head down, fingers moving. I've started to notice he stretches his hands from time to time, and it looks like he's in pain.

My father had trouble with arthritis in his hands. My mom taught me how to massage them when they felt locked up. He was a stubborn man, so he often refused to leave the office or whatever site we were working that day.

I am so tempted to take Reid's big hands in mine and show him some relief.

But only because it's the nice thing to do.

"Just explain what you did today." Patrick nods to the cameraman.

"Well, I woke up," I begin.

The cameraman is named Mike, and he chuckles. "She caught on quickly."

"She's made of sarcasm, like the other one. The one with the computers," Patrick says with a shake of his head. "All right, Harper, could you please explain the trouble you had today and why it's important."

I have gotten more comfortable in front of the camera. Especially when we're talking strictly about work. They sometimes try to slip in questions like "how is it going working with the Dorsey brothers?" That's when I freeze up, but this is the last shot of the day, and everyone seems eager to go home. It's late, and I'm looking forward to having a quiet workplace. I'm looking forward to some quiet because when Reid finds out we've hit a big pause in the kitchen, he's going to… Well, I have no idea what he's going to do. He's kind of been a rock through everything. This might not freak him out at all.

I face Patrick, who stands slightly to the left of the camera. We discovered this is the best way for me to handle these piece-to-camera scenes. "So we got a surprise when we opened up the west side wall of the kitchen. According to the records with the city, Banover Place was rewired in the eighties. Now as all of my Gen X relatives will tell you, the eighties were a free-wheeling time, and apparently that applies to following code. Whoever was responsible for the rewiring not only didn't bother to take out the old knob and tube wiring, they left it live. Knob and tube was used in homes in the States from…the late nineteenth century through roughly 1940. Think first-generation electricity. And it's sitting there still connected while the updated lighting is as well. It's all connected. Like a string puzzle. Except this string puzzle could potentially shock the hell out of you, and it's a big old fire hazard. So it has to be dealt with."

"Can you deal with it?"

Patrick often asks questions during the sessions, but I've been told it's to prompt me for more material since his voice will be edited out. So it's up to me to in some way repeat the question so the viewer knows what I'm talking about. "This is the kind of electrical work that requires a specialist. Molly is a wiz with modern electricity, but she's never worked with knob and tube since she wasn't even born when it was phased out. I'm pretty sure her grandma might not have been born. I mean this stuff is old, and given how it's wired, we need someone with experience dealing with it. We need to basically take everything out and start over again."

"What's the cost we're looking at?"

This was the bad part. Besides taking time, it's going to take cash to fix this problem. A lot of it. "Depending on whether we find it in other parts of the house—and I have no reason to think they properly wired the rest of it—we're looking at rewiring a twelve-thousand-square-foot house. At the very least I estimate a hundred K. It's more than enough to throw the whole project into chaos. This is the kind of news no one wants to hear."

A groan goes through the small crew.

Patrick sighs, and the assistant director calls it for the night. "Well, you are a fount of happy news, Harper."

"Yeah, that's pretty much in the job description." There's a reason people hate contractors, but we have to be realistic. "I already talked to Ani. She's going to discuss it with Luca and their mysterious buyer."

I do not ever mention the mysterious buyer on camera. That's a no-no. We actually don't talk about the fact that there is often a buyer when they start filming, but we're running with a skeleton crew right now, and they all know the truth.

"Tomorrow is going to be a fun day," Patrick says with a huff. "I'm going up to the office. Everyone wrap up. We've got an eight a.m. call."

I step back into the kitchen as the crew starts to put away the equipment for the night.

It's getting late, but it's not like I have anything better to do. I look over at the shelving units that were delivered today. They're lovely. White Oak. Very high end and will go beautifully in what we're calling the great room.

So why is it here in the kitchen? The great room is on the ground floor or what would have been known as the parlor floor. The kitchen is on the garden floor. I have zero idea why these shelves are in here. I need the space to work because I have to take down a whole lot of walls to make it easier to start the rewiring. Ani simply shook her head when I told her and asked me to start the process.

Part of the process includes not having a bunch of insanely heavy boxes in my way.

I pick up the delivery invoice from the large island we're replacing in a couple of days. Maybe more now. The white marble has already been delivered and is waiting for use, taking up more space I'm going to need to get into the walls. It was signed for by one of the crew who I'm going to have to talk to about putting things where they're supposed to go. The elevator isn't working—another thing I need to plan for. So these will have to go back up the stairs. Somehow.

It's actually a lot of shelves. Is Reid planning on filling every spare inch of wall space in the great room with floating shelves? There's art we're supposed to use. Now that I study the paperwork, I can also see it's not all white oak. There's several boxes of walnut with a live edge. These two things do not go together, and I have no idea what Reid is thinking. I especially have no idea since there's a third shipment of cherry shelves. He might be putting floating shelves in every single room for all I can tell. I only know they don't belong here in the kitchen, and I have to do something about it.

I need some help, though. These boxes are super heavy.

I was hoping I could turn on some music and spend a couple of hours tearing out walls for the electrician who's coming in tomorrow to see how bad the situation is. I know it sounds weird but it's soothing. Especially alone, with no one asking me for directions or telling me they found a nest of pigeons in one of the upper bedrooms. True story. But it's going to have to wait because the space is too crowded.

I make my way up the stairs, and I'm surprised at how quiet it is. Although I should have known. The crew can get the hell out of here fast when they want to, but usually Patrick hangs around for a long time after work is over. I make my way to the ground floor and turn down the main hall.

No one. It's perfectly quiet. I sent my own crew home hours before since they don't have to sit around and wait for the director to be ready.

I do not. If I go home, I have to deal with calls from my mother about the upcoming holiday season, and wouldn't it be lovely if the company helped out the family? Wouldn't paying for a car for Cousin Steve be a Christmas miracle?

I'm the Grinch.

I'm weary, working fourteen-hour days because I can't trust Paul to do the right thing for the business. It's almost like he wants it to fail so he can come in and save it from himself. And then likely figure out all kinds of ways to milk the company for his own good.

The real problem is no one else sees anything wrong with it. I'm being forced to save them from themselves, and it's making me tired.

I want a night of peace and quiet where I tear apart stuff and go sleep on the air mattress I set up in the butler's pantry. Is that too much to ask?

I'll wake up, rush to get back to my place, take a shower, down some coffee, and then get back here pretending I'm a normal person who didn't stay up working until long after midnight, got four hours of sleep, and is back for more.

Where did everyone go?

There's the sound of the keycard on the door pinging and it comes open. Through the stained glass I see a tall figure moving to the inner doors.

Reid. I would know those shoulders anywhere. He strides through the inner doors, looking far more casual than I've ever seen him before. He's in track pants and a hoodie. How does he make it look so good? He glances around, and his eyes laser focus in on me. "What the hell is this about the electrical costing a hundred thousand dollars? In what world does it cost that much? What the hell are you trying to do to me, Harper?"

Well, that is one way to greet me. When I saw him I kind of thought maybe he was here to talk. Like a real person. He is definitely not going to help me. It looks like there's no one who will, so I should get started.

"This is a twelve-thousand-square-foot home. Yes, it can certainly cost a hundred thousand dollars to rewire it. If you have a problem with budgeting, talk to Luca." I turn and stride back toward the stairs. He probably came here to look for them anyway. They often stay late, but tonight they have some kind of party at the embassy. He obviously didn't get the memo.

The week had been okay up until now. We sniped at each other from time to time. We sparred over a couple of choices that weren't practical, but for the most part we've ignored each other. We hold to the whole "we're coworkers and don't have to hang or even like each other."

So why the minute I realize we're alone and he's in a mood does something light inside me? Something angsty and twitchy. Something that keeps building between us, that wants let out of this cage we put it in.

We need some distance, so I keep walking.

And he keeps following.

"Tell me you didn't do this to get back at me." Reid sounds way more irritated than I've heard him in forever. It makes me realize he's been handling me.

I don't know that I want to be handled. I turn as I reach the garden level. "You think I went back in time? Am I the one who installed the original wiring, or did I pop back to the eighties and make the terrible decision to leave them all live?"

"You know damn well you could take that wiring out yourself," he accuses. "It would add time, but it wouldn't take a hundred thousand out of my budget when the new buyer is completely insane with her demands."

That was a him problem. "I am not trained to handle this kind of work. I work on modern systems. As you've pointed out so often, I work on big ugly boxes. Guess what big ugly boxes don't have? Knob and tube wiring. I suppose I could try, and then my almost certain death by electrocution could solve your problem. Or I could burn the whole place down. Then I'm sure you would get all kinds of publicity. Think about it, Reid. You could do PSAs on how you should never work with poor people."

"For fuck's sake, Harper. Stop trying to turn me into some robber baron bad guy. This is a project we're both working on. We need to make it successful, and taking a hundred thousand dollars out of the budget is going to hurt," he argues.

"Then do it yourself." I stalk into the kitchen. "That should save money, but I'm not risking anyone on my crew so you can have more money. And you think you're not a robber baron. You know you would fit right into this place. The Gilded Age was great for millionaires. Not so good for anyone who wasn't. Send in the poor kid. If she gets electrocuted, we'll replace her."

A low growl comes from his throat. "Not what I'm saying. Damn it, I'm handling this wrong. I came looking for my brother. I should have turned and walked away when I saw you because there's not one person on this planet who sends me into beast mode the way you do."

"I don't care." His words hurt, but it's not like I've never been told I'm annoying. I don't get it. "I've left you alone. I do what you tell me to do."

"Sure you do."

"Unless it's going to harm the integrity of the structure."

"Oh, I'm not sure how the wallpaper for the powder room harms the integrity of this building."

"I'm trying to defend her dignity, too, and that wallpaper is a crime against my eyeballs."

His fists clench. "That wallpaper was designed from artwork that was originally in this home. I fucking selected it for you, damn it. I didn't even select it. I had it made. The art is now in a museum, but I wanted to tie some elements into the history of the house to please you. But there's no pleasing you."

He did what? I stop, my eyes widening. "You did that?"

His head shakes. "It doesn't matter. I'll chuck it out and go with my first instinct."

I know exactly what he's going to say. "No shiplap."

He gets right in my face, bending his tall frame down so he can stare into my eyes. "Yes, shiplap. Guess what. I don't care what you think."

"You never cared what I think."

He huffs. "Why the hell have I invited you to every design meeting I could? Why did I change my plans for the marbled hallways?"

"So no one dies." I don't back down at all. "It was impractical. It's slippery."

He points my way as though I'm making his point for him. "This house isn't about practicality. It's about design, and I've let you seep into my art."

I groan. "Yes, I'm your muse."

"You're the damn devil on my shoulder, and I'm fucking sick of ignoring you."

I feel my eyes narrow. "Well, you do an excellent job of it."

"That's what I'm trying to say. I'm not. I can't ignore you, and I can't do what I want to do." He stares for a moment and then curses and takes a step back along with a long breath. His fists are still clenched at his sides like he doesn't quite trust himself.

I'm not sure I want to know what he wants to do. I'm worried it's what I want to do, and it will ruin me. "It doesn't matter. You know what. Do your worst. You want to turn this place into some beige McMansion you could find in any suburb, do it."

He turns, and I can tell I've pushed him over some edge. He's a little predatory as he glares my way. "Which one is it, Harper? Am I too erudite, hence the murdering marble, or too bland?"

"You can be both." I hate the me he brings out. I'm not this person. Not in any way. I'm the patient one. I have to be because I work with men all day. I can't lose my temper or I'm emotional. I can't show irritation or I'm probably on my period. I have to be gentle when I instruct the men on how I want a job done because I might hurt their egos. I'm never, ever mean. Except with him. "You can be a boring, erudite prick, and guess what, you can haul these ridiculous bland floating shelves right out of my kitchen."

"Why would I do that? They go in here. They're to be installed on either side of the range."

I feel my jaw drop. "To what purpose?"

"Because they will look beautiful and properly showcase the family's dining ware."

I shake my head and point to the space. "First of all, are you only allowing basketball players to buy this place? Because I'm fairly tall and I can't reach where the third shelf would need to go."

"That's what they make ladders for," he says between clenched teeth. "And the higher shelves are for dishes they don't use every day. The lower levels are for everyday China and barware. It's going to look beautiful."

"But there are no standard cabinets in the kitchen now."

His eyes roll. "I assure you the shelves provide space for all of it. Appliances not considered attractive enough to display can be stored in the pantry."

He has obviously never, ever had to deal with an actual family. "And where do the sippy cups go, Reid?"

He stops for a moment, and I worry he doesn't even know what a sippy cup is. "No one who lives in this home will ever use a sippy cup. And while we're at it, no, they won't save the plastic cups from Yankee Stadium or have a single red Solo cup. And I desperately want to kiss you right now. Like I need to walk away this second or I'm going to do something that will send our director right back to whatever spa he recovers at."

Thank god it wasn't just me. I know I should tell him to run, but I'm physically incapable. I'm standing in front of this man I loathe, and I can't think of anything except getting my hands on him. "I still hate you."

His eyes flash and he moves in, my words not stopping him at all. "And I still think you're a stubborn, annoying harpy. You are not my type."

"And you aren't mine," I hiss back.

Then I can't think straight because his mouth is on mine, those big hands of his on my hips, pulling me close. The kiss immediately goes wild. The flash fire that's been building between us can no longer be denied. He kisses me like I'm water and he's been alone in the desert for days. Eternity. His tongue surges in, finding mine, and we fight for dominance. Every stroke of his tongue goes straight to that part of me that has taken over all thinking. I no longer care that this is a mistake.

This will almost certainly come back to haunt me in the worst way, but I don't care. I do care about getting his shirt off and feeling his warm skin against my hands.

I tug at his T-shirt, and he briefly lets me go so he can drag it over his head and toss it away.

"Now you." He nods my way, and his words come out on the grunty side.

I like caveman Reid. I pull my T off and let it drop to the floor.

He moves back in, towering over me in the sexiest way. "We should go to my place."

That's not realistic. "You have two minutes before my brain takes over again. This is a terrible idea, and if we're going to make this mistake it's going to be in the next five to ten minutes. No one's here. They've all gone home. Kiss me now or we can go back to screaming at each other about floating shelves."

He growls my way. "Annoying woman."

But his fingers sink into my hair, and he practically inhales me. I wrap myself around him, luxuriating in the feel of his body against mine. So long. It's been too long since I had this thrill of lust. If I'm honest, I never felt this way. Never been swept up into anything. I think things through. I do the right thing.

This time wrong feels so right.

When he tugs on my hair, I let my nails dig in slightly, rewarded with a hiss and a nip to my earlobe that I swear goes straight to all my pink parts.

His hands go to the waistband of my jeans, and he unbuttons the fly. I manage to somehow toe out of my boots before he drags the pants right off me. I toss them away, and I hear something crash. My head turns, and his hands come up to bring my attention back to him.

"Not now. This now."

I love the fact that he seems to mostly cling to one-syllable words when he guts lusty. It makes me forget about whatever we broke. Makes me forget about anything but him and the way his hands brush over my skin like he needs to touch every inch of me. "This now."

There will be time enough for me to pound my head against a wall tomorrow. I'll do it anyway, so I'm going to have the pleasure he's promising me now.

Somehow everything seems to go soft and wild. Like the world isn't as hard edged as it always seems. While he's definitely into this, there's something gentle in his touch. And then he'll nip me like he wants a taste. It's a wild combination I've never felt before, and it's got my head spinning.

His hands cup my rear, and he lifts me up. "I wanted this from the moment I saw you. Never wanted anything the way I want this."

He sets me on the kitchen island. It's huge and his pelvis aligns perfectly with the edge. Like someone designed it for a throwdown when the couple who owned the place didn't want to go up two flights of stairs to get to a bed.

He moves between my legs, nestling against my core, and I can feel how much his words are true. "Tell me you want me."

There's no place for lying here. We can do that later. I won't even lie to myself here. "You know I do. You know I wanted you the moment I saw you, and then I discovered what a massive ass you are. And I still want this."

"We need this," he says on a low groan.

"Maybe if we have this, we'll be able to think straight again." Well, maybe I lie a little to myself. Or maybe I'm finally being honest and this is absolutely what we needed all along.

I gasp as his hand finds my breast, thumb rasping over the rock-hard nipple. He traces the areole and then leans over, kissing his way down my torso, starting at my neck and pressing his lips every few inches until he licks his tongue right over that desperate nipple.

I groan and my back flexes, offering him more and more.

He takes it. He takes everything I'm offering him. He plays with my breasts, sucking on my nipples and lavishing them with affection. He kisses his way down my belly, right to the band of my undies before slipping his thumbs under them and tugging them off me. They join the rest of our clothes.

"Lie back," he commands.

"Reid, it's..." I begin, ready to tell him it's chilly.

He gets to his knees and brings my ankles up so my feet are placed on his shoulders and I'm open and utterly vulnerable to him. Also, I'm suddenly not cold. The granite underneath me can't touch my inner temperature, which is skyrocketing because he's looking up my body, our eyes locking even as he lowers his mouth.

"Is there something you wanted, Harper?" He stops, his mouth hovering over my clitoris. I can feel the heat of his breath, know he's so close.

I know when to not complain. "Nope. I'm good. You can proceed."

That arrogant smirk is back, and it's sexy as hell. "Good. I was hoping that was the case since I've been wanting to do this since the moment I fucking laid eyes on you."

When his mouth covers me, I can't think at all anymore. Not about anything but the most important—how this man can make me feel. Powerful. Desired. Needed. Over and over he lavishes pleasure on me. I press myself against his mouth, wanting that strong tongue to lead me where he's promising.

He puts his thumb right on my clitoris and spears me with his tongue, sending me over the edge.

Before I can come down from the high of that orgasm, he's rolling a condom on and pulling my legs around him. "Harper, tell me it's okay."

I like that he's not taking this first time for granted. Later in a relationship things get established but now, he wants to know I consent. I shouldn't, but there's zero way I'm not letting this man have me any way he wants. "Yes."

The word seems to work some magic on him, and he leans over with a smile and kisses me. "You won't regret it."

I'm pretty sure I will, but the feel of him thrusting inside me is all I care about right now. I'm so aroused the tight fit doesn't bother me. He thrusts in and drags out, pulling me up so my arms can go around his shoulders.

"I want you close," he whispers. "I want to be able to kiss you."

And he does. Even as he hauls my hips closer and thrusts inside me, his tongue rubs against mine. We're as close as we can get, and it feels fabulous. It feels warm and right. I hold on as he finds the exact right spot, and this orgasm has me gasping for air and digging my nails lightly into his shoulders. He tightens around me and loses control. I feel the moment he comes and hold him.

And then it's over, but instead of stepping away and letting the regrets begin, he eases me down and rests his head against my chest. "Now that was what I needed. And a great way to send this countertop off. What were they thinking?"

I can't help but laugh and wonder what I have gotten myself into.

Chapter Fourteen

I lay back, not quite sure what the hell just happened.

My heart was racing and now it's finding this glorious pulse that almost feels like it's synching up to his. It's the closest I've ever felt to a man, and he's pretty much my enemy.

Is he my enemy?

I try to wrap my head around the last half hour. I made love to Reid Dorsey on the kitchen island in a Gilded Age mansion we're supposed to be restoring. Yep. I did that and now he's on top of me and it feels weirdly right, and I don't trust it at all. "Uhm. We should probably get dressed."

"Give me a minute, Harper." He sighs and rubs his cheek against my breast. "This is the calmest I've felt in months, and I know the minute our clothes are on we go back to fighting. I don't want to fight right now. I want to pretend you like me because this is the closest I've felt to any woman in my life."

Damn it. This is not supposed to get emotional. This is supposed to be sex. Nothing more. An itch we scratch and then walk away from and don't think about again. I'm not supposed to wrap my arms around him and know I feel the same. I want to pretend it's real, too, and we're not going to go back to the enemies we are in real life.

"Fine. A cease fire." I don't want to fight. I need to understand why every piece of my soul wants to hold this man and start the process all over again. We can have one glorious night before we face reality. "But this is cold, and I have a perfectly good air mattress in the other room. It's got blankets and everything. It's small, though."

He slides off me and doesn't even wince when he picks me up. It's like I don't weigh anything at all. "Then we'll have to cuddle."

He carries me through the kitchen to the massive butler's pantry where I set up an air mattress a few days ago. I put it in the pantry because we're not working in here at all, so no one would notice.

"I knew this was you," he says as he lays me down and climbs in after me. "I came in here looking for a quiet place to take a phone call two days ago and saw the bed and knew Harper Ross was pulling some overtime."

Well, almost no one notices. He's taking up all the space. I'm forced to kind of lay half on top of him, my arm around his chest and leg dragged over his. "I do stay late sometimes."

He kisses the top of my head, and his hand smooths over my hair. "You are trying to work two full-time jobs, and it's catching up to you. You need more sleep. Also, I'm glad you're not walking home or taking the subway in the middle of the night. If you ever find yourself here late and need to go home, call me. I'm a couple of blocks away. I can be here quickly."

"Why would I do that?" How is this the way the day is ending? I should be running. We didn't even pick up our clothes. And yet my head finds his chest and I'm fascinated by the strong beat of his heart.

"So I can make sure you get home okay," he replies. "And don't tell me I'm being sexist. I make my brother call me, too, if he doesn't have someone with him. Now tell me why you're having to work two jobs. I thought you took a sabbatical."

I did, too. "I thought I could leave it in Paul's hands for a few weeks. I was wrong. We've had some major problems on a couple of important jobs. One was an ordering issue. The foreman didn't order enough concrete mix and it was a specialty order, so it's putting us back and I had to handle the client. Paul says he forgot to double-check. The other was plumbing placed in the wrong wall. So we get to eat that cost."

"And you can't fire him?" Reid asks.

"I would love to but he's on the board. Firing me or Paul requires board approval the way hiring us did. I assure you my mother would be haranguing me about taking food from his poor babies' mouths," I reply. "She's worried about everyone eating. I tried to explain to her that he won't be able to feed them if he takes over and runs the place into the ground. Sometimes I think she would rather let Paul have the position so a man is in charge."

He's quiet for a moment. "You know you could get a job anywhere, right? You're not tied to one company. You're skilled, and you're about to be something of a celebrity. You have literal connections to royalty. You're not stuck. You are in a unique position to follow whatever dream you like."

Dreams. I have a weird connection to that word. "I don't know that I ever had one. I knew what I was supposed to do from the time I was a kid. Like as soon as I was capable of holding a hammer, my dad had one in my hand. I guess that's why it hurt so much to find out he actually intended to give the company to my husband."

"He what?" Reid asks, obviously in disbelief.

I haven't even shared this with my friends. "It's something my mom told me. Dad never really thought I would run the company. He thought I would get married and my husband would manage the company. I'm not sure how he intended to find a man who could magically walk into the job. Mom assures me he had a few candidates lined up."

Reid huffs. "I can tell you how he expected it would work. He expected you to teach him. My father...well, I saw it a lot. He was propped up by the incredibly intelligent women he hired. Assistants. They did most of the work for him, and he took all the credit. He would promise them the world and never deliver. There was this woman who came up with an idea that brought company expenses down by ten percent. Would you like to know what he did to her?"

"Probably not. Your dad seems like an asshole." The more I hear about the Dorsey patriarch the more sympathy I have for Reid. Who does actually work well with others. All the people on my crew adore him and think he and Jeremiah are the best. Probably because they often come to set with cronuts.

"He was an asshole of the highest order. He laid her off and announced he'd saved another half a percent and told the shareholders it had all been his idea." He sighs and his arms clutch me closer. "I'm glad he never wanted either of us to take over the company."

Yes, but he still reaps the rewards of owning all that stock. He doesn't depend on working to live the way I do. We are from two different worlds. "Did you ever think about it?"

"Think about sitting in some office plotting how to get more cash out of people who can't afford it?" he muses. "No. I knew I wasn't going to follow in dear old dad's footsteps. The truth of the matter is he was done with us when we turned eighteen. He blew through as much money as he could. I think he somehow knew he wasn't going to make it to eighty and wanted to spend it all if he could. So he left us with the penthouse and the stock, and we had to figure things out from there. The first time I walked into a board meeting they laughed at me."

I cuddle closer, the warmth of our bodies lulling me. If there is one thing I can empathize with, it's feeling shitty at a board meeting. I had to start going to them way too young. "That wasn't fair of them. Did you vote the CEO out? I've been told it's an easy thing to do."

He chuckles, and I'm so close I feel it on my skin. "Not in my case. My father's will was interesting. But I do not want to think about my dad right now. We need to talk about something."

And all that lovely intimacy is gone. I know exactly what he's going to say, and at least one of us is being an adult about this. I should thank him. "This is a one-time thing. I get it."

He turns slightly so I can see his quizzical expression. "Why? I mean, that's not what I was going to say, but maybe we should talk about it. Why would you think this has to be a one and done thing? Harper, that was incredible. Do you really think you never want to experience that again? You must have way better sex than I've had because the idea of never being with you again is not something I want to contemplate."

His words kind of shake me. I sit up. There's some illumination from the window high above us. This level of Banover Place is mostly below the street line, but there are two windows right below the ceiling that let in natural light. Or natural NYC light, which at night is from the streetlights above. It sends a slash of illumination across the room, putting Reid in shadows. "You don't even like me."

He shifts so he's on his side, head propped up with one hand. "I argue with you. That doesn't mean I don't like you. I think I was open and honest about liking you from the beginning. We disagree on things, and we haven't learned each other's languages yet. You, on the other hand, do not like me. I think I can work with it. Honestly, I've had worse relationships."

We're in a relationship? Also, that's super sad. "Reid, we just had hate sex."

He shakes his head. "Nope. We had inevitable, let the steam out because we've been stubborn sex. Hate sex does not end up with the participants cuddling on... Is this an air mattress? We need to get something better if we're going to do this very often because my legs are hanging off. Hey, I've heard there are some tunnels that lead to the hotel across the street. We could get a room and sneak over there when we need to. Think about how much nicer this would be if we could also order room service."

The truth is I am hungry. A charcuterie board after athletic sex might be amazing. My last boyfriend wouldn't even spring for Taco Bell because he was worried about his abs.

Reid might be right about the hate sex. I don't exactly hate him right now. He's completely adorable lying there. But how can I trust him? Do I need to trust him in order to enjoy being with him for a brief period of time? It's not like I'm looking for marriage here. "I don't think it's a good idea."

"Why?" Reid sits up, leaning his back against the wall. This puts his gorgeous chest on display and the sheet is hovering around his hips, dangerously close to showing off that part of him that entirely pleased me not ten minutes before. "I think it's a great idea. I have zero desire to yell at you right now. I'm relaxed and calm in a way I haven't been in forever."

"It'll pass." I take the top blanket with me when I stand. I'm getting antsy again and it's all about the fact that I don't want to get up at all. I want to stay in that too-small bed with him. "I understand what happened was exciting and spectacular, but you have to know it's not the kind of thing that can last. We're a flash fire. It might be hot in the beginning, but it's going to burn us both in the end."

"It doesn't have to." His tone has gone soft.

"What is that supposed to mean?"

"I mean a flash fire can be contained," he replies.

At least he's getting my metaphor. "Yes, by dosing it with a ton of cold water—which in this case is reality—and being put out entirely. Which we did. We gave into the temptation, and we don't have to do it anymore."

A brow rises. "Really? I don't think so. I think you're going to wake up tomorrow and want me every bit as much as I want you right now.

As I've wanted you every minute of every day since I met you. I didn't say you put out the fire. I said if the fire is dangerous, you tame it. No one wants to live without warmth in their lives. I know I don't, but the truth of the matter is I've been afraid of it. I think that's why I end up with the women I date. I watched my father go through woman after woman, and every time he was excited and passionate about the new lady. Obviously, since he often forgot he had children. It always died out, and he cheated on the woman he was so passionate about with a new woman. So the flash fire scares me because I know where it leads. But what if it doesn't have to?"

I can understand where he's coming from. My dad cheated, though he never left my mom and she never made what she would call "a fuss." Sometimes I wish she had. "Where would it lead? Passion like this is amazing, but it's also brittle. It breaks easily. It's a storm that passes and ravages everything."

"Or we could find a way to make it softer. Make it stronger," he says, his words filled with warmth. "I think that's what I'm figuring out. My ideas about love and sex are wrapped up in my childhood, and the truth of the matter is I wasn't surrounded by good examples of love and friendship. I saw my father's world, which was warped by his selfishness. I saw my mother leaving Jeremiah and I behind to find herself. So when I chose a woman as a companion I wanted one I didn't feel too much for because I knew it wouldn't last. My therapist told me if I'm open to it, one day I might find a woman I'm willing to risk heartache over. What if it's you?"

The words…those words. I can't handle them. My brain goes to all the worst places. He's trying to control me. He's using me. We're not alike. I hold on to that one. I shake my head. "We're too far apart."

"How?"

How long do we have? "In every way. You've never had to worry about money."

Even in the dim light I can see his eyes roll. "Of course I have. I assure you, you don't know my whole story. But let's address this part. I was a snob when I met you."

This I can handle. "Yes, you couldn't stand the thought of working with some blue-collar stiff."

"No, I worried Anika was bringing in a friend who didn't have a lot of experience in high-end renovations," he corrects, and he's so calm I can barely stand it because I'm not. "I certainly have zero issues working with blue-collar people. I work with construction crews and contractors all the time, and this will shock you, but they tend to like me. I did a whole series about helping people figure out how to renovate their homes on a budget. I don't have a problem with the circumstances of your birth, but you have a real problem with mine. I can't help I was born into a wealthy family, and honestly, while we're at it, let's talk about how many women your age own their own apartment and are the CEO of a family firm."

He is deliberately misunderstanding me. "My apartment is eight hundred square feet, and I have to fight with the building constantly. You have an AI elevator and a view of Central Park. I have a view of the bodega across the street and regularly watch drug deals go down. We are not the same."

He slides off the cot and does not seem to mind that he's naked. "You have no idea how the same we are, but you don't want to see it."

I try not to look at how gorgeous this man is. "I am nothing like you."

And that's part of the problem. I'm not sure why he's here unless it's to use his gorgeousness and charm to get me to do what he wants. I've seen myself in the mirror.

You should find a man now, Harper. You're not getting any younger. No man wants you for your wisdom, honey.

I don't need to hear my mother in my head right now.

"You are everything like me." He's got a slight smile on his face as he moves into my space. "You are practically the female version of me except without my refined tastes. You are stubborn as hell. You tend to center things around your personal feelings but you tell yourself you're thinking of others. You equate sacrifice with love instead of the martyrdom it actually is. Trust me. I know how that feels."

I take a step back, not liking how he seems to see me. Or maybe it's that he sees through me. "You're a psychologist now?"

"No, I've just had an enormous amount of therapy. We can all use some, but especially when you come from highly toxic family situations," he says quietly as though trying to handle me with care.

There he is. There's the arrogant man who thinks he knows everything.

"I'm insane now. Are you seriously going there? I need therapy?" I don't address the other thing. Because I'm nauseatingly certain he's right. I've never thought of it that way before. Or he's wrong and this is just how my mom is. She doesn't mean anything by it. My dad cheating on her didn't make her leave him, so I can't accept that I won't live that life.

He puts a hand to his head as though the whole conversation is giving him a headache. "I didn't say that, and you know therapy isn't about insanity most of the time. Stop making people feel bad for needing help sorting themselves out."

I take a deep breath. The flash fire is here again, and I have a choice. "That is not what I'm trying to do."

I can push him away. It would be the safest course of action. He's getting way too in my business, and all this crap about turning the dangerous fire into something that might keep us warm is bullshit. I can do what I've been doing and shove this man away as fast as I can. The sex means nothing. The sex is something I can get anywhere.

But the way he held me. Like I'm something precious. Something he truly doesn't want to let go. The way he smiled after. A pure, joyous smile, like he did something amazing and the amazing thing is me.

I don't know if I'll ever have that again. Do I want to throw it away without examining it at all? What if he's right and there are people who are worth the heartache that inevitably comes?

I know one thing. I want to stop hurting this man. I want to stop reacting to every perceived insult and act like the Harper Ross I want to be, and that is not the woman I've been around him to this point. He's been a place where I could put all my anger, and that stops now.

"I'm sorry." I take a deep breath and touch him, wanting him to know I mean it. "I'm glad you went to therapy. You might be right about the toxic family bit, but it hurts to hear it."

His expression softens, and he pulls me into his arms. "I am, too, but I think I need more. So much more because I'm at a loss for what to do with you. I don't want to hurt you. But I also don't want to let you go. There's a lot about my life right now that isn't settled."

"Yeah. You either have a fiancée or a stalker." I turn my chin up with a wince. "Sorry. I didn't mean that in a rude way. I don't know what to call that whole situation."

His hands smooth back my hair, and he presses a kiss on my forehead, a tender gesture that gets to me in a way all that passion can't. "I do not have a fiancée, and Britta only stalks me when she needs something. I promise it won't affect you in any way. She's back in Europe, and I'm sure she used those pictures she got out of me to prompt whatever wealthy boyfriend she's after to capitulate to her demands. That's the only relationship I have with her now. She uses me as a blunt instrument. Nothing else. I haven't had sex in over eighteen months."

That surprises me. "Really?"

He nods solemnly. "I kind of swore it off, and not because I was pining for her. Pretty much the opposite. I realized I managed to get myself involved in the same kind of toxicity my father indulged in and decided to take a break. Everything fell apart around the same time, and I kind of pulled into myself. That was when a friend of mine suggested I go to Dr. Warner. He's helped me see I often take on too much responsibility because I'm still playing out my childhood fears that if I'm not on top of everything, in control of everything, the world will fall apart. That's what I meant about the martyrdom thing. I should have put it better. He would tell me language is important, and I need to speak one you understand. So let me put it better than I did. You have the weight of the world on your shoulders, and it feels like you have to keep it there. But it's not your responsibility, so what if you just…didn't." He kisses me again. "And that's all I'm going to say because I just figured out how to keep you."

"What does that mean?" When he kisses me, I can't think straight.

"It means I'm a ruthless bastard, and I don't care what my brother says. Grumpy and grumpier can find a way." He sounds entirely sure of himself. "And that way is a common enemy. Baby, you think I'm bad. I can give you someone worse. You don't like those floating shelves."

"They're fine for living spaces, but as the primary place to store dishes, they suck," I admit. "And you have them in three different materials. What are you thinking?"

"I'm not. The owner is. And they're for three different kitchens. Apparently she has two daughters and she's decided to…"

I shake my head. "No. No, she did not."

He is not about to say… He can't.

"She's splitting the whole place into three separate residences."

My knees get weak, and not for the right reasons this time.

Reid simply leans over and picks me up, hauling me against his chest. "I think we should get back in that ridiculous bed, I'll blow your mind again, and then we can talk about how we're going to take down the new owner."

That is a plan I can say yes to.

Chapter Fifteen

"Do you think we should…"

I stir in my warm nest. It's so cozy and perfect. I'm wrapped around a furnace and I'm happy here so why are people talking? Whispering. Like they don't want to be heard, but I catch some of what they're saying in this weird dream I'm having.

"I have no idea what to do. I've been standing here trying to process," a familiar voice says. "I thought Jeremiah was pranking us."

"You should have known since he sent pictures."

"Well, I guess I thought he's probably handy with a computer," the voice replies.

"Thank god the crew is running late."

Those words shake my comfort. The crew. My crew. Well, now I'm awake. I sit straight up in bed and then realize it's morning and I'm naked.

"Well, hello, sunshine," Ivy says with a grin that tells me she's enjoying the drama. She always does as long as she's not being the dramatic one.

My best friends are here. And it's daytime and Reid is…yep. He's here and yawning and giving me a super-sexy smile that reminds me of everything we did the night before. What we didn't do was remember to be out of here before everyone showed up for work. I look at Anika and

Ivy, who are both holding coffee cups. Ivy has a kolache in her hand. Like she wanted snacks for the morning show.

"Would you believe this isn't what it looks like?" I try.

Anika's eyes go wide as Reid yawns and stretches and the sheet kind of slips down around his waist. "Really? Uhm, did you find yourself locked in and decide you required body heat to survive the night? You do realize there's a security guard. He could have helped."

I reach down and tug the sheet up because while my friends have absolutely seen me naked—we shop together a lot—Reid's body is a wonderland they've never experienced before, and I mean to keep it that way. I didn't think about the security guy. He's used to me staying overnight. He's probably surprised I invited a friend to stay with me.

Especially one who I would totally have said was an enemy right up until I woke up next to him.

"Dude, the heat's out?" Ivy watches as Reid's eyes open. She gives him a grin. "Hey, there, Dorsey. You're looking good."

I expect my erstwhile lover to freak out and make the same types of excuses I am. Instead, he grins in a wholly adorable way. "Heat's working fine. Morning. Hey, Ani, can you show me where the tunnel is? I want to get a room because this thing is way too small. Can one of you grab my clothes? I would do it myself but I think Harper wants me to be modest."

He's going to be fun. He is taking this in a stride I would not think him capable of. "Clothes would be good, and he doesn't need to get a room because we're not doing this again."

He frowns. "Well, if I'm not on a leash then…"

He starts to push the covers down.

I put a hand on his chest. "You are absolutely on a leash."

His brows rise in challenge.

Such an annoying man. "Fine. It's probably going to happen again, but maybe we can go back to one of our places like regular humans. This thing was not meant for two."

"I'm good with that." He sighs and lies back. "Ladies, if you don't mind retrieving my clothes, I'll leave you to talk this out and go find us some breakfast. I'm feeling hungry today. Oh, and I should check my phone. My brother probably freaked out."

Ani's head shakes, and she turns slightly and picks up a garment bag. "Who do you think called us at this ungodly hour? Jeremiah said he noticed you were still here at three in the morning and came by to check.

He brought you a fresh suit so you don't have to walk of shame it. He also left you a box of condoms and a nice inspirational note."

"Thoughtful guy." If Reid is embarrassed that his brother came by in the middle of the night, cleaned up after us and left a note, he doesn't show it. He simply takes the boxers off the top and manages to put them on under the covers then looks my way. "These are pretty much the same size as swim trunks. I can go get dressed in the kitchen if we're alone and you can talk to your friends. Unless you want me to stay. I assure you I can be entirely amusing."

He's entirely obnoxious. "Go. And you should go home. People will notice if you're early. You don't ever show up until noon."

His nose wrinkles, and he leans over and brushes his lips against mine. "Maybe I'll switch things up. I'll be waiting with coffee. Craft services should be here."

Anika's mom runs the craft services table. It's set up in the ballroom, so they won't wander down here. Reid rolls off the air mattress and collects the rest of his clothes.

"Ladies," he says with a nod and then walks right out of the pantry like he didn't get caught with his pants down.

I sink into the bed because the air mattress did what they do, and now I'm kind of sliding off one side.

"I just… I mean I always thought if one of us was going to get caught sleeping with someone we shouldn't, it would be me," Anika says.

How soon they forget. I drag the sheet with me as I ungracefully force myself off the floor. "You did. You got caught sleeping with the dude you were competing with like a hundred other women for." I manage to get to my feet and look Ivy's way. "And you got caught sleeping with Heath when you wouldn't answer anyone's texts and we all thought you were dead in a ditch somewhere."

"It's New York City. I don't think we have ditches," Ivy replies. She looks Ani's way. "Do we have ditches?"

"You know what I mean." I need to find my lost dignity. I drape the sheet around me and try to appear as regal as possible. "Fine. Reid and I had an unscheduled meeting and we discussed the fact that we might be attracted to each other."

"You discussed it." Ani didn't sound sold on the idea.

"Maybe not so much with words," I allow.

Ivy's grinning. "I think her vagina discussed the situation with his penis."

I grab my clothes and try not to think about the fact that Reid's brother folded my bra and undies. I definitely hope they were dry at the time or Jeremiah Dorsey knows way too much about how his brother affects me. "It's just a fling. You have flings."

Ani shakes her head and passes me a bag. "I went by your place and got fresh clothes. Your mom left a note. Something about meeting with Paul and a reminder that your eggs are shriveling up. Is that how eggs go bad?"

My mother...

"I do not have flings." Ivy ignores the egg convo. "I have had four boyfriends, if you count Kyle Woods in the fourth grade. I do because I spent a lot of time writing out my married name in a notebook when we were supposed to be taking notes. Ivy Woods. I dodged a bullet there. Then there was college."

"The Irish guy." Anika winces. "Henry Plant. Yeah, you did not pick a guy based on how weird your name would sound with his."

"My point is none of us are known for straight on hooking up with a guy. We plan it. We think we can do the sluttiest of things with some dude we recently met and are working with and then we wake up and he's still there and he's offering you a breakfast bagel and it's a good bagel, and he likes tacos, too." Ivy can be weird sometimes, but she's pretty accurately described Heath's courtship.

I shake my head. "I don't think Reid and I are going to bond over food."

"I believe the point that Ivy is trying to make is that you aren't known for having wild flings, and you definitely aren't known for dating coworkers," Ani points out.

I manage to get clean undies on. Even though I'm irritated at being found out, I'm also grateful for the clean clothes. "There's a reason I don't date at work. I'm the boss. It's a bad idea. Reid is not my boss. I'm not his. There are no power issues between us."

"I don't know. His pecs looked pretty powerful to me," Ivy replies. "You know this is inevitable. Emma says so."

Ah, Emma. Ivy and Heath named their AI matchmaking baby after Jane Austen's Emma. I'm certain they only read the CliffNotes since the heroine of that novel was a terrible matchmaker. Or maybe they did since she matched me with Reid.

"Emma is wrong, and you need to check out the code you've written because Reid and I are not a match." I point Ani's way. "Do not make a snarky statement about how matched we looked while we were sleeping. It was cold."

"It looked pretty hot to me," Ani replies and reaches out to the countertop behind her, bringing back another coffee. "To tide you over until your lover brings you some."

I growl her way, but I take that coffee. Now that I'm dressed I'm feeling less vulnerable. Not to them. I can be vulnerable to them, but Reid and I haven't talked and he seemed...weirdly cool with the idea we would do this again. "Not my lover."

"So he was bad?" Ivy asks. "Because you were wrapped around him. Were you looking for a good cuddle?"

He is a good cuddler. I didn't expect that. But then I expected him to finish, shake my hand, and we would both go back to our corners.

I didn't expect him to hold me all night.

I already kind of miss the feel of his arms around me.

"I think that's a no." Ivy's head nods as she studies me. "That's her 'I'm trying to figure out how to answer a question I don't want to answer' face."

I do have one of those. "Fine. It was good."

"*It* being? The cuddling?" Ivy presses on.

Well, she's obviously going to put me in a corner. I give her what I know she wants. "The sex. The sex was amazing. It was the best sex I've ever had."

"Me, too, baby." Reid slides the door open and looks fresh as a daisy in his suit and tie. He winks my way. "I'll save you a croissant. Don't be late. We have plans to make. Ivy. Anika. Sorry for the early morning wake up."

I wish he didn't hear that. It's true, but he doesn't need the ego stroking.

"He's peppy." Anika pats my shoulder. "You keep that up. Now what is this about plans, and I just figured out your mother is not talking about eggs. Not the kind you buy at the store. Eww. Why?"

Two complicated questions. I take the easier one. "Because she wants grandchildren to prove she's...I don't know, a grandmother. I'm ruining her life by not procreating."

"She's on that again?" Ivy asks. "I remember in high school she thought I was a bad influence because I wanted to code. She told me computers wouldn't get me a man. Hah. That's exactly how I lured Heath in. Computers and boobs. They're the only languages he speaks."

"Well, she didn't like me either," Anika says with a frown.

Ivy's eyes roll. "She loved you."

"Only until she realized I was as career motivated as Ivy." Ani sighs and leans against the counter. "I didn't even think about it when I read the card she sent. She told me I made the right choice. I thought she was talking about Luca, but she was telling me choosing marriage over my career was the right choice."

"You still have a career," I point out. My mother has been doing a ton of damage. "You just work with a tiara on your head."

She snorts, an entirely inelegant sound. "Do not. Mostly." She sobers. "What are you going to do about Reid? Because that did not look like a man who was one and done."

A feeling of deep uncertainty washes over me. I'm putting Ani at risk again. "I'm sorry. I'll try to be professional with him. I don't want to bring our drama into this show. I know how important it is, and last night was a moment of weakness."

Ivy huffs under her breath. "Told you."

Anika puts on her "deal with Harper because she's a stubborn asshole" face. Yes, I've seen that one a lot. "Not what I was saying. Look, I know I come off as sweet and maybe naïve at times, and when I read the press coverage about the Banover reno, it's a bunch of crap about it being a vanity project because Luca's a king and I couldn't possibly know anything. He's indulging me. They don't talk about the almost decade I put into my career. I let them because lowered expectations can sometimes lead to great things. I know how to control this narrative. I'll be in the editing room. You and Reid do what you like. Figure out if this is a situation that might work for you both. And then we decide if there's a love story attached to our reno or if I make it look like you and Reid barely spoke to each other through the entire process. It's up to me. You cannot fail me unless you walk away."

This is why I have the best friends. Smart, capable women who know their worth and who always have my back. I hug Anika. "I won't walk away. Not ever."

Ivy joins us. She used to be the one who hung back, but she now joyously throws herself in. "We can't walk away. You guys are my family, and I think my mom is seriously dating CeCe's driver. I heard CeCe calling him Diane's Boyfriend instead of Thomas, and he didn't correct her. You know how important it is to have a name in CeCe's world."

A revelation occurs to me. "Holy crap, you're right. The last time I talked to CeCe she didn't call me Ivy's Friend or Construction Girl. She called me Harper."

It's almost enough to bring a tear to my eye.

"She stopped calling me The Blonde One. I'm Queen Anika, but she told me to never forget who the real queen is," Anika explains.

We all know this answer.

"Lady Buttercup," we all say in harmony.

CeCe's overly privileged Maltese is definitely the queen of Manhattan.

"Though she should have rethought her name. Lady isn't above queen. I know. I had to take a class and everything," Anika says as we break up and she starts for the door. "I think I'm going to join the Dorsey brothers for some coffee. I don't know why CeCe didn't call her Queen Buttercup."

"I think CeCe would say lady feels younger and cuter." Ivy follows her. "She doesn't want to give her dog a complex."

"Uh, hello, queen here," Anika jokes. "Harper, you coming?"

"Yes, because we have some things to talk about, bestie." I can't forget Reid and I have a common enemy now, and it's probably time to declare war.

Anika sighs. "He told you."

"He told me."

Ivy frowns. "Told you what?"

"You know what—screw craft services. I love my mother, but this calls for mimosas," Ani declares.

And we're off.

Chapter Sixteen

"I can't tell you."

I bite back a groan, and Reid puts a hand on my shoulder. It's odd how comforting that hand is. When we moved this meeting to the hotel across the street from Banover, Reid followed along, joined by his brother. I warned Ani that this is New York and seating a large party without reservations is damn near impossible, and then realized that kind of truth is for the normal people of the world as the maître d' fawned all over her and assured her it was no problem to open a private dining room for us.

When Reid slid in next to me and his arm went around the back of my chair, I have to admit my heart did a fluttery thing. It was weird. And warm. I kind of liked it.

I turn to Ivy. "Do you know?"

Ivy shakes her head. "No. And I don't think she does either. Not really. She knows the name, but I doubt she has a relationship with the person."

"I can tell you it was purchased with cash, and the new owner sounds very British. At least her husband does. He's the one I've been communicating with over the phone. She is strictly emails to me and Reid," Anika explains. "And we had to sign nondisclosures. I think it's either a celebrity who wants to do this under the radar or some royal.

Maybe from the British royal family."

"I thought she was doing it for her daughters." I'm extremely confused as to why this is so hidden. Property records would have to be filed. "Can't we look it up ourselves?"

"Technically the sale doesn't go through until we're finished, but the couple has been more than happy to pony up cash for some of the unexpected problems we've found." Anika takes a sip of her mimosa. "The good news is the owners agreed to pay for the whole electrical fiasco. So Reid's budget isn't blown."

A long sigh goes through my guy. "Thank you, rich people."

Like he's not one of them, but I'm grateful, too. "Excellent. I already put a call in to an expert. I sent him the full scale and he thinks he can have the whole place done in two to three weeks."

Reid nods. "We can focus on the rooms he's finished. There's plenty to work on. Especially now that we're building out three separate residences."

It makes my heart hurt. "Does that mean what I think it means?"

Anika looks my way. "I told her the ballroom was nonnegotiable."

The ballroom. The heart of entertaining for that magnificent home. But Reid's right. It's impractical for today. There are plenty of spaces for entertaining. No one throws grand balls anymore, and Anika needs this sale. It sounds like the owner is actually being helpful if they didn't blink at 100K for electrical. I've known clients who would spend thousands and thousands on things like marble bathtubs and skylights and heated floors, but mention how much an HVAC unit costs and it's like I'm trying to bleed them dry.

The truth is it's not my house. "Ani, I'll do whatever you need me to do."

"I thought we were sticking together," Reid whispers.

I turn to him, seeing him differently than I did before. This man held me all night. He didn't have to. I certainly didn't expect him to. The night before was a weird revelation that's starting to sink in. "You honestly care about keeping the historical integrity of the ballroom?"

He's quiet for a moment. "I care that you care. I meant what I said. I'll back your play."

Damn it. He's supposed to be an asshole. He is not supposed to make me tear up. I'm supposed to be questioning all of my choices.

I'm not supposed to lean over and kiss him in front of my friends like we're together. He's not supposed to make me feel all warm and gooey. He's not supposed to utterly distract me from my goals.

And yet I let my lips brush over his.

A long sigh comes from the end of the table. "I thought I wanted my brother to find a nice girl, but it's kind of icky, isn't it?"

"Only a little," Ivy says. "But I do admit I'm not the most romantic sister."

Anika gently slaps at Ivy's arm. "Don't you make her feel bad about this. Jeremiah is jealous because Patrick is not moving."

Oooo, gossip. I sit up, and Reid sends his brother a stare. I look at him because he's got to have the goods. I've been ignoring everything except work, and now I wonder why. Life has become such a ritual because I'm holding myself apart. That stops now. If I'm in, I'm in. "He hasn't cracked that code yet?"

Reid's lips curl up. "He has not. I'll be honest. I took one look at that grumpy asshole and knew my brother was going to lose it over him."

"I have lost nothing," Jeremiah insists, but he's pouting a bit. It looks super cute on him. "We spent some time together, but he says I'm not being my authentic self. What is that supposed to mean? How do I be anything else?"

Reid turns thoughtful. "He said that?"

Jeremiah sips on his coffee. He and Reid both skipped the mimosas, as did I since I work with power tools. But Ani and Ivy are making up for it. "Yes, and it's ridiculous. We even had the hottest make-out session of my life, and let me tell you it did not happen on an air mattress. What were you two thinking? So it's obvious the man is attracted to me. I catch him looking all the time, but he's playing hard to get. I don't understand. This is not the way of my people. Emotionally hard to get, yes. But physically? I'm at a loss and I would simply move on to the next cutie patootie, but I really want this patootie."

Ivy's eyes go wide. "Maybe you need a therapist."

Anika huffs. "Patrick is not that bad."

"He's grumpy, but I kind of like him," I admit. "I've come to appreciate his honesty. I did look like a ghost the first couple of days. Now I make sure I have blush on even though it's weird to put on a bunch of makeup when I'm installing drywall."

"You look cute installing drywall," Reid says, and I feel his hand on the back of my neck.

Jeremiah is staring at us like he's never seen his brother with a woman before. Though I know he has. I've seen tons of pictures of him out with Britta and Reid.

Britta. I am not letting her ruin this. Reid told me they aren't together, and he doesn't have a reason to lie to me. I'm going with the flow, and the idea of her is not going to get in my way.

"Well, it's going to be his loss," Anika says, giving Jeremiah a supportive smile. "I thought the two of you would hit it off."

"I'm intrigued by the use of the word *authentic*," Reid says as his fingers move over the nape of my neck like he can't make himself stop touching me. "My brother is generally the person he presents to the world."

"I don't know. I think I have my secrets like anyone else," Jeremiah replies.

Reid's gaze softens. "Your secrets are your own. You don't owe them to anyone, brother. You don't lie to the world. You don't pretend to be someone you're not."

Jeremiah suddenly seems to find his plate interesting. "I don't know about that." He takes a long breath and seems to shrug off whatever emotion he was experiencing and he's back to peppy. "But we should talk about the ballroom because splitting it up will cause as many issues as keeping it. What would that space be for?"

Reid sits up. "This is supposed to be for a mom and her daughters. We've been treating this like a normal property. When we do that, we have to consider things like the resell value of the space and if we're creating a design that will speak to the most buyers we can find. But what if instead we consider this a multigenerational home?"

I'm not sure what he's talking about, but it causes Jeremiah to sit straight up and a gleam to come into his eyes.

"I like that," he says. "It opens up a world of possibilities."

Anika looks my way. Ivy just keeps drinking. "Any idea why they're so excited?"

Reid moves to the opposite end of the table, pulling a chair around, and suddenly Jeremiah has a pen in his hand and they're jotting things on one of the notepads Reid always seems to have.

I shake my head. "I don't know. I make things structurally sound and they make them pretty."

Anika moves down to take Reid's seat. "You're taking this better than I thought you would. Unless you're hiding it and you're going to have a meltdown later."

"Why would she melt down?" Ivy shifts, too, her voice going low. "I think Reid's made himself plain. He's not acting like a dude who's embarrassed by his one-night stand with the contractor. He's been all over you. I think he's under your sexual spell."

I snort. "I'm not going to melt down. And he is not under a spell. I don't have a spell."

"But you do have really strong thighs," Ivy points out. "I've seen you do that thigh master thing at the gym. All the guys drool."

Ivy could totally watch me because it wasn't like she was going to actually work out. "I don't think he's attracted to my thighs."

"You don't go with the flow." Anika looks worried.

"I'm trying something new." I steal a sip from Ivy's mimosa. One sip won't make me go crazy with a sledgehammer, and we're veering back into uncomfortable territory. "Look, we've got two months tops on this project. We don't work well together when we're sniping at each other. Let's see how it goes when we're both loose and relaxed. He's already looking peppier than he's been the whole time he's been here."

"I don't know if it was only the sex that pepped him up," Anika begins. "I've talked to Jeremiah, and he thinks the turning point was meeting you. Says Reid has been more himself since that day than he's been in years. Since the accident."

I'm sure there's more to it. "I think he's feeling like himself again. The accident was bad." He showed me the scars the night before. I traced them with my fingers and then kissed my way around them. "His hands still hurt from time to time, but I think his recovery is finally solid."

Ivy's head shakes. "No, there's more to that story. I've held off asking some questions."

I don't like the sound of that. "You think something's wrong with the accident?" I glance down the table, but Reid and his brother are still deep in conversation. "I don't think he would hide something."

"I don't think they're bad guys. I like them. I do have some questions, but I think I'm going to back off because like Reid said, they don't owe us explanations," Ivy finishes.

"I think they wanted to avoid a lawsuit," Ani says quietly. "The palace did do some questioning. They have to run a deep dive on anyone Luca works with. They found Reid didn't do anything but get distracted while driving at night. He was sober. It was an accident, but it somehow led to everything going wrong for him. I think his injuries are why he ended the show."

Nothing they've told me makes me think I'm wrong. "I can imagine having a life-threatening accident like that could affect you for a long time. He went to therapy. Both physical and emotional." The more I think about it, the more I admire him for it. "He's back on his feet, and maybe being with me for a few months will be good for him."

The way I hope it will be good for me. I might have walked into this restaurant thinking this was all a huge mistake, but his tenderness won me over and I can't even think that way anymore. Something warm opened inside me, and I have to see where it takes me.

Anika gives me a little smile. "That sounds good."

I nod. "I'm going to try to not get in my own way. Maybe this is a bright spot in an otherwise dim time of my life."

"Yeah, I hate that you think that way." Ivy's mood seems to shift. She's way more serious now and has a look that lets me know she doesn't particularly want to have this chat. "Because it's not. This should be a great time in your life. You're young and financially stable. You have a great group of friends. I think we should address what's dragging you down. It's not Reid. It's not this project."

"It's your family," Anika says.

Ivy's head shakes. "It's the business."

I send her a pointed stare because that feels like hypocrisy. "Really? You spend all of your time working."

"Not so much these days. Heath doesn't let me. At first it was that he needed to rest on Sundays, and wouldn't I like to lay around and watch a movie or go for a walk by the food trucks? And then I didn't work on Sundays anymore. Then he attacked Saturdays. I'm only working a couple of hours on Fridays now. Huh." She looks up like she's having a revelation. "He's kind of lazy."

Heath is anything but lazy. Heath provides balance to Ivy's ambition. Ivy is happier now.

"Not the point," Anika counters. "What Ivy is trying to say is that while we're all about our jobs, we can't make our jobs everything."

Ivy's head shakes. "Not my point at all. Look, I've literally built the whole ship and gone down with it before. When I built up Jensen Medical it was eighty-hour weeks, and I was passionate about it. I sometimes wonder if I would still be at it had my boyfriend at the time not been a dickwad. I did find purpose in that work. And now I find it in building Emma and having this life with Heath. But both of those things serve me. They place value on my quality of life. I'm not saying you shouldn't sink into your work. That can be a magnificent thing to do when the work is right for your soul."

"Like rebuilding a country," Ani says with a sniffle. "I feel the responsibility, but I also feel the love from the people we're working for."

"I'm trying to save a company, too," I point out. I don't understand what any of this has to do with my soul. It's business and family and responsibility. I honestly don't know how they think any of that is supposed to feed my soul. It mostly drags me down, but I know how disappointed everyone will be if I fail.

Ivy nods. "Yes, and how is that serving you? Is the responsibility worth it because of the love you get out of it? Does it fill your soul or suck it dry?"

"You don't understand. It's a family thing." No one does. No one I know was left with a whole family to take care of. Ivy only had to deal with her mom. Anika's parents split when she was in school. Heath has the greatest grandmother in the history of time. Luca has a country. Okay. I'll listen to Luca about this because he does understand. But I'm the one with a family's life hanging over me like the sword of Damocles. A stubborn family who doesn't understand how badly it can go. They don't know what it would mean to not have the company to fall back on. I don't know why, but apparently my cousins' parents didn't tell them all kinds of horror stories about what it was like to live without a dime to their names. I can still remember my grandfather telling me how two of his siblings died because they couldn't afford adequate medical care. He told me it haunted him because he was the oldest and his siblings were his responsibility. Then he told me I was the smartest and had to take care of things now.

Why is that your responsibility?

I try not to listen to the voice in my head. It's nothing more than selfishness.

"I understand far more than you think," Ivy says and seems to come to some kind of decision. "But you're right that I don't understand the whole family thing. It was just me and mom."

Damn. I didn't handle that well. Ivy's family life was hard in a different way. Diane Jensen only recently got her shit together and with the help of therapy. I sometimes wish my mom would get some therapy.

Reid mentioned it. Therapy. Had he gone in to deal with his awful father and the damage he left him and Jeremiah with?

How much damage did my dad do to me? Is my mom still doing it every time she tells me I'm failing her?

It doesn't matter because I'm tough and I can handle it. I am handling it. "Ivy, I didn't mean to say something hurtful. I don't want you to worry about me."

"Hard to do when you're my sister," she replies. "If there is one thing I've learned by being kind of alone the majority of my life it's that you make your own family. We spend all this time thinking blood is thicker than water, but sometimes that thickness is something that drags you down. Can I ask you something?"

"Of course." I hate that I put that serious look on her face. I love how much she smiles now, how comfortable she is in her own skin.

"I call you my sister. I truly think of you and Anika that way. If anyone asks about my family, it's you two and Heath I talk about. How do you think of me? What place do I hold in your heart?" She holds out a hand. "It's okay to say I'm a friend. It won't make me love you less or think of you in a different way. I don't have the ties you have so I might not understand them. I'm just curious."

Tears prick at my eyes, and I reach for that hand. I need her to hear me. "You are my sister. I don't need blood to know you two are my core family. Hell, I'm the one who poked and prodded when you were in San Francisco. I did everything I could to keep us all connected. I love you and I appreciate that you're worried, but I have this."

Even as I say the words and she squeezes my hand, I doubt them.

Do I have this? There are days when I want nothing more than to never have to think about my mom and cousins again.

Ivy nods and leans over, hugging me. "I know you do. But if you ever want to talk, I'm here."

"You ladies look serious," Reid says from the opposite end of the table. "Everything okay? Is this a sister thing?"

At least my temporary boyfriend understands. I sniffle. "Definitely a sister thing. We're fine."

"Good." He gives me a brilliant smile. "Because we figured out how to save the ballroom."

Now that is a plan I can listen to.

Confessionals

Reid

The electrical is done, so we're hoping for smooth sailing from here on. The ballroom is going to be shared space for all three residences. An inner courtyard, so to speak. Harper and I have been working on how we'll deal with access, but we think the garden should be a shared space as well, and the ballroom would be the back door for all three residences. She's got some great ideas. I'm sorry. What did you ask? Oh. The team. I think we're all working very well together. Certainly Jeremiah and I work well, but Harper turned out to be a great fit with us once we found our groove. There's something special about Banover Place. It's got both a historical feel, and it oddly seems like home. I can't put my finger on it. I've never lived in a place like this. I've spent my entire life in a high-rise. I've designed hundreds of interiors, and not once did I get attached. I'm definitely getting attached to Banover.

Jeremiah

He said that? He said he was attached? He said that to the camera? Does Harper know?

Harper

Well, I'm attached to Banover Place, too. I don't think it's weird for him to say that. I think it's rather lovely. It's kind of a magical place. Now that I'm over the shock of splitting it into three residences, I've grown to kind of love the idea that a family gets to live here. They get the best of both worlds. I like my apartment, but I have to say I've started thinking about how small it is. I think it would be hard to have a family in. Not that I'm, like, planning a family or anything. It's just...you know... Banover Place makes you think.

Reid

She said she's thinking about a family? Seriously? Why am I smiling? I don't know. I guess the weeks I've spent on this place have maybe made me start thinking about a family, too.

Jeremiah

I think I liked it better when they were yelling at each other. Has anyone mentioned where we're putting the sippy cups? That seems to set them both off. Also, could someone explain to me what a sippy cup is?

Chapter Seventeen

"Good morning, sunshine." Reid walks out of my bedroom looking ridiculously delicious in a pair of PJ pants and a T.

It's the third straight night he's spent with me, and we're weirdly functional as a couple. Not that we are. We're playing around. That's what I keep telling myself.

Except we're only days in and it doesn't feel like play. It feels like comfort.

Don't get me wrong. We have been screwing each other's brains out, and I expected that. What I didn't expect was sitting around and watching old movies with him while he works on his never-ending scarf. I knew he would be sexy. I didn't think he would be so adorable sitting on my couch with knitting needles in his hands.

I'm fascinated with his hands. With the scars he took in the accident. With how he's working so hard to regain his mobility.

I look up from the plans I'm working on. Redesigning a home to be three separate homes is a lot. The architect might be the one doing all the technical plans, but I have to figure out if it can actually be done. "Morning. There's some coffee, and I made some toast and eggs."

"You are a busy bee this morning." He kisses the top of my head.

I glance up at him. "Have you even been home in the last couple of days? I saw your brother brought you fresh suits. We can stay there if you need to. I would suspect Aggie is lonely."

He chuckles. "Aggie will pour all of her attention on Jeremiah. He loves it when I'm gone. He plays the lonely boy, and she makes him all his favorite treats. If I stay away for a couple of weeks, he'll get pudgy. But I like it here."

I snort at the thought. "It is as far from a beautifully designed space as you can get. None of my furniture matches, and the most expensive piece is from IKEA."

"Hey, that desk you're sitting at is a Nakashima," he points out. "I think it's real. If it's a knock-off, it's spectacular. That is some mid-century modern elegance."

"It was my grandmother's. When she passed they let the grandkids take a few mementos. My cousins naturally took anything they thought was valuable. But the desk was old and used, and it's not like my cousins spend a lot of time working at a desk. I always loved it. I guess I didn't think about the designer until one of my friends mentioned it. I like the wood. It's plain but not plain, if you know what I mean."

"I do." He puts a hand on the top of the desk, running it over the smooth, elegant lines. "George Nakashima didn't like the idea of industrially produced furniture. He preferred to have his designs crafted by true artisans. He wanted his designs to represent the trees he worked from. Elegant. Natural. Peaceful. And that's why I like it here. You see a piece of my soul in the way I designed the penthouse. Masculine. Ultra modern. Designed for form over function. This place is a piece of yours. Comfortable. Functional and yet warm and inviting."

I tilt my head up to look at him. "I'm functional?"

He gives me a grin. "Very functional, but I like your form, too, baby." He leans over and kisses my nose. "I like your form a lot. In fact, I could show you how much I like your form."

I playfully push him away. He's insatiable. "We are due at Banover in an hour, and I have to go into my office and tell my cousin I need an extra couple of weeks since I now need to oversee a lot more work. Though I talked to Lenny, and he can handle some of it. He's excellent, by the way. I like working with him."

"He's a good man, and I'm glad he can give you some flexibility, but I hate that your cousin keeps calling you." He moves to the kitchen and pours himself a cup of coffee. "I would think he would use this time to show everyone he can run the company."

"The problem is he can't. So he's trying to use this time to show everyone how little I care," I explain. "I've got my head wrapped around the idea of three residences, but the timing is hard. I'm supposed to start an office complex upstate in six weeks. I'm pretty sure we won't be done in six weeks."

He huffs. "There's no way. I mean we'll likely be doing the finishing work, but you still need to be there. We'll be doing a lot of filming in those weeks."

I don't like to think that far ahead, but it seems as though I need to. I need to remind myself that we have an end date. "Did you have another job lined up? I don't suppose you need it. How long do you usually take between jobs?"

He takes a sip and leans against my counter. "I'm heading out to LA as soon as this is done, and my brother and I will be taking meetings. Since we shut down *The Dorsey Brothers* show, we've been doing a lot of private contracts, but the truth of the matter is the show pays so much better and we're getting to the point that we need to consider money."

"You?" I raise a brow.

He nods and gives me a "what are you going to do about it" shrug. "My father was in a considerable amount of debt when he passed. It was why we first agreed to do the show."

We've talked a lot about work in the last couple of days but not about his past. I'm insanely curious, but I've been trying to play it cool since we're involved in a casual fling. It's the opening I've been waiting for. "I kind of thought you liked being on TV."

"I don't mind it. I did at first. I enjoyed the actual work. I quite enjoyed working with the families. When we were strictly private design consultants we worked for very wealthy people. Half the time they didn't appreciate what we did. Doing homes for working-class people is different. I know we joke about how deeply urbane my tastes are, but making things work for a family while staying within a budget is far more rewarding."

"Why did you stop?"

His eyes go to the floor, and he takes another sip of coffee. "After the accident I couldn't work for a while, and we had some trouble with the production studio. I was in physical rehab for months. I shut down after the accident. I let things go. We had been almost ready to sign a deal with a company to design furniture and household goods. I regret not signing that deal now. New York City property taxes can be draining to a bank account. Since the accident I've had some unexpected expenses, and the world of reno TV moves shockingly fast. I was grateful to Luca for thinking of us. It gives us a real step up in getting back in the game."

It's good to be reminded that he won't be here for long. It even sounds like he might sell that gorgeous penthouse of his. I don't blame him for that at all. It's far too big, and no matter how he decorates it there are bad memories there. "Well, I hope you get what you want."

He studies me for a moment. "Lenny isn't coming with us. Says he's too old to travel around the country. This is his last job before retiring."

"Oh, I'm sorry to hear that." I've come to like Lenny.

He stares as though waiting. "Harper, we'll need a contractor."

"Oh, you want me to introduce you to some people? I don't know if Samantha is completely ready. She's pretty young and needs more time, but she's going to be great one day and she looks…" I'm interrupted by him chuckling and leaning over to kiss me.

"I don't want Samantha. Nothing against her, but I like to hire the absolute best," he whispers against my lips. "And you are the best."

The idea sparks something deep inside, but I can't give up my whole life to follow some man around. "I have a job."

"Unless they oust you, and then you'll need one." He straightens up and genuinely looks like he would enjoy the scenario. "Think about it. No more big boxes. No more huge crews. And all the orgasms you can handle."

I'm about to argue that making orgasms part of the job is unprofessional—and really hot—but then I hear someone opening my door.

I groan as I realize who it is. "I'm so sorry, Reid. That is my mother."

"Harper," she calls out. "Harper, are you still here?" She walks into the living room, lips pursed as she looks me over. "I thought you would still be here. Those Hollywood people are making you soft. Your father was always at work long before the sun rose."

I stifle a groan. "They're not from Hollywood. Many are hardworking Canadians, though this one is New York born and bred. Reid, this is my mother, Margie Ross. Mom, meet…"

"Why on earth is Reid Dorsey in your house?" She smooths back her hair and is suddenly smiling. "I'm sorry, Mr. Dorsey. I'm completely forgetting my manners. It's so lovely to meet you. Oh, I wish Harper had cleaned up more. I assure you I taught her how to keep house properly."

She starts to straighten up the mail I chucked on the end of the bar.

"Mr. Dorsey is here because we…" I begin.

"Are dating." Reid moves to my side, his arm going around my shoulders. "And her place is perfectly lived in. I can't stand it when a house is neat as a pin. It lets me know the person who lives there doesn't have a life."

I turn my head to stare at him but he's serious. This man never has a thing out of place. His home is immaculate. "I should tell Aggie," I say under my breath.

His lips kick up slightly. "She knows I don't have a life."

"You're dating Reid Dorsey?" My mother looks shocked. It's good to know I can still do that to her. "And you didn't tell us?"

I never planned to tell her. Reid has zero idea the can of worms he's opened. "It's pretty new, Mom. And also casual."

"Not so casual I didn't wake up here this morning," Reid offers. "So you should also consider the fact that having another whole human being in a place can make it messier. It's not bad. You keep a fine house."

I didn't consider the fact that he is defending me. He doesn't even know my mom but he's telling her to lay off. Ivy and Ani stopped a long time ago because the fight's not worth it. I'll tell Reid the same thing once she's gone but… I realize how alone I've been feeling. Maybe I won't tell him. It's dangerous because he told me he's leaving for California, but I can't help but revel in the warmth I feel right now.

My mom stops fussing. "Well, I guess Harper works, so it's hard to keep up both. Harper, I wanted to talk to you about having a big family gathering before the meeting in a few weeks. I know there's been trouble, and everyone is anxious about the new changes you've made."

I step away from Reid because suddenly my shoulders are up around my ears. I am anxious. Everything seems to be slipping through the cracks, reminding me how much I'm needed there. Paul is sloppy and he puts his buddies in lead jobs on the sites rather than the person with the best experience and skills. "I've explained to you that they aren't arbitrary changes because I'm some kind of evil oligarch trying to take all the wealth for myself."

She sighs. "Harper, no one thinks that. Everyone knows how hard you work. I know some of the things your father did weren't perfectly legal, but he did them for the family. We need to sit down and figure out how to help. Aunt Elaine needs a new car."

"Aunt Elaine is ninety-two, and they took her license because she smashed into a fire hydrant the last time she drove."

"Well, she was trying to get to church."

Oh, how she rewrites history. "She was right outside the liquor store. There was a case of beer in the back seat."

"I'm sure she was buying that for someone else." My mom's lips purse. "Harper, I didn't teach you to judge people like this."

"Yes, you did. It's literally all you did my whole childhood, up until right this second."

She shakes her head. "You and your precious sarcasm. You are going to give your new boyfriend the wrong impression. Oh, Reid... Can I call you Reid?"

"That's my name." He looks entirely too amused by the situation.

Mom nods primly. "Reid, you will have to come to our family dinner. You're always so gracious on the television. Very masculine, but in an old-school way. A veritable knight. You might soften up my daughter's image."

Reid gives her a bland smile. "Harper doesn't need softening up. She's the CEO of a company that people depend on. She's too soft if you ask me since she keeps people on the job who are clearly not competent. Otherwise, she wouldn't have to rush from her passion project two or three times a week in order to save her cousin. Who has been doing this job for every bit as long as she's been, so he should know how to handle a client. It's almost like he wants her to fail."

"Paul would never put the company in jeopardy," Mom insists.

"And yet he keeps doing stupid things that upset the clients," Reid replies, and I'm surprised that he's been keeping up with my day-job problems. I wonder who's been talking to him. "Suddenly the man can't read his own bids and overbuys for a site and has to ask the client for extra cash?"

I groan. Yeah, I handled it. "I called the provider. They let us return the extra materials, but they don't usually do it. I barely scraped out of that one, and the client is still upset Paul came to them."

"He's overworked, too." My mother stares at me. "He has children."

She's making my argument for me. "And a wife who does all the work. You know I've actually been to Paul's place. He works. He golfs. He drinks with the guys. So please don't tell me Paul works harder than I do because I don't have children. Go talk to his wife because she's the expert. And Mom, I don't have time for some reunion party where I'll be inundated with requests I have to turn down."

"That's the point. Don't turn them down," Mom orders. "Give on a few of them and I promise the board meeting will go exactly the way we need it to. You need to stay in control of the company. I think if you would give Paul a raise so he makes what you make, it could go a long way to get the two of you on the same page."

"Why would a site manager make as much money as the CEO?" Reid asks, crossing his arms over his chest and studying my mom. "Harper does almost all of the administrative work, on top of being in charge of all the sites and planning. And dealing with the unique problems of a family owned and operated business."

Ah. Now I know who he's been talking to. I had lunch with Lenny a few days back and went over all of my day-job problems. He's the one who pointed out that dealing with family members would be even worse than a bunch of board members since at least you knew the only thing the board member wants to do is make money. I get to deal with the fact that my cousin Susan, who works in accounting, hates my cousin Deanne, who handles buying and billing and shamelessly stole Susan's boyfriend in eleventh grade. They are still at war to this day, and who gets to mediate? It sure as hell isn't Paul.

"Oh, Harper has people who help her, and also it's important to consider the fact that Paul has a family to take care of," my mother says primly. "He has two beautiful children. They have to be considered."

"Harper, I might need to start drinking early today," Reid announces. "This is what you deal with?"

"Pretty much. It's the 1950s with my mom," I reply and again, I can't say how good it feels to have someone back me up unashamedly.

He leans over and kisses me briefly. "I'm going to finish getting ready because I am incapable of not mansplaining feminism right now."

He's wrong about that. "Oh, it's not mansplaining if the person who the man thinks needs the explanation actually needs the explanation. It would be mansplaining to me. It's just explaining to her. But I would save my breath. She lives in denial, and there's no talking her out of it."

He smiles, an expression that sends a thrill of heat through me. "Thanks for the advice. I'll get dressed and we can go in together. I might call and tell CeCe's butler there's an emergency and he'll send a car and we can skip the subway."

I'm about to ask why CeCe would send us a car, but she does enjoy ordering people around, and she likes Reid. She doesn't even hit on him, so I know she likes him. Oddly, she does hit on Jeremiah, but I think it's because he's gay.

"Well, he's ruder than I would have thought," Mom says with a frown. "I guess he puts on a good show for the TV."

This is why I didn't want them to meet. No one is ever perfect enough for my mother. "He's a nice man. You were being mean to me, and he likes me."

Her head shakes. "I wasn't being mean. I'm trying to help you."

"I don't want help." I take a long breath and pray for patience. "I want Paul to be able to do his job. The whole point of this was me getting time to work on something I've wanted to my whole life and Paul getting the chance to prove that he's better than me. Something he's wanted to do his whole life. He's screwing it up. No one is going to oust me, Mom."

Tears pool in her eyes. "That's how they're talking. Your cousins are going to back Paul if you don't at least listen to them."

She clearly doesn't understand. If I give in once, I'll be doing it the rest of my life. My dad was lucky he was only audited once, and I was able to work it out. But beyond asking for cash, my family has other asks. "Mom, they want me to fire people who've worked for the company for decades so they can give their kids jobs when they are not qualified. I offered them internships so they can learn the business and be ready when a couple of our older guys retire. I've offered them daywork. They want their sons to walk in as managers. I can't do it. It would hurt our productivity and our morale."

She shakes her head. "You won't listen to me. Well, I hope you get out of this what you need. I'm afraid if you're not careful you're going to lose your family. I don't suppose you want my advice on your new boyfriend."

I so do not want that. "Nope."

She ignores me. "He is not like the boys you've dated before. He's a serious man with a serious career and a lot of eyes on him. He's been seeing a model for a long time. I overheard some of my friends talking about the fact that they broke up, but they seem to do it a lot. It's only a matter of time until he goes back to his real life. With models and parties and wild times. You can't hold a man like that."

The words don't surprise me at all. They still hurt, but I'm starting to turn to other people for the support I should be able to expect from my mom. "I probably could. You need the right rope, and I'm good with knots."

She huffs. "I mean it, Harper. You're going to get your heart broken or worse, you'll look like a fool and it will be all over the papers. Everyone will know. I've seen pictures of his ex. She's considered one of the most beautiful women in the world. How do you expect to compete with that? He's being kind about the apartment. It's a mess. You have to offer a man a safe, clean place. You have to treat him like a king, and you can't even be kind to your own family."

"It sounds like she's trying to be smart about her business so it still exists for her family. Also, Britta is gorgeous on the outside but like a painting, there's not a lot beneath her surface." Reid is buttoning up his dress shirt as he stands in the hallway, a deep frown on his face. "Well, there's a lot of selfishness and narcissism. Don't believe the gossip about me, Mrs. Ross. I'm quite a homebody, and your daughter is far more beautiful to me than any other woman I've ever seen. Knew it the first time I met her, but she's a little stubborn. So I'm going to ask you to never again speak that way to your daughter. Certainly not in my presence."

There's something deeply sexy about him right now. But I also know this is going to bite me in the ass because he won't be around to defend me forever.

"Well, I certainly haven't given a good impression of myself." My mom starts for the door. "I'm only trying to spare my daughter, Mr. Dorsey. When you have children you'll understand that sometimes you have to be cruel to be kind. The truth is often hurtful but it's best to get it out there and deal with it. Harper, when you come to your senses, I hope your family will still be there for you."

With those loving words she's off. I sigh. "And that is my mom."

He turns me so I'm facing him. "That was a lot. Does she always talk to you like that? Who does she think you are? Also, you don't have to tie me up to keep me, but we could discuss tying you up. I think you would look extremely hot tied to my bed."

I go up on my toes and kiss him. I don't think he'll be around the next time my mom ambushes me, but I'll remember this moment for the rest of my life.

He picks me up and starts to carry me to the bedroom.

Work can wait.

Chapter Eighteen

"Hey, you want to go back to my place or are we going to yours?" Reid stands in the doorway to the primary bedroom in what I've started to call residence one. It's the easternmost of the three brownstones.

We've spent the last month making huge changes to Banover Place. There are now three kitchens and three primary bedrooms and three great rooms. Each residence has four bedrooms, and the good news is none of them have bad wiring now.

I glance up from the crown molding I've been working on all afternoon. I want to make sure I don't damage the original wood. "Oh, I think we should put Jer out of his misery and spend the night at your place. Your brother is needy. He fell asleep on the couch last night. I thought he was going out."

Reid looks superhot in his perfectly tailored suit. It appears he's spent some time in front of the camera. "He was supposed to meet this new guy Anika set him up with. He called it off at the last minute. I swear I've never seen him so hung up on a guy before. It's not like Jer's a player or anything, but he tends to take his shot and move on if it doesn't work. He's hung up on Patrick."

"I don't get it," I admit. "Not the being hung up on Patrick bit. I don't get why Pat won't give him a shot. They're adorable together. They get along great on set, and it's not because Pat's hiding something.

He thinks Jeremiah is. It's weird."

Reid moves into the room and holds a hand out to help me up. "So my place it is then. Do you need to pick up fresh clothes or did you stash some last week? I found a pretty pair of undies sliding around with my boxers the other day."

I am so crazy about this man. I tilt my head to look at him, giving him wide eyes. "Why, Mr. Dorsey, do you have some floozy you're hanging around with?"

He grins and moves in closer. "Nope. Just one gorgeous contractor who is awfully good at stretching the truth about timelines." He kisses my nose, a sweet gesture. "You do not need a full week on that second-floor bathroom in residence three."

Okay, I probably don't, but we all stretch timelines. It's nearly inevitable that something will go wonky, and then we're on time. If everything is smooth sailing, then we look like superheroes. "I stand by my timeline. Also, the soaker tub isn't here yet, so I can't even start. I think you should rethink the flooring in the primary."

He looks down at the parquet floors. "I would think you would love these floors."

I kind of thought that was why he was keeping them. "They aren't original. These babies were put in no earlier than ten years ago, and they were done pretty cheaply. The original stops at the doorway. I pulled a little up and I see some evidence of water damage. I think the foundation fixed the problem as cheaply as they could. So you can happily put some plush carpet in."

He sighs and stares down at me, his hand coming up to caress the line of my jaw. "Because I like something warm on my toes in the morning. But it's not ours."

I like the way he's started to use the term *ours*. This project feels like ours. "I think we should design it like it is. I was told this unit is for the oldest daughter. She and her husband have an appreciation for the finer things. They're both interested in architecture and history. They sound lovely. So let's surprise them with a stunning-looking home that's also functional and comforting. I like the carpet at your place."

"Huh. I kind of thought you didn't like my place." His hands smooth over my hair.

"I guess I don't feel like I belong there. It's gorgeous. Don't get me wrong. It's stunning, but it doesn't feel like a home. I'm always worried I'll break something."

"Then you wouldn't mind if I maybe moved," he offers.

Oh, I'm not sure I like the sound of that. "Depends on where you're moving."

He stares at me for a second like he's trying to figure out what he really wants to say. "I want to talk to you about something, but there's part of the story that isn't mine to tell."

"Okay. Does it involve you moving to, say, LA?" There's another possibility. "You got a new show and you're moving to Toronto." I've learned a lot of the home and garden TV world is centered around Canada.

I know I said I was going with the flow, but it turns out I like the flow. I don't want the flow to end when we finish this thing up in a couple of weeks.

"I'm not leaving New York," he says. "I'm going to maybe down-size."

I breathe a sigh of relief. "That's good. Downsizing can be refreshing." Something about the way he says it makes me think it might not be his choice. "It's a lot of condo for two of you."

He nods. "And a lot of bad memories that turns out can't be glossed over with new paint and furniture. Maybe you can help us find a new place. Anything up for sale in your building?"

"My building is a dump," I point out. "But Lydia's is more your style, and I happen to know there are two units up for sale there. I know because I was kind of thinking about looking at the smaller of the two. I probably can't afford it, but I thought I'd look."

"Then we can look together," he says and kisses me again. "But tonight we'll go to my place. I'll call and let Aggie know we're coming. I think she said she wanted to make meatloaf sometime this week. She thought we could use some comfort food."

"Sounds delicious." I'm all about someone feeding me. "Let me finish up here and we can head out."

"Not staying late?" Patrick stands in the doorway, a clipboard in his hand. "Sorry to interrupt. I need to check on the camera in the corner. It needs a battery refresh."

It's so easy to forget about the cameras. I take a step back. Reid frowns but moves to my side.

"We were about to head out," Reid responds, "Unless you need us for something. I finished my to-cameras with Tony. We're shooting at the design studio tomorrow."

Patrick nods and reaches up to pull the small camera in the upper corner of the room. "Nope. We have everything we need. And don't worry about the cams, Harper. Anika is taking care of you in the editing room. I sat in with her last week, and if you don't know the two of you are hooking up like crazy pants, you look like congenial coworkers. It's all bland, if you ask me."

"Bland?" I don't like the word. I think Reid and I are anything but bland.

He shrugs as he opens the camera's battery pack. "I think a hint of romance would spice things up a bit. She and Luca have the laid-back royals' thing going, but everyone knows they're together. We have enough footage of the two of you yelling at each other for an excellent enemies-to-lovers storyline, but Anika says no."

"We're not hooking up," Reid argues.

"We're not?" I was kind of looking forward to hooking up with him tonight. After some of Aggie's delicious food. Ooo, and I bet she makes a hell of a breakfast, too. I threw a protein bar Reid's way this morning because we were running late to catch the train that took us from Hell's Kitchen to the Upper East Side. Aggie will probably be able to shove crêpes in my mouth.

"That is not how I would prefer to refer to our relationship. It makes it sound cheap," Reid admits.

"What would you call it?" I'm interested in hearing this. I've been careful to not refer to him with anything that sounds permanent. Even though we've taken to going out as a couple with Ani and Luca and Ivy and Heath. A lot. He weirdly fits right in with the supernerd and the king of a small European country.

"You're my...Harper," he says and then sighs. "You're my girl-friend."

"Huh." Yes, I'm at the stage Ivy talked about where he feeds me enough and I'm used to him and I kind of go with it. Past Harper urged me to fight this. Current Harper is surprisingly cool with it. "Okay."

"So you don't have to jump ten feet away from me when you remember there's a camera on us twenty-four seven." Reid reaches for my hand and pulls me in close.

"It's not that bad," Patrick insists. "It's only in the rooms that are actively being worked on, and they're all motion activated. The ones filming the actual work, that is. If you two decide to go at it here, please use one of the closets. Or the attic room. That one's finished and not due to see a camera until the big reveal."

We do all our sex stuff in real beds now. I do not say that to Patrick, but Reid's eyes catch mine, filled with humor. We're thinking the same thing. We've been good since that first day in the…kitchen I was actively working on at the time.

Yep, we've got a psychic thing going because his eyes go wide.

"I didn't think about that," he whispers. "The kitchen. There was absolutely a camera in there that would have been able to see the island."

The island where he'd made a meal of me. And then climbed on top of me.

"What?" Patrick asks when he turns and sees the shock we're going into. "I'm serious. So you kissed a little. You're not the first couple to kiss on camera. Ani's never mentioned it, so it's not a big deal. You can call her. I know she's on a plane to Ralavia but I've heard they're using CeCe's, so I bet the cellular coverage is spectacular. Now, see, if I was going to worship a woman, it would be CeCe Foust. That woman knows how to live."

"Who would have looked at the tapes from the residence one kitchen reno?" My voice is as tight as the rest of my body. I made a sex tape. I didn't mean to make a sex tape. It might be no big deal if I made a sex tape with some random dude, but I made a sex tape with a reality TV star.

"It must have been off," Reid says, squeezing my hand. "If that footage exists, we would have heard about it. Ani would have told Ivy, and Ivy would never stop ribbing you about it."

"What footage?" Patrick asks.

"My brother would poke me with it twenty-four seven," Reid insists. "So it doesn't exist."

I'm not so sure. Oh, he's right about Ivy, but Anika might have kept her mouth shut. She's a queen now. She's learned decorum and grace.

Patrick's gaze moves from Reid to me, and his jaw drops. "Holy shit. You two did it in the kitchen? Like out in the open?"

I shake my head. "It was over a month ago, and it was way after hours. No one but the security guard was still there, and we all know how he likes to get his naps in. Where would the footage be stored? It's wireless, right?"

Patrick nods. "Yeah. It goes to a mainframe that the editing staff and director can access. We have literally thousands of hours of footage. We don't go through all of it. The cameras are on simply to catch footage we need. If we don't have a place in an episode for Harper working on the kitchen, then the likelihood is no one's even seen it."

I let loose a long breath. He's right. The work I was doing that night was all prep work for the next morning. Boring stuff. I wasn't even supposed to be working. There would be no reason to go through it.

Reid leans over and kisses the top of my head. He's a deeply affectionate man and while it surprised me at first, I've gotten to where I crave his kisses and touches throughout the day. "It's okay, baby." He looks to Patrick. "It's important that we erase that footage. If it gets out, it could cause an enormous amount of embarrassment for the network and Anika and Luca."

I feel a flush stain my cheeks. I didn't even think of that. "Yes. We need to make sure it doesn't exist."

Patrick nods. "Yeah, I'll need permission. Let's go to the office and I'll call her directly. I assure you Tom will be all for not having a sex tape associated with his pretty renovation film. I'm not even going to tell him. *House of Skanks* still haunts his dreams. What were the two of you thinking?"

He stalks out of the room.

Reid follows, gently tugging me along. "We weren't."

"Obviously," Patrick mutters. "I know it's practically blasé in Hollywood, but we answer to Toronto, people. Toronto and Ralavia. Ralavia is like a Disney movie. It is very PG. Toronto is… Well, it's full of Canadians, and they are not used to scandal among their beloved celebrities."

"I'm American," Reid points out as he follows along. "And a New Yorker. I assure you we are used to scandal. She's my girlfriend. It's practically boring sex." He winces when I punch him in the arm. "Baby, I don't want anyone else watching it. You know how hot it was. We don't have to share it with the world. But for our own personal record it was filthy and glorious."

Patrick turns toward the great room we're using as a mini production office. "I do not need to hear that. Do you remember what day it was?"

"It was like a Tuesday. Maybe Wednesday." I realize I don't have to wait for Patrick. I have a direct line to the woman herself, and I don't even have to worry about Ivy listening in. This is a quick trip back so

Luca can sign stuff because, well, king.

"October fifth around midnight," Reid corrects. "For the record it was a Friday."

I stare at him. "You are very concerned about records."

"I'm sorry. When I get nervous I fall back on all the procedurals I've watched over the years. We might need a lawyer," he says.

Patrick pales. "We do not need a lawyer. This is not freaking CSI. This is a tiny show about a home renovation. It is supposed to be easy. This is where my blood pressure is supposed to go to flatline, Dorsey. There is not supposed to be any excitement here, damn it. I am absolutely not supposed to need hacking skills to go into the production files and delete what is considered company property."

I push the number for Ani's cell. "I'll get you the go ahead from the boss herself."

"I would assume you want to hide the whole 'I made a sex tape' thing," Patrick points out.

I'm about to explain when Reid waves him off. "She was always going to tell Ani, and she'll ask Ani not to tell Ivy because Ivy will tease the hell out of her. Ani will agree to keep it quiet, but Ivy will take one look at them and know she's been left out and they'll tell her anyway. There's no point. Look, I know I seem like a vault of toxic masculinity wrapped in a designer package, but I'm going to tell my brother, too, because I'm going to need someone else to know. The key is to keep it in the family, so to speak."

I kind of want to make out with him right now. The man knows me.

"Well, I don't want to be a part of the family, so to speak," Patrick complains. "Tell Ani I need the editor code."

"Hey, Harper," Anika says. "I was about to call you."

She sounds…concerned. I put aside my own worries because my bestie has a whole country and a brand-new production studio on her back. It's a lot. "Everything okay?"

She pauses. "I don't know how to tell you this. Harper, I don't even know what happened."

Shit. "I made a sex tape with Reid and it's gotten out, hasn't it?"

Reid curses beside me.

"Yes, how did you know? I got a call from the palace public relations office that one of the French gossip rags is going to run a story about it. The actual tape itself isn't out, but they're planning on running stills from it. Luca's on the phone with our lawyers," Ani says.

Patrick groans. "I'm going to go and get something to knock out Tom. Where is a drug dealer when you need one? Who thought it was a good idea to clean up Manhattan?" He starts walking toward the door. "My kingdom for a Xanax."

"Whoa," Jeremiah says as Patrick brushes past him. "It must be bad if we're talking sedatives. Can I help?"

"Can you go back in time and make your brother not create a sex tape that will forever be associated with a family show?" Patrick asks with a syrupy sweet grin. "No? Then you're useless to me. Oh, hey the gang's all here. Ivy, you should know that Harper..."

Ivy holds up a hand. "Made a sex tape." She gives me a thumbs-up. "Way to go, sister."

"How?" It's the only thing I can think to ask because this is moving way fast for me. Not five minutes ago I was a normal woman whose superhot encounter with a design star wasn't about to be placed on the Internet for the whole world to see.

Ivy strides right to the computer. "Ani asked me to come in and fix the problem here so no one else can access it. Do you want me to put it on a thumb drive for you?"

"Yes," Reid says.

"No," I reply at the same time.

"Ivy's there?" Anika asks.

"I don't understand what happened." Jeremiah looks around at the chaos.

"Yes, Ivy's here, and she apparently knew before I did. I'm not sure I like that," I complain.

"Well, Jer," Ivy says as her fingers start to fly across the keyboard, "when two people who pretend to not like each other go at it on a kitchen island in front of a camera, the inevitable happens. I'm just saying, Harper, shouldn't you have a copy for posterity?"

"Does she need the code? Tell her I texted it to her," Anika says in my ear.

"Well, I thought you would be smart enough to like put a little cover on the camera." Jeremiah sounds prim. "Like a cap or something. Maybe some tape."

"I was not thinking about the camera at the time," Reid admits. "They're easy to forget. You get used to them."

"Anika says she texted you a code," I tell Ivy.

It's chaotic, and I should be way more upset. I'm more irritated than truly worried. I don't want this to upset Ani, but honestly, I'm not ashamed of anything except not covering the camera. We should have thought about that.

"I don't need a code," Ivy says with a huff. "I'm already in, and I've got the login for the fucker who downloaded it. Tell her I'll send it to her, and I've got some hacker friends who can probably figure out who this person sent it to." She looks up with a frown. "Tell her I'll handle it. Keeps the feds from coming after her. My friend might not be the most law abiding when it comes to information. Although... Hey, does diplomatic immunity cover this? Can we make me a duchess or something because it would free me up."

I don't think that's how it works, but I agree with leaving Ani out of the less than legal parts. "Ivy's got this and we'll keep you up to date. I'm so sorry if this is going to cause you trouble. I would offer to fall on my sword..."

"You already fell on Reid's," Ani quips. "I'm not letting you quit, but it might be for the best if you hang in public and look like you're together. We can add in a romantic subplot and all will be well. I'll let you know what our lawyers say. It's going to be okay, Harper."

"I'll do whatever you need me to," I offer.

"Tell Ivy to send me that name so I can fire the asshole and then I don't want to know what she does. If she can cut this thing off at the pass, I would love it. Remind her CeCe has a ton of lawyers who would find getting her out of jail genuinely amusing," Anika says and then hangs up.

"It's one of the assistant editors." Ivy's face is lit by the screen. "I've got his email and I'm in. Gosh, why do people bother doing criminal stuff if they're not even going to try to hide their tracks? Huh. That's weird."

"You're awfully calm." Jeremiah's arms are crossed over his chest. "I thought we were trying to avoid scandal."

"I suppose I don't think it's all that scandalous. I was fucking my girlfriend. We do a mea culpa interview and we're cool." Reid huffs like he just thought of something. "We could get married and then it's even more boring."

"What?" Now I am shocked. Did those words come out of his mouth? "We can't get married."

"People have gotten married for worse reasons," Reid replies.

"Name one," I counter, my head still reeling.

"I don't know. What was the last *Dateline* I watched?" he muses and then snaps his fingers. "Oh, yeah. Man marries an heiress and she mysteriously falls off a mountain on their honeymoon and he inherits everything. See. Worse reasons than publicity and saving some money on an apartment. Think about it. That building is expensive."

"We've been casual for a month," I point out.

Reid snorts. "Sure. We've spent pretty much every second of the day together, and then we go back to your place or my place. The only time we're not together is when you have to go to a site to deal with your cousin's screwups. And I offered to handle him for you."

I can imagine how my cousin would deal with Reid Dorsey. I'm going to keep those two parts of my life separate. Especially since one of the two parts won't be around forever and I'll have to sink back into my real life. These days with Reid feel like a dream sometimes. Getting to work on this magnificent house is the same. I keep getting reminded I don't belong in either world. Reid is joking with me. He has to be. "We're not getting married because of a sex tape."

"Of course you're not," Jeremiah says, and I swear he breathes a sigh of relief.

That stings, but I move on. "We do have to consider how this is going to affect us if it gets out in the public."

"Already snagged it from the French magazine editor's system." Ivy never looks up. "I'm pretty sure I got every copy. They had it locked down, and I pulled some of the emails concerning it."

"You what?" Jeremiah is staring at her like he can't quite believe it.

"She's good at her job," I explain. "She's been hacking systems since we were kids. I'm pretty sure I passed Spanish because of Ivy."

"No, you magically made an A on your final," Ivy shoots back. "Anyone read French? I think this email is about the tape. It's from another company. Skonhet. Hmm. That doesn't sound French, but the rest of the email is absolutely French. I think."

The only other language Ivy speaks is code.

"It's the Swedish word for beauty." Reid looks grim as he replies.

"I told you she was planning something," Jeremiah says under his breath.

"I'll handle it." Reid turns and starts to walk away.

I rush to catch up to him. "Hey, what's going on?"

I'm confused. One minute we're kind of blowing it off, and now he looks like a man on a mission.

"It's nothing you should worry about," Jeremiah says, moving in beside his brother.

"I told you I'll take care of it," Reid replies, but he doesn't look me in the eye.

And it hits me. "Britta."

In the weeks we've been together he hasn't mentioned her once and I haven't brought the subject up. I don't like thinking about the fact that the guy I'm rapidly falling for used to date supermodels. Well, a supermodel. But just the one is enough to make me heinously insecure.

He hasn't done anything to feed that. He hasn't talked about her. There are no photos at his place. By all accounts he's not thinking about her at all when he's with me.

But the closed-down expression on his face kicks me in the gut. It's like a wall has gone up between us, and it's all about her. "I think we should talk about this. Let's go somewhere, get a drink and talk this out."

His fists clench. "I can't get a drink and talk this out, Harper. I've explained to you that I will handle it, and that's all I can say."

"Reid," Jeremiah begins.

Reid points a finger his brother's way. "Don't. Don't you even dare with me right now. You know exactly what's happening and why, and I'm not bringing her into this. Let's go."

Jeremiah puts his hands up like he's holding off a predator. "I know."

I don't like how he's pushing his brother. "Hey, he's done nothing wrong here. We need to take a breath. I know this is terrible, but we should calm down and talk this out."

"Of course. He's done nothing wrong. It's all me." Reid's eyes close briefly, and when he opens them I realize I've lost some battle I didn't even know I was fighting. "Harper, I'm sorry I dragged you into this. I won't allow that tape to be released or that story to run. If it does, I'll explain to the press that I'm entirely in the wrong."

I'm so confused but he's shutting me out, and I can't stand it. "Or we could talk about it."

He turns and walks away without a second glance.

"I'm sorry. I'm so sorry," Jeremiah whispers and then he's gone, too.

I'm left alone and wondering what the hell went wrong.

Chapter Nineteen

Two hours later I'm on the couch at Lydia's, a cup of tea in my hand and the delightful smell of Lydia's cooking in the air. It's kind of perfect except I've been crying for most of the time, and I hate crying. It sucks and I'm not good at it.

"I bet Britta cries pretty," I say with a frown, hating the fact that I know I don't. And that I've cried more over Reid Dorsey than I should.

"Okay. I don't know if I'm supposed to agree with you or tell you that she likely had her tear ducts removed in one of her numerous plastic surgeries." Darnell has babysitting duty since Anika is out of the country and Heath and Ivy are all wrapped up in their laptops trying to ensure they shut down everything. I know supposedly once something like this is out there it's out there forever, but Ivy assures me it didn't hit the Internet. They had the footage on lockdown so they would have the exclusive story. CeCe is in the office with them fueling the whole enterprise with vodka martinis and her joy at taking down the Euros, as she calls them. Darnell showed up for dinner and Lydia asked him to sit with me. I'm pretty sure he wishes he ate a PBJ at his place now.

He sighs and reaches out to pat my hand. "There, there."

I roll my eyes. "You don't have to comfort me. I'm fine."

Darnell sits back. "You're not fine. You have that look."

I wish I went back to my place, but the thought of heating up something frozen held little appeal. Although once Ivy's married and Ani's in her magical kingdom, there will be a lot of that. "I have a look?"

"Yeah, the one that tells me you're about to blow. Look, Harper, I'm going to be honest with you. You're absolutely my favorite. Ivy is bossy and surprisingly open about her feelings. Heath ruined her. She was all about business and cold, hard capitalism, and Heath was her Hallmark Christmas movie and now she wants to celebrate joy and shit. Anika is a walking ball of emotion. But you...you remember all those times when we would sit beside each other and never feel the need to talk?"

I sigh because I do remember. "Good times, man."

He nods. "Yes, they were, my friend. Yes, they were. So if you want to sit in our comfortable silence, I am here for you."

The problem is the silence doesn't feel comfortable right now. It feels like anxiety and making a mistake. I want to send angry texts to Reid telling him what a massive ass he is. This is why I'm really here. If I was home, I would probably drink too much wine and drunk dial his ass. "I don't need a man."

Darnell's head shakes in that "you are preaching to the choir" way. "No, you do not. You do not need a man to talk to."

"I can handle my own business." I did it for years. I don't need to talk to Reid about things. I don't need his opinion on how to handle my cousin. I don't need him to simply sit and listen and hold my hand the way he has the last month. I'm not weak.

"Yes, you can," Darnell agrees.

I don't need Reid for anything. Anything at all. I can take care of myself. "And by business, I mean orgasms. Does he think I'm going to go back to him after he refused to talk to me?"

"You should not." Darnell sounds firm in his agreement. Then he leans toward me. "Unless you want to. I can hail you a cab."

Asshole. I ignore him. He's my only sounding board right now, and I'm going to get all of this out of my system because I have to work tomorrow. "He made himself clear. He doesn't want to talk to me. He never wants to talk about this woman he spent years with. I can't tell whether they're star-crossed lovers or if she's stalking him."

Darnell groans, and his head drops back against the couch. "Are we doing this? Fine. We're doing it. What is the situation? All I know is you're sad because the guy in the suit dumped you."

He wasn't told much. He was handed a beer and told to take care of me. Poor guy. "He didn't dump me, exactly. He said he would handle something that I should really be a part of."

Had he meant to dump me? It didn't feel like he had but I was definitely dumping him because I won't be treated that way. He can't walk away.

We only agreed to sleep together while we were working. A short-term situationship with an end date. Except we kind of stopped talking about end dates. He even mentioned I should come to LA with him after the filming. I won't, of course. Although I thought about how nice it would be to walk on a beach with him and sit in one of those Hollywood restaurants with Jeremiah and listen to all the gossip he knew about the stars.

Why would Reid talk to his soon-to-be ex?

Darnell seems to make a decision and sits forward. "What is he handling? I need to know since if we're talking about, like, taking out the trash, you're overreacting."

Reid is very good about taking out the trash. I was a little surprised at how domestic he is. He even helps his housekeeper in the kitchen. "We made a sex tape, but it should have been lost in the hours of boring footage of me restoring cabinets, and according to Ivy the assistant editor went through it about a week ago trying to find some setup footage for one of the early episodes they're working on. He finds the footage and decides to cash in because he knows Reid's ex is always looking for a way to screw him over. Apparently this particular editor used to work on *The Dorsey Brothers* show."

"I'm sorry, Harper." Darnell gets extremely serious. "I thought we were talking about some run-of-the-mill breakup. I had no idea we were talking sex tape and potential international scandal. You're right. This is some serious shit. I am here for you. I might take a couple of notes because this sounds like a great plotline. Please continue. So the Swedish twig gets the footage of you and Reid going at it hard and what is she doing with it?"

This is probably going to go into one of his novels, but I don't care. He writes sci-fi so he'll turn me into some alien princess fighting to save the galaxy. I'm kind of on a roll now, and it helps that Darnell isn't looking at me with nauseating sympathy like Lydia or vowing bloody vengeance like Ivy. I did have to tell her she couldn't go after Reid. "She took it to a French publication."

"You mean a scandal rag."

"I do mean a scandal rag," I reply. "They were planning on running a story about how Reid found an American floozy, except in French it's something that means chicken. I don't know. Ivy ran it through a translator. Anyway, it was all about how he betrayed the beautiful model who loves him so much and I'm after his money."

"That sounds awfully predictable. They could come up with something better," Darnell says. "How did Reid handle it? Did Mr. Uptight lose his shit?"

"He's not that uptight when you get to know him. I think it's the suits that make him seem that way." Although I've come to think those suits of his are sexy as hell. "So when it first came out, Reid was cool with it. I was surprisingly chill. Like I'm in good shape. I don't know what the angles were or if the lighting was right, but I'm pretty comfortable with my body and I like Reid."

Darnell shakes his head. "Get to the good stuff. Reid was truly cool with his sex tape getting out?"

I shrug. "I thought so. He said we should go to the press together and maybe we should even get married."

A snort comes from Darnell. "You have not known each other long enough."

"That's what I said." But now I wonder if I shouldn't have taken him to the courthouse right then. Maybe he would have talked to me if we were married. That is such a ridiculous thought and exactly why I need to get all of this out of my system before I have to see him again. "Anyway, then Ivy announces it's Britta who has the tape and he loses his shit. But in that very Reid controlled way. He announces he'll take care of it."

Darnell waves the idea away. "Ivy already took care of it. The girl is thorough. Britta will be lucky if she comes out of this with her dignity intact. She's going to be put on a lot of mailing lists. Maybe a couple of watch lists, too."

I can't worry about Britta getting endless rounds of spam concerning male enhancement and tractors. Those are Ivy's go to's for some reason. "I know, but he didn't stick around to hear that part. He walked out and refused to talk to me about it. When his brother tried to slow things down, Reid yelled at him."

Darnell blinks as though he has to think the information through. "That does not sound like the Reid I've come to know. He practically treats Jerry like he's a sick toddler."

"No one calls him Jerry."

"He looks like a Jerry to me," Darnell continues. "So he blew up at the brother he adores and ices out the woman he tried to sneakily marry? All because of an ex."

I nod. At least he gets it. "See. That's it. He's either still in love with her and I'm in the middle of this twisted game they're playing, or he hates her and I'm in the middle of this twisted game they're playing. But in the last scenario he doesn't want to play."

"I like this." Darnell seems to think for a moment, and he's probably already plotting the book in his head. "So you're not upset that the sex tape has likely been viewed by both perverts and journalists who are probably perverts? You are upset that your boyfriend yelled at his brother and walked away. See. Another reason to like you. So I'm going to come down on the side of Reid doesn't want to be playing whatever games she's playing."

Or maybe he doesn't get it. "You can't know that."

"His actions speak louder than words," Darnell counters.

Ah, but Darnell is forgetting the most important part. "Mostly because he doesn't actually say words."

His lips press together as he looks me over. "Harper, I do not give relationship advice. It actually physically pains me to be saying these words to you. Like deep down in my gut where dinner should be right now."

I don't like receiving relationship advice. The only one who ever gives it is my mother and that's mostly to tell me I'm going to die alone. "Just say it."

"Has he given you any reason to doubt him?" Darnell asks.

"So many."

"Name one."

"All right. He hated me at first. He thought I shouldn't be working on a project like this."

Darnell's head shakes. "Nope. That was an opinion he had in the beginning. He's apologized. Has he given you reason to doubt that he doesn't want to be with you?"

I think about how to answer. "He tells me how much he likes me. It's weird and comforting. He's liberal with the praise, but why would I trust that? It could be how he gets me to do things for him. I've seen it happen before. Things can look good from the outside..."

He interrupts me again. "Nope. We're not talking about your rough childhood and your mom being a walking, talking mouthpiece for the patriarchy while your dad treated you like a son he needed to toughen up and had affairs behind your mom's back."

"Why are we talking about this?"

He stares at me. "Girl, get thee into therapy, as my friend Shakespeare would say. Seriously? You don't see the connection between your childhood and your inability to believe that your relationships can work out?"

He's not listening to me. "This is about Reid walking away. Not my dad."

"Everything is about your dad," Darnell insists. "Everything. Give me one thing Reid has done in the month you've been basically living and working with him that tells you he wants to walk away."

I love the way he put that. It lets me pivot back to my original point. "The fact that he literally walked away."

Darnell's eyes roll. "No, just let me make an appointment with my therapist guy."

I am so frustrated. "He walked away."

Darnell sighs and sits back. "It sounds to me like he ran away, and until you understand why you can't know what's really happening between the two of you."

And he's neatly summed up the issue. "He won't tell me. Believe me, I've asked."

He considers me for a moment, and I almost think he's going to leave it at that. It might be for the best since he doesn't understand. Or maybe I don't. Instead, his voice goes soft. "How much does he mean to you?"

I don't want to admit how much, but I guess honesty is the best policy here. "I care about him."

"Do you see yourself having any chance at a future with this man?"

"No." I groan and lean forward, setting my mug down on the coaster. "That's the thing. I don't see us together. How would it work? He wants to put together a new show, and this is my one and only. I'm worried about the next board meeting and the vote. If I take more time off, I lose the company to Paul. Even if Reid stays in the city most of the time, I work so much. I put in fourteen-hour days most of the time."

"How will any relationship work if you have that mindset?" His expression softens. "And this is what I mean when I talk about therapy. It's great for figuring out why you do the things you do. Especially the things that make a person miserable, that sabotage our growth and happiness. Have you considered the fact that working as hard and long as you do means you can't have a relationship?"

"Yes. Of course. I told you." I wonder if that's why Reid went into therapy. He said he did it after the accident. It's the one thing he likes to talk about. Not the accident but how he got help.

"Have you considered that's precisely the reason you choose to work the way you do?" Darnell asks. "I know in your head you don't have a choice. I know in your heart you have to do these things because they're your family and it's been drilled into you that family comes first. Even when it hurts. Even when they actively harm you. That's what your parents taught you. But if you were my kid, I would only want one thing for you."

"To be happy," a familiar voice says.

I look up and Lydia is standing there still wearing the bright yellow apron she dons when she's cooking. Lydia Marino is five foot nothing, with dark curly hair and big brown eyes. She has a loveliness that defies the marks of aging. There's something infinitely warm about Lydia, and I realize it's why I avoid having these talks with her.

Because I don't understand. Because her love and affection are unfamiliar to me.

It's easier with Diane and CeCe because while they're wonderful and supportive, they don't hug me and make me want to hug them back. They don't make me wish things went differently as a kid.

Darnell might be right. I might need therapy.

"Thank god." Darnell stands and waves a hand around. "I thought I was going to have to handle the whole thing. Lydia, you know I adore you, but I am not good at this mushy stuff."

Lydia walks right up to him and puts a hand on his cheek, her head turned up because he's got a foot on her. "I think you were handling that really well. But I'll take over now. You go and make sure my rolls don't burn."

He smiles and practically runs out of the room.

Lydia turns to me. "I don't like to criticize other people's parenting styles, but I'm going to make an exception for you. Your mother should want one thing in the world for you. Your happiness. Your family should want the same. Your father raised you to think that all of this is your responsibility, but it's not. What Darnell is worried about is the fact that you're using your workload, all that responsibility your parents gave you, so you don't have to do the scariest thing of all."

"Actually be in love with someone." I at least get that part. It makes my eyes water. What I've been avoiding all this time is examining my real feelings for Reid. I tell myself it's all just fun and we're passing time and having good sex, but if I'm honest with myself, it's more. It's the deepest relationship of my life, and I'm going to lose it.

Lydia sits down beside me. "Yes. Honey, you know when we had all those talks about your questionnaires? Do you think I didn't learn something about you? We talked about your past relationships. You weren't in love with those boys. You selected men you couldn't fall in love with. Even this relationship you started with Reid follows the pattern. You are running under the impression that it's an affair and it has an end date so it's safe for you to enjoy it. Except a woman who was merely enjoying an affair wouldn't sit here and cry because she doesn't know why her lover is hurting. Can you admit that? You're not crying because you're angry. You're crying because he doesn't trust you enough to let you help him."

The words open an ache inside me. She's right. "I don't think he loves her."

Lydia's eyes are bright with tears, too. "No. I think he might love you and he might worry that whatever he's hiding could infect you. So, my darling girl, the question is do you have to know? Do you need to know why he keeps going to a dark place whenever this woman shows up? Or is it enough to be his light until he's ready to tell you?"

The tears fall pretty freely now. "Will he? Will he tell me?"

"That's the risk you take when you love someone," Lydia explains. "I think he will. I honestly believe this has more to do with his brother than he's willing to say. I've spent some time with Jeremiah and he's such a sweetheart. But there's something dark about him. Not dangerous. We all have our darkness. He hasn't reconciled his yet, and so it's his brother's burden. Rather like your family business is yours, and you rarely allow anyone to help you with it."

She's not wrong. I hid it for so long because I felt like I should be able to handle it. I was ashamed. I only asked Ivy to help me when I thought the whole thing would go under. "But, Lydia, he walked away. He doesn't want me around."

"So change his mind. One of the things that I believe could make you and Reid an excellent couple is the fact that you come from similar places. You both bear a deep and abiding sense of responsibility that isolates you. But what if you didn't have to be alone? What if you opened up to him and allowed him to help you? It might be what he needs to feel okay with asking for his own help. But you have to make the decision."

A gut-wrenching decision. A terrifying decision because if I'm wrong, then the heartache I feel right now will be an ache forever, but I'll compound it with feeling like a fool.

How much is my pride worth? My father taught me it was worth everything. My mother believes appearances are far more important than honesty. Maybe it's time I learn from the people who truly have it together. "You think I should go to him."

"I think the man you love is hurting and you left him with something else to worry about. If you're brave you can tell him you won't leave him. You can say it doesn't matter and he never has to tell you a thing but you trust him."

"Do I?"

Lydia's voice goes low. "My darling girl, who do you not trust? Reid? Or yourself?"

The question hits me squarely in the chest, threatening to suck all the air from my body.

I don't trust me. I don't trust that the ground I walk on is firm and won't crumble and shake beneath me. I don't trust that I can build something strong enough to last because the one marriage I had as an example had been rotten at the core.

I don't have to choose between being my mother and being alone. I can choose a different path.

"Whoa, Nonna, what did you do?" Heath stands beside Ivy in the hallway.

Ivy puts a hand on her boyfriend's chest. "It's okay. It's good for her to cry. She doesn't cry enough." She steps toward me, a soft look on her face. She kneels down in front of me. "Harper, I think we got it all. Unless Britta has a copy I couldn't find, we have the only one. Now that doesn't mean they won't run the story. We deleted all the files I could find, but I can't be certain."

I sniffle. "You could get in trouble."

Ivy waves off the idea. "They won't be able to find me."

"And if they do Lawyer is very bored right now." CeCe joins Heath, a fresh martini in her hand. It's her favorite accessory. "Honestly, Harper, it upsets me seeing you like this. Should I purchase the magazine? I can have it razed to the ground." She puts a hand to her chest and grimaces. "Oh, I don't like this feeling at all. Perhaps we should go to war with France."

I sniffle again, and a laugh huffs from my chest. It's good to know the sight of my tears can make all the moms upset. "I think it should be Sweden."

Ivy's eyes widen. "Don't encourage her. She's dealing with a lot of emotions, and they aren't her strong suit. I asked her if she would walk me down the aisle along with my mom and she teared up. Like I didn't know she could do that."

"Neither did I," CeCe admits, swallowing another sip. "For a moment I thought I was having a heart attack. Now to the problem at hand. I rather like Sweden. The people there are extremely standoffish. No one smiles. I enjoy it. So I shall forgo bombing Sweden and simply hire on a new man. Assassin. Ivy, I need you to find a couple of potential assassins and I shall interview them. Make them attractive, please. Do you think we can find an attractive assassin?"

Ivy shrugs. "According to all the romance novels I've read it won't be a problem."

Lydia stands and points CeCe's way. "You are a menace. And you're out of martini. Harper is going to be fine. She needs time and some dinner."

I hear Darnell's groan from the other room.

He gets hangry.

I stand. "No, what I need is to go and tell Reid that we don't have to worry about the tape getting out."

"I've also threatened to sue the magazine. The film they have is the property of Ralavia Entertainment and technically of the royal family," CeCe announces. "I've explained there will be an international incident if they pursue the story in any way that shows the footage."

"She came up with that one herself," Heath explains. "Lawyer was impressed."

I walk up to CeCe. Such an intimidating woman. "Thank you."

She holds my hand for a moment. "You're welcome, my dear. Now go and be brave. Be the Harper Ross we all know you can be. Just remember that sometimes the bravest thing we can be is patient."

I stride out and hope I can find a way to make him believe.

Chapter Twenty

I'm walking in the door while Jeremiah is striding out. We nearly bang into each other.

His eyes widen when he realizes it's me. "Harper. I thought… Well, I didn't expect to see you." His expression goes distinctly sympathetic. "Are you okay?"

I'm being honest. Old Harper would smile and say sure thing. Nothing phases me. But I'm trying something new because Darnell is right. The old me doesn't get what I need because the old me would never, ever ask for something. "No. I am completely overwhelmed, but I'm going to hold it together because I think Reid needs me. Are you okay? He was pretty harsh with you."

"Not harsh enough," he says under his breath. He steps back and invites me into the lobby. "Harper, I don't think you should go up there. He's in a state."

"I need to tell him that it's going to be okay. Ivy and CeCe took care of it," I explain. He's not going to scare me off. I need to do this. Even if Reid sends me away.

He seems to think about that for a moment. "Good. I can tell him. That might help but you should know Britta probably won't stop. We're trying to figure out what her angle is this time."

"Angle?"

Jeremiah's head shakes. "I shouldn't…or maybe I should. Maybe I should tell you everything and get my brother out of this mess."

He seems so upset, so anxious. It's odd to think that an hour before I would have begged for information. But I'm taking Lydia's words to heart. I put a hand on his shoulder. "No. If Reid wants me to know then I'll know. I'm going to go up and talk to him. I'm going to let him know I'm not about to leave him."

"I can't tell you how much I love hearing you say those words, but I don't think he'll allow it. Harper, if he says stupid, hurtful things, he's trying to protect you. He's trying to push you away so she can't hurt you."

She can't hurt me. Not really, but Reid can. Reid can tear me apart with some casual words.

But they won't be casual. They'll be planned and used like a weapon.

They will also be a lie.

"I can handle Reid." I notice his hand is shaking and I reach for it. "Jeremiah, where are you going?"

A few suspicions have been playing through my head. Jeremiah never drinks. Not even a glass to taste the wines the rest of us try. He could simply not enjoy alcohol. But then why would Reid keep the liquor locked up like a gun? Why did he get so worried when his brother was out late? Lydia told me there was a darkness in Jeremiah.

"I don't know." He looks haunted. "I haven't decided yet."

"Why don't you come back up? Or let me call and find someone for you to hang out with."

He shakes his head. "No. I don't think Reid wants to see me right now." A long breath and then there's resolve in his eyes. "Tell him I'm going to a meeting and I'll spend the night with a friend. Tell him I won't break my promises. And that I'm sorry. Are you sure you want to see him tonight? He'll likely be better in the morning. More in control."

I need him to understand that he doesn't need to be in control all the time. "I'm going to see him. Will you get me on the elevator since I don't trust him to not lock me out?"

He nods and when he puts in the code for the elevator, I give him a hug.

"You're good for him," he whispers. "Don't let him convince you otherwise."

I wave good-bye and hope he finds some peace at his meeting. His

AA meeting, if I'm right. I'm still processing the information when the door opens and I walk into the darkened foyer. I make my way into the living room, but someone's gone all broody and left off the lights. Moonlight filters in and I see the shadow of Reid standing by the window. A lonely god watching over his kingdom from high.

Or simply a man who feels like the world is crashing in on him.

"Jer, I don't want to talk about this again. Please. I know how it makes you feel, but I need to stand here and drink. Please let me." He doesn't turn around.

"He's going to a meeting. He wanted you to know. He's not going to a bar," I say quietly.

Reid turns. "Harper? What the hell are you doing here?"

Not the welcome I hoped for, but I knew this wasn't going to be easy. "Well, my boyfriend is upset, and I thought I would come over and comfort him. Have you eaten anything? I skipped out on Lydia's dinner, so I could eat. Pizza? Or should I hunt around and see what I can make? Warning. I'm not a good cook so you're probably looking at sandwiches. I can make sandwiches."

He sets down the glass he's holding and moves toward me. "You should go. I'm not capable of playing the nice guy tonight."

"So don't," I reply. "How about we both stop playing and be who we are? I think we've actually done a lot of that, but I also understand people are complex and you can be nice most of the time and also something of an asshole."

"I'm all asshole tonight, Harper. And if you've come up here to point out all the ways I've wrecked your life, don't bother. I've already made a list."

Oh, my tiger has a thorn in his paw, and he's going to fight me to take it out. "You haven't wrecked my life. We made a mistake. Ivy corrected it. She and Heath think they have all the footage. Even if it gets out, I'm not ashamed."

"It wouldn't get out if you had been with anyone else. No one would care. There would have been some immature giggling, and everyone would have moved on."

He's missing the point. "But I don't want to be with anyone else."

He grips me by the shoulders as if he can shake some sense into me. "She's not going to stop. She'll get what she wants out of me or she'll break me. Either way, I can't let you in."

Maybe we should revisit the whole assassin plan. I step into his space, putting my arms around him. "I'm already in. Reid, don't fight me on this. We can do it the hard way or the easy way, and I would rather go easy. It's been a hell of a day."

He stands there stiffly for a moment. "I'm not talking to you about it."

"You don't have to."

"I don't know what you want."

And that's the problem. He thinks I want something. "I want my boyfriend to feel better. I want my boyfriend to know he has me no matter what."

"You don't know what you're saying."

I tilt my head up. "I do."

"And if what will comfort me is sex?" He makes the words a challenge.

"Well, I would probably find it comforting, too."

His hand snakes up my neck, and his fingers tangle in my hair, twisting lightly. "You would let me do it to you again?"

"You're being dramatic. It's a whole other side of you." I'm not going to let him push me to anger. "I let you do it all the time. We kind of fuck like rabbits."

"I'm not the man you think I am."

I run my hands up his chest. If this is what he needs, I'll give it to him. "I'm under no illusions that you're perfect. I'm well aware that you might rip me up tonight, but I'm still here."

"You should run because I'll take everything from you," he promises.

But it feels more like a plea to my ears. One I can't deny. I go on my toes and press my lips to his, and that seems to be all he needs. He takes over, hand tightening in my hair as his tongue plunges in. Like he needs to make sure I don't run despite all his advice. Like he can't stand the thought of me walking away.

I have no intentions of leaving him. I can take some damage. If you asked me a month ago how I would handle a man who said the things to me Reid did tonight, I would have said I would leave. I would walk out because no one is going to treat me like that.

He's more important than my pride. Lydia is right and Darnell is, too. I've been trying so hard to avoid living my mother's life that I forgot to define what I want for my own. Something beyond working and keeping my head above water. I want this. I want to love someone, to go through life with these people who fill my soul. With people I can't leave alone to face the storms inside them.

"Take off your clothes." He steps back, dragging his shirt over his head and tossing it aside. Again he looks at me like he's sure I'll walk.

I would have seen it as arrogance once, but I know him better now. It's not bravado or anger. It's fear. In some ways he's accepted that he'll have to do everything alone and so he would rather get it over with. The me walking out part. From what I can tell, the woman he's spent the most time with is a blackmailing asshole, so I have some walls to get around.

I pull my T-shirt over my head, and it joins his along with my bra. I kick out of my boots and make quick work of my jeans and stand in front of him completely naked.

"Just like that?" He asks the question with one raised brow.

But I think I'm starting to understand his secret language. One day he won't need the arrogant tone. One day he'll feel safe with me. What he's asking is if he can trust this. If he can expect me to turn on him. There's only one way to show him. Don't leave. "Just like that."

He forgets how often in a day he does nice things for me. He brings me coffee every morning and makes sure I have a sweater. If I forget one and get cold because I'm working in a part of the house that isn't heated, he wraps me up in his and kisses me on the nose and tells me to stay warm. When I get involved in a job and forget lunch he shows up and sits and eats with me.

So no, it's not just like that. What I'm doing is the culmination of weeks of tenderness from him.

"Sit on the couch, Reid."

His eyes flare, likely because he realizes what I want to do to him. He pulls the belt from his slacks and undoes his fly before lowering himself to the leather Chesterfield. Yep. I know a little about furniture now because my boyfriend is obsessed with making things pretty.

Because design was the one thing he could control. When everything in his childhood seemed unruly and chaotic, he could make his space comfortable and safe.

He's about to find comfort in more than expensive furnishings.

I lower myself between his legs, my knees cushioned by the soft carpet beneath us. I look up and his face is all planes and angles in the moonlight, his emotions stark.

"Harper, I want to tell you to leave. I should. I should force you out, but I want you." He shoves his slacks down enough to free his cock.

I reach for it, sliding my hand over soft skin and hard flesh. "My point is you can't force me out. Or maybe you can shove me away, but you can't make me not worry about you. You can't make me not care."

Before he can reply, I lower my head down and give his big cock a long lick, and he doesn't seem to feel the need to talk anymore. He groans and his hands find my hair, though he's gentle now. He strokes my hair even as I suck and kiss and lick. I love the way he tastes, the way he feels under my tongue. The way his thighs tense and his eyes get hot. I watch him while I work my way down his dick, lavishing it with affection.

"I could take this and then throw you out," he says even as his breathing picks up. "I could show you who I am."

I know who he is but he needs to growl and howl for a little while longer. I simply whirl my tongue around his cockhead, drawing him further and further in.

"Stop." He growls the word and tugs on my hair. "If you don't stop, I'm going to come."

"That is the point," I say, pressing kisses on his skin.

"I want to be inside you," he admits. "I want to see your pretty face and know you're with me."

There he is. My Reid is still here. He's simply at war with the one Britta created. I plan to win. I get to my feet as he finds the condom in his wallet and rolls it on. His hands come out, waiting to guide me down. I straddle him and feel his cock against me, heat sparking through my system. I've never wanted anyone the way I want him. I suppose that's why I've been so afraid of him. I'm diving into the deepest pool, but I can't back out now. I'll learn to swim.

He sighs as he thrusts up and our bodies fit together like they were made for each other. His hands are on my hips, but he leans forward to kiss me as I start to ride him. Slow at first, and then building heat and friction. We kiss until I can't stand it a second longer and I give in, pleasure pushing aside all the tension we feel and replacing it with nothing but joy. Reid grips my hips and swings me around so my back is against the couch and he's on top. He takes over, thrusting in and out. Over and over until I feel it build again and ride the wave one more time. His whole body tightens, and he holds on as his orgasm takes him over the edge.

He falls on top of me, and I hope we've survived this storm.

Hours later I realize the sex was kind of the eye of the storm, and we're definitely still in it.

"You should go home, Harper."

The words are cold, but I can see his hands shaking slightly. He rolled out of bed after the last time he gave me a mind-blowing orgasm. He went straight to his dresser and pulled on a pair of boxers. I notice he didn't bother with actual pants. He paces at the end of the bed.

I yawn and turn over. The drama is ongoing, it seems. He has way more energy than I do. I'm all happy and sated and sleepy, but does Reid Dorsey let me rest? Nope. "I think I'd rather stay here."

He stops and puts his hands on his hips, looking judgmental but also hot. "And I want you to leave."

"Then you should pick me up and throw me out because it's the only way I'm leaving this bed." He isn't thinking straight. It's two in the morning, and he'll get anxious when he realizes I'll take the subway. Then he'll hail a cab. Then he'll worry about me getting into my building. Then he'll come with me. Trust me. This happened before. It's best I stay in place. "And I won't let you dress me, so if you don't mind chucking a naked chick out of your place, go for it. I bet the security cams will get some footage of that, too, and I'll have to wake up Ivy. She can be cranky if she doesn't get eight hours."

He frowns. "I'm serious. You can't control me with sex."

I yawn again and pat the place beside me. It's a good bed. Very comfy and warm. "I'm not trying to control you, babe. I'm trying to get you back into bed so you can get some sleep. You have a design meeting about the ballroom in the morning, and I'm installing crown molding. Gotta be sharp."

"I have to go to Europe. I'm going to find a flight tomorrow."

The thought of him going to see her makes my heart ache, but probably not for the reasons he thinks. "Then you should definitely get some sleep."

"Are you listening to a word I say?" Reid asks, obviously exasperated.

I wish there was an easier way to do this, but I think Reid needs to understand he can't move me. "Of course, but you're not saying anything that makes sense. Hence the need for sleep."

"Me sleeping with you won't change the fact that I'm going to

Europe to meet with Britta." His gaze turns steely, and I realize we've come to the nasty part of this drama we're playing out. This is when he makes what he thinks is his big play to save me. "I've been lying to you. You were right back in Ralavia. I'm in love with her. When she came to see me that night, we made love and talked about how we could fuck with you. We came up with this whole plan to draw you in and make you believe. I'm sorry. This is just what we do. We play games. It's exciting."

I can't help but smile. He's so bad at this. "Ah, we're going the *Cruel Intentions* route."

He winces. "It's *Dangerous Liaisons*, Harper. One is a brilliant play and the other is for teenagers. But I suppose you could say it's an inspiration. Wealthy, bored people like to play games."

I've started to wonder about the wealthy part, but I leave that for another day. "Yeah, you look like you're having a ton of fun."

He's back to pacing, every lean line of his body tight with anxiety. "Whatever you believe, understand that I am going to see her. I'll leave the project we both love, the one we're both committed to, for her."

"Jer and I will hold down the fort, sir," I vow.

He ignores my jaunty salute. "I'll take her places I would never take you. Fancy places. Expensive places."

I groan at the thought. "Good. CeCe already makes us dress up when she takes us out. She thinks denim is for mountain people. What are mountain people and how do I become one because I think they get to wear boots? Those heels are torture devices. I'm with Ivy. I like a food truck."

His hands are clenched around the bed posts. "I'll be photographed with her. You'll have to see it online. You'll read about our love story."

That is where he's wrong. I'm perfectly happy to stop stalking him online. It leads to hurt feelings and does no good. "I'm not much of a reader of magazines. Now a good romance is another story. If she can get Jen Armentrout or Kristen Ashley to write it, I'll have to rethink my stance."

He sighs and stops and plays what is likely his last card. "Harper, I won't ever marry you."

I sit up. "See, I knew I should have taken you up on it this afternoon."

"This is not a time to joke," he scolds. "She will always be in my life. She will be known as the love of my life, and for that reason alone you need to leave."

We're back to this. I don't bother with the sheet. I let it pool around my waist, and for a man who claims he loves that supermodel, his eyes go right to my chest. "I'd rather stay. Reid, I care about you. I think I'm falling in love with you. I don't know what's happening with her. I do know she's got something she's holding over your head and it likely has to do with your brother."

Reid's eyes narrow. "Why the hell would you say that?"

"Because if it was about you this would be over. You would never allow her to put you in a corner over something that embarrassed you or hurt only you. You would put it out there and take whatever happened. But you will go to the ends of the earth for him. So here's what's going to happen. Jeremiah is going to figure this out, and he'll do the right thing in the end. I don't know what you're both hiding, but I think he's almost there and when he proves he loves you, too, I'll be waiting. You say you're not going to marry me. If you don't, that's okay. If you don't because you don't love me and you think someone else will make you happier than I can, then it's good. But if it's because some chick in Sweden is blackmailing you, I'm not okay with it."

He stares at me for a moment. "I don't understand you."

"I know. I don't think I understood until earlier today. I think this feeling I have for you is more important than being loved by you. Your love isn't something I can control, but I can decide how I want to treat you, how I want to honor this feeling inside me that only you have ever brought out. You think we're alike because we had fairly awful parents, but I had these amazing friends. I wasn't responsible for them. We were equals. Ivy and Anika… They're my touchstones, and I would never leave them and they wouldn't leave me. Reid, I won't leave you alone in this. You don't have to ever tell me what happened between you and Britta if you don't want to. You don't have to marry me and promise to love me forever. I'll still be your friend if I can't be your lover. Damn. I think I figured out what love is. So odd. Turns out love is just putting someone ahead of you not because you were taught to or because you're obligated. You do it because their happiness is the most important thing."

He's silent, and for a moment I think he's going to find a way to kick me out.

Then he moves to the bed. He shuts off the light and crawls in beside me, his arms wrapping around me. He holds me close and I feel something wet against my cheek. My heart threatens to break.

"I can't tell you because I promised my brother," he whispers. "But I want to because I'm almost at the end. I can't pay her off much longer."

I kiss the top of his head. "Then we'll figure out another way. No matter what, I'm with you."

I hold him until we both fall asleep.

Chapter Twenty-One

I'm walking back to Reid's building with coffee and croissants the next morning. Not early morning. We slept in, and Reid is still in bed. I went and checked in with Patrick to ensure we're not needed for filming this morning. Apparently my crew working on laying tile in the guest bathroom isn't all that interesting.

When my cell rings, I give serious consideration to not picking up. I only look at the screen because it might be a friend who needs me.

Paul.

I definitely consider not picking up. I consider chucking my phone into the East River. But the truth of the matter is he'll find a way. "What do you need, Paul?"

"I need some fucking support is what I need," he grumbles. "I need a CEO who actually gives a damn about her job, but I'm not going to get that, am I?"

I'm so tired of this. Reid has real problems. Jeremiah has real problems. "Buck up, buttercup. The board meeting is coming up. Maybe you'll get lucky and be named the CEO and then you can deal with all of this. Except that's what you're supposed to be doing now, and you call Mommy at least twice a day. By the way, I'm talking about me. I'm Mommy in this case. Be careful what you wish for."

"You're such a bitch, and you should be the careful one. When I'm the CEO, I don't think there's going to be much of a place for you," he threatens. "Look, I called because I need to know if you're about to cause some kind of scandal that's going to bring down the company."

"What? The only scandal the company had was improper tax prep and misuse of funds. I assure you that's not happening on my watch."

"I'm talking about your sex life."

A pit opens in my gut. Well, we knew Ivy might not get everything. "My sex life has nothing to do with work."

"Oh, but it does according to the reporter who called your mother. You're sleeping with the designer on your vanity project. According to her, he's a celebrity. I never thought you were that kind of a woman. Do you realize what a shock it was for your mom? She wanted a quote on how your mother felt with you being the other woman," Paul practically snarls. "Do you realize how much you hurt her? How much of an embarrassment you are to all of us?"

I hang up because I'm incapable of dealing with him right now. I need to talk to Reid before this hits the news. I'm not even sure what's hitting the news and why I'm suddenly the other woman.

I realize I'm out of time when I see the photographers. There are three of them, and they appear to be waiting for something.

Luckily I'm wearing a ball cap and no makeup and a fairly shapeless sweater. I let out a long sigh because I have to get past these guys who seem to be waiting for someone to arrive and then I have to tell my boyfriend that apparently Ivy didn't get everything. Or Britta decided to go to the press without the tape. It was a long shot. We fell asleep in an excellent place, but knowing the press is here might kick him right back into save-Harper mode.

I think seriously about turning right around and running because if the tape got out, they might recognize me. I should have asked Paul more questions.

But I can't leave Reid alone, so I continue walking. It's like they always tell you. Pretend like nothing's wrong and nothing will be wrong.

"Harper Ross," one the photographers yells, and suddenly there are cameras everywhere and dudes shouting questions at me and proving that all those people who told me that lied.

"How does it feel to be a homewrecker?" one of them asks with a ghoulish grin.

"I don't wreck homes. I fix them." I realize this could be bad for my business. "Please excuse me."

I try to get around them.

"What do you have to say about allegations that you sent a sex tape of yourself and Reid Dorsey to his fiancée?"

"I did? Dude, I didn't even know there was a sex tape until yesterday. I assure you I didn't send it to anyone."

"That's not what Britta Olensoff is saying," Man Number Two explains. "According to a report out on *Celebrity Today's* website this morning, she received the tape along with some taunting words from you. Something along the lines of you have him now."

"Did she release the tape?" I ask.

"No, of course not," Guy Three says. "She's a lady."

She's something else, that's for sure, and she definitely doesn't have the tape. She's pivoting for some reason, and I need to figure it out. "Well, good for her, and I'm not commenting further."

The door comes open and the doorman looks frazzled as he manages to pull me in. "Are you okay, Ms. Ross? I don't even know what's happening. Those three showed up right after you left. Then a limo pulls up and this blonde woman walks in like she owns the place. I'm pretty sure she knew the photographers were going to be there because she talked to one of them like they were friends. I told her Mr. Reid didn't want to be disturbed, but she called him and he let her up."

My heart hurts. "Did he tell you to keep me out?"

He shakes his head. "Didn't say anything about you."

"Then I'm going up." I'm not about to let him fight this battle alone. Even if he gets anxious and kicks me out, he'll know I want to be there with him.

I can barely breathe the whole way up. I wish we went back to my apartment the night before. Now that I know more about Reid, I see the penthouse for what it is. Carefully designed to show the world what he wants them to see. Perfectly designed. He's not actually comfortable here. He seems happier and more at ease at my place.

The doors come open, and I realize he is absolutely not comfortable right now.

"How much, Britta? You know there's only so much I can fucking give."

"I don't know about that. You still have this place." Her voice is soft but with a hint of mocking. "Poor little rich boy. I don't want money this time."

He goes quiet, and I move into the living room.

"Hey, babe. If I knew we were having guests, I would have brought more coffee." I act calm, cool, and collected even though I'm trembling with rage on the inside. I believed him before, but now I have confirmation that this woman is nothing but an albatross around my guy's neck. I need to find a way to permanently remove her. "I brought you some croissants, but I bet you lost your appetite."

Reid stares at me like he can't quite believe I'm here.

But Britta can. She's dressed in slim slacks and a white shirt that's unbuttoned down almost to her navel, showing off some barely there curves that would look fab on a magazine cover or a runway. Here in the apartment in the middle of the morning, it's a bit much. "What are you doing here?"

It's said with a disdain only Europeans can achieve. American disdain is a whole other thing, but the force is strong with this Swede. "Well, I spent the night here with my boyfriend, so I should be the one asking why you're here."

Britta's hair is up in a high, sleek ponytail that sends her hair whipping around with a swish when she turns back to Reid. "Send her away. I'm not talking with your sidepiece here."

"She is not a fucking sidepiece," Reid says, his voice going dangerously low. "You mean absolutely nothing to me and you haven't for a long time. I've had nothing but disdain for you since the first time you blackmailed me for a million dollars in exchange for your silence. Harper isn't here for my money."

"Well, apparently she shouldn't be if you're running out," Britta says with a wave of her hand. "Letting the show go was a mistake."

"One I didn't have a lot of choice in. I couldn't work," he pointed out.

"Well, you'll find a way. This new show might have gotten you another. I've heard from some people on the inside that it is wholesome and sweet. I guess this sex scandal will derail it," she says with a shake of her head.

Damn it. I did not think of that. I thought about Anika and how it would affect production, but I didn't think about the fact that Reid and Jeremiah were trying to get someone to back their family-based restoration and rehab show. "We should talk to CeCe about getting a crisis publicity firm. I can call her, and she'll have some shark in the water by this afternoon."

"He can't afford someone like that," Britta huffs. "I do keep up with him. I know he's bleeding money and he's going to have to sell this place soon if he can't get another gig. That's what happens when your brother..."

"Don't you say another fucking word or I won't care," Reid warns. He's flush with anger, but there's softness in there, too, as he reaches me and takes my hand. "Baby, it's not..."

I shake my head and hug him. "Not your story to tell. I don't need to hear it. I'm here. I'm right here without reservations or questions."

He holds me so tight and takes a long breath before letting me go. His hand is in mine when he turns back to her. "What do you want? You don't have the tape or you would have released it. By the way, your guy on the inside has been fired, and you're lucky we're not prosecuting."

I squeeze his hand to let him know I'm with him. Lawyer would love to. Damn it. I need to figure out that man's name.

"I'm not sure how you managed that, but it makes no difference," she says, regarding us with a cool smile. "The tape was merely to humiliate you. I can certainly get out the word that it exists and I'm far too much of a lady to ever put such a thing out there. The fact that you're cheating on me is enough. I have an excellent reputation among my fans. They're women, by the way. Women who watch home and garden shows. Women who like to boycott men who cheat."

"Except it's not cheating." I do feel the need to point that out.

She ignores me. "So you can move ahead with this...worker person."

"Contractor," I correct.

"Fine. You can move on with this contractor and you'll lose your chance at the show. You'll be vilified, and no one will work with you or your brother. Especially after I put out the truth about him. You can sell this place and move to Arizona or wherever poor Americans go."

"Hey, the Phoenix real estate market would like a word." Because those prices are soaring. I should know. I tried to convince my mother she needed some sun. Then she told me I need some sons, and I went back to drinking heavily.

He sighs and frowns down at me. "You can't help it, can you?"

"Sarcasm is how I deal with stress," I admit. I am feeling stressed because I know whatever Britta says next is going to be terrible.

"Or we can change this narrative entirely," Britta offers. "I think you'll find I sat down with a couple of journalists to talk about my epic love story and how many times I've forgiven you since you're the love of my life."

"You don't love anyone but yourself," Reid replies, but he seems calmer now.

"No one else needs to know this." Britta shrugs it off and settles her designer bag over her elbow. "Now, if you choose to work with me, I think you'll find your image rehabbed and all doors open to you within a year or so. Of course, you'll need to quit the show you're working on right now. I can't have my husband working with his former mistress."

Reid drops my hand. "I'm not going to marry you."

She gives him a chilly smile. "Of course you are, and the truth of the matter is this is the best course of action for you as well. Your brother will fuck up again, and you'll lose it all."

"We lost it all because of you." His eyes narrow, and he moves toward her.

"Hey, babe. If we're going to murder her, we should do it when there aren't a bunch of photographers she hired downstairs." I'm pretty sure this is what they mean by being the voice of reason. "We should wait until we have excellent alibis and she doesn't see it coming. I would say poison, but we all know she doesn't eat. Maybe we could sit a Birkin bag out on a frozen lake and then oops, she falls through the ice."

"I am unamused by you," she says, her eyes rolling before she looks back to Reid. "I suppose you have to decide between your ordinary-looking contractor person and the brother you spent your whole life protecting. Also, you should know I intend to tell the press I'm pregnant."

"You're pregnant? Whose baby is it?" Reid asks, sounding shocked for the first time.

I'm not. I know this play. "She's not pregnant. She'll tearfully put out a statement in a couple of months that she lost the baby and either the story will be that her husband is by her side or he ran off with the help. Either way she gains sympathy, and that makes me wonder. What are you trying to hide?"

For the first time Britta looks slightly unsettled. "I'm not hiding anything. I'm simply done waiting. I've always known Reid and I are endgame, as you Americans like to call it. Think about it, Reid. It's your choice. It always has been, and you always come back to me. Hooper, you should think about that. Did you know he made love to me in Ralavia? He left that part out, didn't he?"

"Yes, he did, because it's not true. Now you should leave, and you'll have our answer soon." The only reason I don't throw her out on her skinny ass is I think Reid needs some time to process.

"Your answer means nothing." Britta turns, and her heels click along the floor. "Oh, look. Here's sweet Jeremiah. He looks a bit haunted. I wonder how he will deal with the whole world knowing his secret."

She walks past Jeremiah, who is wearing last night's clothes and looks stark white.

"What did she want? We can sell the penthouse. At least my part." Jeremiah seems to be deep into the bargaining state, and I wonder how long he's been there. Years, it seems.

"Jer, I love you. I can't. I can't marry her. I love Harper," Reid says, his voice shaking. "I'm so sorry."

Jeremiah stops, and his shoulders relax. "You love Harper? You really love her?"

Reid nods. "Yeah. Though now that she sees how bad my baggage is I don't know that she'll think I'm a good bet."

He loves me? It's stupid how those words wash away all the anxiety of the last few minutes. We can get through this if he loves me. I might be able to get through anything if he loves me. "Yeah, I'm bad at gambling, so you're good. I mean it, babe. I can walk by a slot machine and it never pays off again. Did I mention sarcasm is also how I handle strong emotion since I love you, too."

Jeremiah tears up. "I'm so happy to hear that. I can't tell you. I'm happy for you."

He hugs his brother and then me. I hold him close. "How was your meeting?"

He backs up and gives me a weary smile. "Well, I spent most of the night in a coffee shop with my sponsor talking about how to keep my sobriety."

"Jer," Reid begins.

Jeremiah waves him off. "She figured it out. Besides, she's probably going to be my sister-in-law. Let me think for a couple of hours."

Reid nods. "Of course."

"Or we can sic Ivy and Heath on her and figure out what she's trying to cover up." It is obvious to me that the Dorsey brothers aren't big on conspiracy theories. Lucky for them I'm pretty good at them. "Think about it. She doesn't love you. She's not really pregnant. She said it herself. She needs to change the narrative."

"She said I could change the narrative," Reid points out.

"No. I think Harper's right." Jeremiah paces while he considers the situation. "She normally wants money or she wants you to short term look like you're back together. She doesn't have feelings for you beyond using you. So why would she be willing to tie herself to this family?"

"She's jealous of Harper," Reid offers.

He is a beautiful man, but I don't see it. "She's the one who needs to cover something, and the tape gave her the idea she needed. The fact that she lost it and is still pushing means she's desperate. If she's desperate, then we can use it against her. We need to figure out what she's hiding, and Ivy is our best bet. She knows people who can get pretty much anywhere on the web. I would like to do a deep dive into Britta's life for the last six months. If we can get leverage to make her drop whatever hold she has on you…"

Jeremiah's jaw squares. "You should know…"

I hold a hand up. "Nope. Don't need to know. I need to figure a way out of this situation so she doesn't come back to annoy me every few months. We can do it this way or I hand it all over to CeCe and we have to interview and vet assassins. She's got a whole plan. But I need you to understand that I don't have to know what you did in order to help you."

"That is naïve," he says with a sigh.

"Did you brutally murder someone in cold blood?" I ask.

"No. No one died," he shoots back and then frowns. "Would it be okay if the murder wasn't brutal?"

I shrug. "Look, there are times when I think death is justified. So if you didn't kill anyone, did you ruin someone's life without care or thought?"

He looks almost apologetic. "No, but that doesn't mean it wasn't a bad thing."

"Swindle old ladies out of their retirement? Not pay your contractor? That could be a deal breaker." I gasp because I do realize something that could give me pause. "Did you kick a dog?"

Jeremiah steps in front of me and puts his hands on my shoulders. There's a serious expression on his face as he looks down at me. "I need you to know that you are the absolute best thing that ever happened to this family, and I will be so grateful to call you sister."

"Don't push her," Reid warns. "She needs time, but I agree that she's the best thing that could have happened to us."

Jeremiah draws me in and hugs me. I take a deep breath and realize I have what I need. I have my sisters and three incredible "moms" who care about me and are willing to make lasagna/talk through a plan/hire an assassin when I'm down. If I play my cards right, I might get the coolest brother out of this. Tears pierce my eyes, and so many of the hurtful, harmful things I heard growing up seem to drift away.

"It will be okay," I promise him.

Jeremiah takes a step back. "Yes, it will be. I'll make sure of it. I'm going to get some sleep because sometimes staying sober is tiring, but I want to talk later. I want you to know."

He gives his brother a long look and then walks away, moving toward the bedrooms.

Reid steps in front of me, a grave look on his face. "Harper, I know what I said, but I need you to think about the ramifications. She's not wrong. If she does what she says she's going to do, I will likely be unemployable for a while."

I shrug. "I have an office with your name on it, and then you can deal with Paul's whining and make all my big box stores beautiful."

A hint of a smile hits his lips. "I have been thinking about this. I know you take your family obligations seriously, and I don't know if I want to go to California without you."

"Babe, you're just taking meetings there. You're not moving."

"I know, but we would be on the road all the time," he says. "That never bothered me before. Now the thought is only joyous if you're with me. So maybe I will take you up on the job offer."

I'm floored. This man doesn't belong in an office picking out paintings for rando motel lobbies. And he's forgetting the most important part. "What about Jeremiah?"

He nods slowly as though processing the words. "Yeah, I'll have to have a hard conversation, but he'll understand. I need to put you first. I love my brother, but you're going to be... I told him not to push you."

"How about we agree that we're both happy in this relationship and it's likely going to end in marriage and a couple of kids who we'll be terrified we'll screw up the way our parents screwed us up, and so we'll fuck up in totally different ways."

The sweetest smile lights up the room, and I'm shocked at how we can go from the abyss of Britta's dictates to this amazing, sunshiney place where we have a future. "We can agree on that. And in honor of our accord, I think I'm going to sell the penthouse, give my brother his half, give Aggie her pension, and then I'm going to bribe your cousin Sheryl to sell me her stock so your position at Ross Construction is unassailable. They won't be able to vote you out. You'll own fifty-two percent of the company."

The Dorsey brothers seem determined to put my jaw on the floor today. "What? You can't do that. I know it's a small company, but Sheryl's stock is worth a million easy, and she can't sell it to someone outside the family."

He nods and proves he can pivot. "Then I'll give you the money and you can buy it. Or I can push you. We could upend all of Britta's plans with one trip to the courthouse."

"You can't. You can't give up your dreams for me."

"What if I just figured out you are my dream?" He asks the question so simply. As if something's happened and all of his previous anger and anxiety are gone now and he's been left with peace.

I wish I was. I'm a swirling ball of emotion right now. I...I'm so happy I have a chance with him, but what if he resents staying here with me? He's used to money, and a lot of it, and I know it's mostly gone now, but will he be happy in my tiny apartment? Will he be okay with not working with his brother? Can he ever be happy in a family I'm not happy in? "You can't stay here. You need to be out there doing the work you love."

He sighs and leans over, pressing his forehead to mine. "I love something more than work. Harper, you don't get to tell me what my dreams are. You can tell me you don't share them. You can tell me you don't love me. But you don't get to break us up because you're afraid, and yes, I sound like the biggest hypocrite of all time. I learned something from you when you refused to leave our bed last night. I learned that I'll go through whatever fire I have to in order to keep a woman I can trust the way I can you. I'm going to figure out a way to get you what you want because making you happy is the job I would like to do for the rest of my life."

"I don't know what to say." He's right. I am terrified. Terrified that I'll love him and it will all go to hell. Terrified that he'll love me the way he says he will and I won't be worthy of it.

He kisses my forehead and steps back. "You don't have to say anything at all, baby. I'm going to give you time, but I'm serious about buying the stock. If what you want is to continue to be the head of Ross

Construction, I won't allow them to hold their votes over your head every single year. I can take out a short-term loan, and then we'll get this place ready to sell. We should get more than enough out of it to pay for the stock and get me an apartment in your building."

"Or we could buy something new." I know why he said it. I'm acting skittish, but I don't want to. I want to be brave. Right now living together is as brave as I can be. "Something a little bigger. Maybe closer to the office."

He draws me close. "It'll be fun to look. Now let's eat these beautiful croissants and then go talk to Ivy. It's helpful to have a hacker friend who doesn't have any real fear of prison."

"Oh, that's because she knows CeCe would just, like, buy the court and get her out," I assure him. "See, it's also nice to have an oligarch on our side."

He chuckles and then sobers. His hand smooths back my hair. "I love you, Harper."

I stare at him for a moment and then wrap my arms around him. "I love you, too."

"We will get through this, and so will my brother," Reid vows, holding me close.

I have to pray he's right.

Chapter Twenty-Two

"I don't know," Anika says a few days later. "I think pretty much any press is good press. Right? That's what they say."

We're standing in the ballroom at the close-of-day filming. Patrick is helping Tom get good shots of all the changes Reid and Jeremiah have made, putting the finishing touches on what is now a grand salon that connects all three brownstones.

"I hate the fuckers," Luca says. "I want to know when we can get rid of them. Has Ivy found anything?"

Anika and Luca got back yesterday, and while they're completely pleased with how the work is going, they don't appreciate the photographers who've taken to hanging around.

"The last I heard she thinks it's got something to do with a fashion line Britta started a year ago," I explain. "I've been keeping her fueled with tacos and coffee."

Reid grins as he sets down the stack of coffee table books on the big, gorgeous table that looks like he time traveled back to Versailles to get. This whole space has a palatial feel to it, but the individual homes themselves are much more modern and functional. There's one with a Northern European style. One that's mid-century modern, but with all the luxury touches that make it comfortable. And one that's sleek and ready for a gamer, weirdly enough. Like there's a massive game room, and the Internet connection is platinum. "Ivy is treating this like a CIA op. I worry they'll recruit her. I don't want to lose her. I now know who to go to when I want to destroy my enemies via laptop."

"He can't do it himself though," I say to Ani. "He's not actually very good with one."

He shrugs and wraps an arm around my shoulder. "I find your sisters endlessly useful. One is a queen and the other is the queen of the Internet." He looks to Anika and Luca, sobering. "Though I am sorry for the mess. I promise we're going to figure this out before Britta's interview."

She called the night of her power play to inform Reid that she had an interview with a major entertainment news outlet set for next week, and it would air sometime soon after.

Luca frowns, arms crossing over his chest. "She's truly doing this interview where she's going to tell the world she's pregnant and you've left her?"

Reid sighs, and I know how weary he is of this. "That's her plan. She sent me the instructions on where the interview is taking place. If I join her, she'll announce our engagement and life goes on. If I don't, she's going to trash my reputation. I should have been smart enough to tape her."

I might have mentioned that a couple of times. "It doesn't matter. We're ready for the storm. I'm sorry it might upset production. I honestly think the guys outside right now are being paid by Britta herself. I worry what happens when the actual interview comes out. For you, though. Not for me. I've been practicing my sarcastic comebacks."

Reid laughs. "She has. Every morning. She runs them by Aggie, and they select the best zingers."

Luca's head shakes. "You seem oddly calm about this."

"I'm willing to deal with the fallout," Reid admits. "But I am worried about my brother. Jeremiah is a part of this, too, and since I announced I'm staying here in New York with Harper, he's been supportive but quiet."

Patrick's head came up the second he heard Jeremiah's name. Those two have spent the last couple of days circling each other like wary sharks. I'm waiting to see if they pounce and what pouncing will mean for them. I happen to believe in a good pouncing. Just take my advice and cover up the cameras. I notice that Patrick stays close even though the director has moved on to another part of the room.

He's still interested, but I worry once filming is done, he and Jeremiah won't see each other again.

"Well, I've talked to him about redoing a couple of rooms at the palace," Anika admits. "It might do him some good to get out of the States for a while."

"Oh, I assure you the European press will be interested in the story," Reid replies. "But we have some plans in place. I want to keep the focus on me. I'm the bad guy."

"Hey," I say, reminding him.

He chuckles. "We're the evil couple. She says being a Disney villain is a life goal of hers. The point is, Harper and I feel like we can handle the heat, but I worry Britta's going to push this further when she realizes we won't break."

Luca considers him for a moment. "I know we haven't talked about the situation, but from what I've gathered she's been holding something over your head for a long time. This should be your worst nightmare."

Reid stills for a moment. "If it goes to hell and the world hates me, are you going to stop being my friend? I'll understand, you know. You have a reputation and a country to hold up."

Luca waves the idea away. "Of course not. You're with the woman who is basically my sister-in-law. I assure you there is only one point of view my family will consider. Even if you weren't, I would believe you. Especially since I've met Britta. She talks openly about never settling down. She doesn't believe in monogamy. I don't understand why she's doing this."

"I do." Ivy walks in with Heath, and she's got the biggest grin on her face.

Oh, that is her gotcha grin.

Anika rushes to my side and we welcome Ivy. "Tell us."

Heath joins the guys, and they look so comfortable together, this family of mine. "Before she does, you should all know that I put her on the right track. She kept looking for a lover Britta was hiding or a shit ton of cocaine. I figured it was something way more ordinary and way worse."

"So money?" Luca asks. "That's where I would look. It's all she's concerned about."

"Bingo," Ivy announces. "Turns out there's some reporters sniffing around a manufacturing plant in Cambodia where Britta's fashion line is made. She's been working hard to cover up the fact that she signed off on paying far below normal wages and has seen reports on the safety situations in the workshops, but I got the receipts. I think she decided if it comes out, she can do an 'I had no idea' tour while announcing her engagement or terrible treatment by a powerful man, and guess which one would get the most airtime?"

"I do not like this woman." Anika looks down at the tablet Ivy's holding. It's got a ton of information about the working conditions, and none of it is good. Including the child labor going into Britta's two-hundred-dollar pairs of jeans. "I consider myself a girl's girl, but sometimes girls are awful, too."

"We can take her down like we used to take down the mean girls in high school," Ivy says with a grin.

I stare at the information and realize something sad. We can't use it. "Guys, let's not get ahead of ourselves. We have to think."

"Or we could upload it all to the Internet and let the world decide," Heath counters. "This could get her in serious trouble, especially in Europe."

I look to Reid, who seems to be thinking the same thing I am. "And then she won't have any reason not to release what she knows. I talked to Jeremiah and we're going to see a lawyer, but I still worry about what it's going to do to his mental health."

Ivy's jaw tightens, and I know she's biting back all her questions. I asked her not to look into Jeremiah. It's killing her to not know, but she's been a good sister.

"So we need to sit down and figure out how to leverage what we've found," Reid says with a nod. "We could use this to get her to keep her mouth shut about what she knows. I think we'll still have to deal with the interview. We have to give her something."

"Or I can do what I should have done all those years ago," a familiar voice says. "I can tell the truth and shame the devil." Jeremiah looks tired as he walks in wearing stylish clothes and a weary smile. "The sad thing is I figured out I've been the real devil all along."

"Jer, you have not," Reid insists. "I agreed to all of it."

Jeremiah holds up a hand, staving his brother off. He has his laptop, and he opens it. "I put this up on social media. I've already got a bunch of requests for interviews, and I'm probably going to need a lawyer for when she sues me for libel. The good news? It's only libel if it isn't true. Anyway, this is it."

I stare at the screen, and Jeremiah is sitting at the dining room table in the penthouse. He gives the camera a smile before talking.

"Hey, guys. My name is Jeremiah Dorsey, though I suspect you already know that since you're following me, but I expect I'm about to go viral, so I thought I would introduce myself. Two years ago my brother, Reid, his girlfriend at the time, Britta Olensoff, and I were coming home from a party in the Hamptons and had an accident with a family of four. My brother was injured pretty badly, and the driver of the other vehicle ended up needing some medical attention for soft tissue injuries. There is a police report that states my brother was driving. This report is a lie. I was behind the wheel. I was also drunk, though I was excellent at hiding it. I started drinking at a young age, and I was always good at deflecting. I suspect my brother caught me a dozen times over the years and never thought there was a problem until he found out that night. I panicked. Utterly panicked. We had a hit show, and no one knew that I was not only an alcoholic, but I started trying drugs. Pot at first, and then cocaine. I was also high that night. We got my brother out of the car before the other car could see us. We placed his injured body in the driver's seat. It was Britta's idea, but I went along with it, and it was Britta and I who told the police he was the driver."

Reid's hand is suddenly in mine, but he looks his brother's way. "Jer. What did you do?"

"What I should have done a long time ago," his brother says, tears in his eyes. "I should never have allowed you to take the fall."

"It wasn't a fall. I would have done it if I'd been conscious," Reid admits.

"And if I'd been sober, it would never have happened." Jeremiah gestures to the screen where he continues his tale.

"My brother and I offered the other family a settlement that included a nondisclosure agreement and hoped that was the end of it," Jeremiah says on screen. "I quietly went into rehab. We decided with the producers of *The Dorsey Brothers* show that it was for the best to shelve the series. That was supposed to be the end of it, but we found ourselves in a situation where the person my brother should have been able to trust decided to blackmail us. Yes, I said blackmail, and I have the receipts. Literally, since mostly Britta wanted money. However, she would also force my brother to perform for the cameras when she needed publicity. All because I was too scared to tell the truth. Lying on a police report is a crime, and I'm willing to step up and do whatever it takes to fix this situation because my brother is in love and he and his girlfriend deserve far more than the trap Britta Olensoff is trying to put them in. So I will be surrendering myself this afternoon. My name is Jeremiah Dorsey and I am an alcoholic and an addict, but what I will no longer be is a coward. To all the fans out there, I am sorry for letting you down. I'm sorry for not coming forward and sharing a story that might help people in my situation. I don't know what the future will bring. I only know that I will face it with love and courage and hopefully sobriety. I love you all."

I'm crying at the end. Big fat tears that feel full of love and not sorrow. Despite the idea of Jeremiah facing charges, these tears are filled with hope because it's out in the open and he can deal with it. We can all deal with it because he's part of us now.

"You did not have to do that," Reid says, his voice hoarse.

Jeremiah's head shakes. "I did. I have to face what I did so it doesn't bury me. I'm an addict. I have to be honest and open or I'll go under, and I swear I don't ever want to do that to you. I'm sorry it took this to get me to do the right thing, but it won't happen again. I won't let her hurt you and Harper."

"Lawyer is going to have so much fun," Ivy says as she pulls out her cell phone. She points Jeremiah's way. "You do not go to the police without Lawyer. Am I clear?"

"As crystal," Jeremiah replies. "I was going to grab a lawyer on my way in, but I bet whoever CeCe brings in will be better."

Reid looks Ivy's way. "We will do everything CeCe tells us to do when it comes to this. I think we need to talk to more than a lawyer. Tell her she's completely off the leash when it comes to this. Raze the earth, and I'll have a martini waiting for her at the end."

Ivy's grin lights up the room. "Will do."

"Well, that's going to be fun," Heath says. "I don't know it's a good idea to use the words off the leash around CeCe. She's been weirdly emotional lately. She even called me Heath the other day. Jer, good on you, man. Anything you need, we're here for you."

"So are we," Anika says. "I'm going to call the publicist and have her write a statement that says our company fully stands behind you."

"That's all well and good, but there are no receipts," Reid argues. "She was careful. She'll say the money was a gift or a loan. This is why I should have recorded my last conversation with her."

"You didn't," Jeremiah agrees. "But I did. I was the one who told security to let her up. I used the security system we have in place to record the entire encounter, both audio and video. Father was paranoid and had cameras everywhere."

"I remember, and we turned them off," Reid counters.

"And then I turned them back on." He holds up his phone. "Heath taught me how to do it on my cell."

"I built an app," Heath acknowledges.

"She can fight me on it or I can release the tape where she admits what she was about to do. As for the accident, I have several text conversations and a couple of emails where she admits what we did and that it was her idea. There's a lot of stuff about me being weak and her being strong, but it should be enough to prove what happened. I also have the driver cam. She was smart enough to hide it before the cops came, but I was smart enough to take it from her. I could have stopped this at any time, but I didn't...I didn't want to be known as your addict, screw-up brother."

"You could be known as a man who has the courage to correct his mistakes and take his rightful place in the world." Patrick stands at the edge of our group, his eyes steady on Jeremiah.

The saddest smile hits Jeremiah's face. "You were right. I was hiding something. I know you won't believe it but it was especially hard to do this now because I have feelings for you. But the me I presented was a lie. This is it. This is me. I'm sorry..."

"Fuck sorry." Patrick walks right up to him, plants his hands on either side of Jeremiah's cheeks, and kisses him then and there. We all stand around watching because what else are we supposed to do? Patrick comes up for air, staring at Jeremiah like he's something precious. "Hi, there, sunshine. I'm grumpy. You want some company at the police station? Maybe we can get a coffee afterward. Or if you're anxious we can find you a meeting and when you're done, I'll be waiting."

A tear spills from Jeremiah's eyes as he nods. "Yeah, I'd like that."

Patrick steps back and gestures to the crew. "That's a wrap for today. Go home and enjoy the afternoon with your families. We'll do pickups tomorrow, and then we're sliding into home. We've got inspections and last-minute stuff and in a couple of weeks, we'll be back to do the big reveal."

Reid looks to Jeremiah. "Are you sure you want to do this?"

He's holding Patrick's hand. "I have never been more sure of anything in my life. Brother, I cannot thank you enough for everything you've done to love and support me, even when I maybe didn't deserve it. So I'm going to ask you to sit back and let me do this for you. For me. For our suddenly larger than I expected family."

"Okay," Reid says and pulls his brother in for a hug. "I love you."

"I love you," Jeremiah whispers.

"Uh, we need to walk over to CeCe's," Ivy says as she enters the room again. "I might have started World War III. The good news is Chef is making lunch, so we won't be hungry while we make our war plans. CeCe's words, not mine. I already called the other moms. They'll meet us there. It's nice to be so close. I usually have to fight my way here via subway when she calls me in."

"This should be amusing." Luca takes his wife's hand. "But I could definitely eat. She has to understand that Ralavia must remain neutral in this war. I'm sorry. We have good relations with Sweden."

"Oh, I'll work on that," Anika vows.

Heath and Ivy along with Patrick and Jeremiah follow, and suddenly Reid and I are alone.

I squeeze his hand. He's less happy than I would expect, but I'm sure he's worried about how this whole thing will go. "CeCe really will take care of it."

"He could go to jail," Reid says. "The crime of lying on a police report is punishable by one year in jail, and if it's considered bad enough, up to seven years in a federal pen. I can't. He won't survive in there."

He's panicking. "I think that's for filing a false report or lying about critical information when it comes to a serious crime. Lawyer will point out that this is Jeremiah's first offense and he's clean and sober and willing to help others do the same. You might have to write a big check, but there's no way they send him to jail. You didn't use insurance to pay for the other car."

"I did it myself to avoid insurance fraud," he admits. "Harper, I know this means Britta can't force her way into my life anymore, but it's still a scandal. If she takes this fight to the press, I likely won't be able to work in TV for a while. I'll have all the problems I had before."

I'm going to have to play a role I never thought I would play. Sunshine. My grump is anxious and needs some optimism. The good news? I'm feeling optimistic. "Then we'll figure them out. Together."

I go up on my toes and brush my lips over his.

"Together," he promises.

"Hey, what's this about some viral video with your brother?" Tom, the director, has his hands on his hips and looks ready to face

Armageddon. "If this is another sex tape, I quit."

Poor Tom. He thought he was doing a staid little reno show and he got us. "It's him admitting he swapped places with his brother after an accident because he was super drunk and likely high and then he got blackmailed by a supermodel."

A long sigh comes from Tom. "Finally something normal. All right. Carry on."

I can't help but laugh.

"We should get to the war room then," Reid offers.

I let him lead me out, but I wonder deep down if he'll ever be truly happy working at Ross Construction.

Chapter Twenty-Three

"So now this Swedish chick is threatening to sue, but the lawyer says it's all a smoke screen because once she sees the evidence Jeremiah has, she'll drop it."

I'm sitting in the boardroom in the Ross Construction office, surrounded by cousins who are treating me like a rock star. Who would have guessed all it took was dating a reality TV star and getting mired in scandal to become popular in my family? Although I should note that popular doesn't mean they like me.

"It sounds messy," Aunt Helen says with a disdainful sniff.

"That's what we're hoping." Reid sits beside me. "The lawyers seem to think this isn't something we should worry about."

It's weeks later and Jeremiah has already made his peace with the police. He pled to a misdemeanor, paid his fine, and is doing PSAs about drinking and driving. He's so at peace and staying at Patrick's place in Brooklyn when he's not traveling. Reid's at my place. Again, when he's not taking meetings since surprise surprise, no one is blackballing the Dorsey brothers. They're actually hotter than ever and have several companies vying for their next show.

Which Reid claims won't happen since he's staying here with me. He's only taking the meetings for Jeremiah's sake. He plans to leave the show to him and sit here in an office and waste all of his talent.

It's making me crazy. I can't convince him to leave me. Or that we can manage long distance for a while.

"Margie, I don't even know how you're dealing with this." Helen pats my mother's hand, and I can see my mom nearly preen under the attention.

"Well, I for one am shocked." My mom makes her presence known. Not that she needs to be here for the meeting. She doesn't have stock in the company, but she does like to bring cookies and sit in judgment of everyone. It's what she lives for. "I guess I suspected someone who acts as nice as Jeremiah Dorsey would be upstanding." She blushes slightly as she turns Reid's way. "No offense meant, of course. And you turn out to be the loyal one. I wouldn't have expected that. I'm honestly shocked you're here. I would have thought you would have moved on once the job was over."

I barely manage to not roll my eyes. I want this meeting complete so Reid and I can figure out what we want to do.

We.

The word plays in my mind.

"My brother is very loyal, but he also doesn't care what small minds think of him," Reid shoots back, proving he knows how to deal with pettiness. "As to moving on, there's no moving on from Harper. I love her and we're going to be together, so you can have this relationship with me where you snipe and swipe and I call you on all your shit or you can start being polite. If things go the way I plan, I'm going to be in this office every day."

"What?" Paul sits up straight, a frown on his face. "We're not hiring your fuck boy, Harper. We don't even know if you'll have a job at the end of today. The way you've ignored this company needs to be addressed."

"Ignored?" Reid sits up, his jaw squaring. "She's been on a sabbatical and yet she's had to be in this office or on site every single day because of your mismanagement."

"I inherited a mess," Paul announces. "We're down from last year, and I'm dealing with all the stupid changes she decided to make. So, no, I can't promise she'll have a job at the end of today, but I can tell you if I'm the CEO, I won't be hiring you, Mr. Hollywood."

I put a hand on Reid's wrist, silently begging him not to engage with my cousin. He's not worth it.

I'm starting to wonder why I'm here at all.

"Well, of course, she'll have a job." My mother ignores Reid's testy ultimatum about their future relationship, but then she's good at ignoring things she doesn't want to deal with. "You can't fire her. She's invaluable to the company, and she owns a good piece of stock. If you decide to go a different way, perhaps she can take over something like human resources or accounting."

In other words more feminine departments, though I'm sure she would say girls aren't good at math, so maybe she'll put me in charge of janitorial. But only until I marry my somewhat surprisingly loyal boyfriend who will still probably leave me for someone prettier and more feminine than me. According to my mother that's pretty much all women.

"Will she? Or if she survives the vote and I can't save us, will she hand the company over to this celebrity person?" Paul asks, looking Reid up and down. He's sitting at the opposite end of the conference table, his sister, two cousins, two aunts, and an uncle between us. My uncle Jed is half asleep. He's eighty-two and once was really salty since his two younger brothers formed the company and didn't give him a job. He moaned and complained enough they let him buy in, hence the extra cousins. He doesn't care anymore and comes around because he likes to vote.

"I thought only relatives could be on the board," Claire says with a pout. "If we're bringing in anyone, then I want my boyfriend here."

"I don't understand why we're hiring this man when Harper told me she couldn't find a place for my Gavin," Aunt Helen says, pressing her glasses up her nose and giving me serious side eye. "I don't think positions should be given to anyone unless the family doesn't have someone to fill it."

"Gavin is a twenty-two-year-old college dropout whose only professional experience is harassing customers at a Wing Stop." This is well-worn ground, but it looks like I'm going to cover it again. A weird sense of fate comes over me. I'm always going to be here, sitting in this chair, fighting for my place, but I'm not as anxious as I should be because he's here beside me. He'll stay right here and take every blow they throw at us. "I'm bringing Reid in as a designer. He's got a degree from the Parsons Institute, and I think having him on board will bring us an entirely new class of clients. Has Gavin worked in the field for years?"

"Gavin doesn't end up in the tabloids," Susan says primly. Gavin is her brother, and I'm pretty sure she's helping pay his rent.

"Because no one cares about him." I'm not being mean. It's just the truth. Gavin is a massive tool.

Susan waves me off. "It doesn't matter. He can learn. You can teach him like you've taught the others. Face it, Harper. You're doing exactly what you always say the rest of us shouldn't do."

"That is hypocrisy," Aunt Flora says, pointing my way. "You wouldn't even let me borrow money for a new boat and yet here you are paying your little boy toy."

Now my back's up because while Reid is an excellent sex toy, I'm the only one who gets to talk about him that way. There's a wonderful brain in with all that hotness. Also, I'm not sure how Flora's husband's second fishing boat is important to the company.

"Excuse me, I'm all man." Reid sits back like none of this bothers him in the least. He also looks gloriously sexy in the early morning light. "Man toy, please. The things I do to her... No boy could handle her."

He's ridiculous, and I'm in love with him. I'm mad, crazy, head over heels in love with him.

I hate that he's having to see this side of my family. I hate that there is this side to my family.

I love that he's willing to be here. Willing to take this freaking abuse with me.

Huh. It is. I know Ivy and Ani tell me all of this is abusive behavior, but I grew up in here. Sometimes it's hard to see what's normal and what's toxic.

"Paul says there's more than enough money to go around," Aunt Helen insists.

"There is," Susan agrees. "I did the books this year and it's our best year ever. Definitely better than the last couple of years when Harper forced us to do that tax thing."

"So no one would go to jail." I don't even try hard anymore.

"We should have fought that," my cousin Cliff says, leaning forward. "We should have ousted her then, when she stopped caring about the family and our needs. I believe I mentioned that. No one listens to me. We could have fought that."

Sheryl smooths back her hair and sits in her chair. "Well, isn't this what we're here to discuss? How Harper is running the company and whether someone else would be better at it? I know poor Paul has been working his ass off to cover for her and she barely pays him anything."

"He's the second highest paid person in this firm." It's a halfhearted attempt, but the truth of the matter is I don't want to be here. I want to be with Reid having breakfast and talking about how cool it's going to be to meet the owner of Banover Place and show her and her daughters around. We think the mid-century modern home is hers. It's mature and understated. It's also my favorite. I went with Reid and Jeremiah when they bought the furnishings for it. Typically we would simply rent furniture and let the new owner bring their own after the filming is done. This owner was insistent that everything be ready to go. She sent a message that she wanted everything perfect for her girls.

So we tackled it like a team. Ani, Ivy, and I each picked a house and with the Dorsey brothers as advisors, we furnished these glorious dream homes. It gave me such satisfaction to step back and see these places we all worked on, these places where people will live and love and work. Where they'll raise kids and have friends over for dinner. Where they will truly live. There is so much of the original left, but with places for the new owners to make it their own.

It gives me this sense of peace. Like I did what I was born to do.

"I mean if we can all take sabbaticals to follow our foolish dreams, then I would like to be paid to try my hand at being a chef," another cousin volunteers. "Maybe the company can pay for culinary school."

"I don't understand why she needed the sabbatical at all," someone else says. "It's not like what she does is difficult."

I stare at Reid while everyone around me complains. I can see he's getting pissed, but he promised he wouldn't say anything. No matter how bad it got.

He's out of place here.

I think I might be out of place here. Lately, I've been wondering who gets to tell me what my place is.

"Now Harper does some nice things for the family," my mother is saying. "But I agree she can do more. I'll talk with her. I'm sure I can get Gavin a job."

She's wrong. "I'm not hiring Gavin. He's a little shit who'll bring a harassment suit down on our heads within his first three months of employment."

Flora gasps. "How could you say that about your own blood?"

"Because it's true. But I'm sure if you vote for Paul, he'll probably hire him today." That feels good to say.

"Now, wait a minute," Paul says, and for the first time he looks slightly confused. "I think we should talk about this. Harper, you do know this company well, but I think we should have some new rules in place. I think we should elevate my position to be the same as yours. A restructuring might help us function better."

Reid huffs. "That's your game, isn't it? You want to get everyone mad at Harper so you can move your position up, get all the benefits, but she's still here to run the company. Because you know damn well that you can't do the job. You know if you're left in charge and she's not around to fix things for you, you'll run this company into the ground."

Paul's eyes narrow. "I'm trying to be nice. I'm trying to forgive and forget."

But they never do either in this family.

What do I owe them? My whole life? My soul? Am I obligated to take their abuse for the simple fact that we share blood?

What do I owe the man I love? The friends who are more of a family to me than anyone in this room but Reid?

What do I owe myself?

All those questions roll through my head.

What would happen if I just...didn't?

Reid turns to my cousin Sheryl, the one with the exact right amount of stock I need to stay in my position. "Sheryl, Harper would like to offer to buy your stock."

Sheryl's eyes go wide. "What? I'm sure she would. What's she offering? Like a couple grand?"

"I don't think that's necessary," Paul replies. "Also, I don't know if it's legal given the company bylaws. Harper doesn't have money, and no one can sell their shares outside the family."

"Babe," I begin.

But he's pushing on with this plan he has to save me, to give me the thing I told him I need. "The shares will be in Harper's name. I'm giving her the money, but I won't have anything to do with the shares. When we marry eventually, we'll have a prenup stating clearly I don't get any stock in case we split."

"We're not splitting." Of all the things he's said, that's what I can't stop myself from responding to. "We don't need a prenup."

I say that because I know he won't protect any of his assets. He's selling his penthouse and plans on using the proceeds to buy us a new place and save this job I don't even know why I'm doing anymore.

No one wants me here. Not really. Or if they do, they only want me if they can control and use me.

Reid gives me a smile. "We'll do what it takes to satisfy your family."

"Now see, that sounds like a sensible plan." My mother nods Reid's way. "I always knew Harper would come around in the end and see sense. She needed to find the right man since she won't listen to her mother."

"I still don't like this stock plan." Paul stares at me. "I think you're trying to buy out family members so you can consolidate power."

"Or I could not," I say.

"I'd like to hear this offer." There's pure challenge in Sheryl's voice. "So I can laugh at you and refuse you because this is nothing but a silly way to try to keep your job."

"I agree." It hits me that I'm here when I could be anywhere else. Anywhere. I think Lydia's making pasta this afternoon, and Ivy and Heath are testing out the AI at her place. We could be there.

"One point five million," Reid says, his tone serious and unwavering.

Shock goes through the room.

"Million?" Sheryl lights up. "You're serious?"

"Now, Sheryl, we should talk about this," Paul begins.

"He's not serious." I know he is, but I can't go through with it. I turn to him and reach for his hands. "Babe, has Jeremiah hired a contractor for his new show yet?"

He's still for a moment. "You don't have to work with me. I'll come here."

"But if I want to? What if I want to do something for me? Not just us, though falling in love with you is why I'm here. What if I want to try something that fills my soul?"

"Uhm, I'd like to talk about the one point five million," Sheryl says. "I say yes. I will sell to you."

"Are you sure?" He ignores my cousin, and his hands squeeze mine. "Oh, baby, be sure because there is nothing in this world I would love more than a *Dorsey Family* show. We can fight and argue and collaborate and make my brother crazy and do so much good for people who need us. And when we make enough, I promise, I'm going to find another Banover Place and I'll let you do whatever you want with it. You can restore it to its Gilded Age glory, and I'll happily live there with you."

That sounds like paradise but with one compromise. I think that's what I learned about love. Or maybe compromise is the wrong word. When you love the person you're in a relationship with, you want to make them happy because they make you happy. And everyone wins. "How about we have some glorious details and places we can show off, and the rest of our house is infinitely warm and comfortable and beautiful. But, babe, I'm going to need a place for the sippy cups."

He stands, and the smile on his face is like sunshine. "I'll design the most functional pantry in the history of time. Shall we?"

I stand with him. Like I always will.

"What is happening?" Paul asks, his face a florid red.

"Yes, Harper. What are you doing?" My mother is a nice shade of pink, too. "Sheryl said yes. Now you'll have what you need to keep your position. I'm sure we can find something for Reid to do."

This actually feels good. Like I'm taking off a way too heavy for me coat and moving freely for the first time in my life. "No, Mom. I'm not letting Reid spend money on this company when we have our own to build. Paul, it's all yours. Good luck. Mom, I'll have Lawyer draw up the transfer of my stock to you. It's where Dad should have left it."

"No. That's not what he wanted at all," my mother sputters.

"You can't leave." Paul is on his feet and looks like he realizes he entered the find-out stage of his life. "You're the CEO."

"Not anymore," I reply. "I quit, and I divest myself of all stock in the company. My mother informed me that my father never wanted me to be the CEO. He intended to train my husband to one day take over." I tilt my head to look Reid in his gorgeous eyes. "You want to take over, babe?"

"Absolutely not. You chose poorly, but I'm holding you to it," Reid replies with a grin.

I turn back to the family I probably will be going low contact with. "See, I chose poorly. Like my mom always says I do. She can have the stock and Paul can have the joy of heading the company, so please direct all of your complaints and requests to him. Also, I'll be taking some of our employees with me. The people who worked on Banover Place will be getting offers."

"We're going to need a crew," Reid agrees. "And I think we already have a head of production, even if he is on the grumpy side. What's up with that?"

Patrick is way less grumpy these days. Jeremiah has the man actually smiling from time to time.

"Harper, this is unacceptable." My mother stands, her whole face rigid with outrage.

I take a long breath because this speech I'm about to give is a long time coming. I never thought I would give it in public but here we are. "Mom, I love you. In many ways you were a good mom, but you don't like me very much and I'm unwilling to sacrifice my whole life so you approve of me. I am going to marry Reid and we're going to start a new career, one I'm so excited about. If we choose to, and I think we will, we'll have a couple of kids and we'll likely raise them here in the city. I'd like for you to be in their lives if you can be good to them."

"And their mother," Reid adds. "If you're not good and kind to their mother, their father will have something to say about it."

"If you choose not to, know that they'll have wonderful, weird and wild women to take your place. They'll have my sisters, and they'll have Lydia and Diane and CeCe to spoil and love them. So even if you can't ever forgive me for not being what you thought I should be, know my kids will be loved. I will be loved." Tears pulse behind my eyes. She's been terrible but she's still my mom. She still held me as a baby and rocked me and went with me to buy my graduation dress and showed up at all my recitals.

"You cannot walk out that door, Harper," my mother insists.

"She won't have to." Reid leans over and scoops me up and starts for the door as everyone is freaking out behind us.

"What are we going to do?" someone asks. Probably one of the aunts.

I don't answer because it's not my problem anymore.

I choose me. I choose us.

I let Reid walk me out of that building and into our future.

Chapter Twenty-Four

I stare up at Banover Place and wish so much we had more time with her.

"It feels like the end of an era," Ivy says, threading her arm with mine.

"And the start of something new." Anika does the same on my other side.

Behind us there are cameras and cranes and everything the crew needs for sweeping exterior shots. They've set up the interior shots as well, and we're simply waiting for the owner to arrive with her daughters. We've been told they know nothing about the gift their mother is about to give them.

I'm excited, but there's a bittersweetness to the day because in some way we started here as young girls, these sisters of mine. This was the place where we first spoke our dreams out loud and vowed to help each other achieve them. Those dreams changed over the years, but what never wavered is our love for each other.

That is what makes a family.

"I know," Ivy says, "but maybe we can sneak in one last time before they move in. I'll make the PB&Js and Harper can bring the juice boxes and Ani can bring some of her mom's chocolate chip cookies and we can sit in that room and talk about boys and the jobs we're going to have."

I chuckle at the thought because we really are at a crossroads. "We're all starting something new."

"We can talk about weddings," Ani corrected, "Because I intend to be invited to two of them soon. Ivy is set for this summer. Do you have a date?"

"Well, Reid technically hasn't asked, but that's because we agreed on giving it six months. We're hoping by then the press around him will have died down." I don't mention the press around me since it's already beautifully dead. Britta's been doing a mea culpa tour blaming everything on bad advice and a medication she's taking that apparently caused her to blackmail two brothers for years. I try not to pay attention, but I do know her agency dropped her.

I also stay completely out of Ross Construction since I divested my stock. Lawyer drew up the paperwork to legally give it all to my mother. She tried to refuse and sent message after message about how I was abandoning her and the whole family. Apparently Paul is already fumbling.

I took that up with my new therapist. Dr. Logan Warner is a funny man. He's one of those people you can tell has been through some stuff but managed to come out of it all with light and hope and love. I'm going to do the same. Starting with setting boundaries.

I got a new number because I'm not ready to deal with my mother yet. I will be one day, but I need space and time to heal. So we're engaged to be engaged. Hopefully by then we'll have a new place to live and steady jobs.

I also don't want to take away from Heath and Ivy's wedding. We're going to be in production meetings for the next couple of months, but Anika and Luca want to talk about producing our show. We're weighing our options, but I know which way we'll probably go. "I'm thinking winter. I like a winter theme."

"That sounds perfect," Ivy says and then her sweet smile turns a little ruthless. Her businesswoman smile. "Now let's talk about getting testimonials from both of you. We're launching Emma soon, and I want to show off how perfect she is. She's three for three in weddings in our family. Also, I ran my mom's questionnaire through and guess who she matched with? Thomas. I think my mom is going to end up marrying CeCe's driver. I'm going to have a British stepdad. I'm also pretty sure he once was a wheelman for the mob."

Wouldn't that be perfect?

"You should expect my mom to want to oversee all the catering," Anika says. "She was super upset that the palace wouldn't let her serve mini corn dogs at our reception."

Ivy practically vibrates. "Can she cater my whole wedding? I was thinking...now hear me out..."

"Food trucks," Ani and I say at the same time.

"Yes," Ivy agrees, and I swear she glows a little.

"Well, I'll take Lydia then," I offer because I don't want to leave a mom out. CeCe doesn't cook, and Diane would order pizza. But Lydia will prepare a feast for the ages. "I want it to be us. Just my little family."

"Your family is about to grow," Anika points out. "You know a crew feels like a family. We've gotten close to this one and we only worked together for a few months. What happens when you work with the same people for years at a time?"

I'll get new friends and people to care about, but this group will always be my core.

"Our guest is three minutes out," Patrick informs us. He's got his clipboard in hand and competently gets everyone where they're supposed to be.

Except us, of course. Reid and Jeremiah are both in stylish suits, ready to show the new owners their gorgeous spaces. They'll be the ones walking them through, explaining all of the finishing touches. I don't have to film today but I wanted to be here to watch. "Where's a good place for us to sit while you get your exteriors?"

Anika promised us we can watch the reactions through the many laptops set up to handle the more technical aspects of the production. I'm nervous. I hope they like it. I hope whoever walks in here will love this place as much as we do. I hope this is the start of a beautiful time for everyone who lives in this space I and my friends and loved ones put so much of ourselves in.

This. This is why I left. This feeling of love and hope for people I've never met is the reward of this job.

I thought I might regret walking away, but I know I won't. Not ever. This is what I was born to do.

"You're fine where you are. Though you really should have put on some blush, Ross," Patrick announces and suddenly Reid and Jeremiah are here.

And so is Heath. Luca appears next to Ani.

"Hey, guys," I say, happy but confused. "Aren't we going to crowd the shot?"

"Yeah." Ivy is obviously with me on this one. She looks around. "If we're all here, where are the new owners going to be? Harper's right. We're going to ruin the shot."

I see a limo approaching, and the camera on the crane swoops in, getting the angle they need.

Ivy's hand comes out, gripping my wrist. "Oh, you're wrong, Patrick. I know that car. That's CeCe's car. I'll tell her she can't be here right now. Or maybe I'll see if she'll take me to lunch. I'm sorry for the confusion. She's been weird lately. If I wasn't certain this could never happen to CeCe Foust, I would say she's having a midlife crisis."

"She's not going to lunch with you." Heath has the biggest grin on his face. "She's got some work to do. And you're not going to screw up the shot."

Anika looks at me, and there are tears in her eyes. "We are the shot, guys. I'm going to need you to look surprised about all the stuff we're about to see."

Reid is beside me, so I turn to him. Like I do all the time now. "What is happening? Do you know what's happening?"

He nods and looks very emotional. "I do, but you should know I only found out toward the end. Why do you think we suddenly wanted a woman's opinion on the furniture? We had Ivy pick furniture for one of the homes. I had to put a futon in my gorgeously designed house. Why on earth would we do that? Because this place...this stunning home is ours. All of ours."

I'm still in shock when the limo stops and Thomas hops out, looking smart in his suit. He gives us a grin and then opens the door and the fabulous CeCe Foust emerges in all her glory. She's gone all out, wearing a classic suit and a gorgeous Chanel jacket, a pair of Louboutins on her feet giving her height she does not need. She sweeps from the limo and shakes out her long, rose-gold hair. I have no idea how she gets the color, but it's always perfect.

This woman will always be perfect.

"What did you do?" Ivy asks.

CeCe smiles, and for a moment I forget the cameras are on us. CeCe takes off her sunglasses and reaches out for Ivy's hand. "My dearest love, I did what any good mother does. What I could. George and I were not blessed with children, though we did try. After he died, I put all of my attention into the business, and that rather changed one day over a decade ago when I went to a school to talk to high school girls about getting a STEM education and I found the three of you. Ivy, of course, was the one I was closest to for years, but when she returned from San Francisco, I truly got to know Harper and Anika as well. Because of you I've found a group of friends I never had before. Diane and I bicker from time to time and Lydia makes peace, but we take care of each other. And I realized this was what it means to have sisters. Harper…you said something to me a few months back. You called me one of the moms. I know you joke about it, but I realized how very much I wish I had daughters like you. And then I realized I don't have to give birth to love you like daughters. I can simply decide to and make it reality. So, daughters of mine, would you like to see your gifts? You never have to worry about having a home. I've set up a trust that will pay the property taxes. The real gift is to myself. To keep you close to me and Lydia and Diane. To keep my family together as it grows."

Tears stream down my face. This is everything I ever wanted. Us together. The people I love safe and happy and secure. "CeCe, I…"

"Darling, we're on camera. Do you not have waterproof mascara?" CeCe leans in and pats my shoulder. "We'll get a makeup artist for you."

There she is. And I wouldn't have her any other way.

"Come along, my loves," she bids us. "Diane and Lydia are inside with Lady Buttercup. Let's do this thing and then we have reservations at Cipriani. We'll celebrate. And I swear if they try to put us in the back, I shall force them to move the table. Nothing but the best for my girls."

I stand there for a moment, completely floored that this is my life.

Reid smiles down at me and leans forward to kiss my forehead. "I would do it all over again. All of it just for this moment. I love you, Harper. The guys and I are going inside. You come in with your sisters when you're ready."

"She better be ready in two minutes because I have a shot lined up," Patrick says as he walks by.

"Don't listen to him." Reid winks and steps back. "You take your time."

The guys walk into the entrance to the house that will be…mine. Ours. I'm wrapping my head around the fact that we get to live here. Together.

I feel Ivy's hand in mine and I take Anika's, all of us looking up at the place where we started. "I can't believe it."

"I can't believe Ani's known for so long and didn't tell," Ivy complains. "The crown did something to her brain."

"It was hard. Especially when Harper was so freaked out about splitting the place," Anika admits.

"Well, I probably wouldn't have been upset if I knew it was for me." I can be honest with myself.

"Guys, you won't believe the futon I put in the game room." Ivy squeezes my hand and starts to lead us toward the stairs. "I was so jealous I told Heath we have to get one. I've got the coolest game room. We're going to have so much fun."

"Then we should get started," Ani says with a smile as she walks through the door.

"Yes, because I'm ready for lunch." Ivy follows her

I stare at the door for a moment, thinking about what is waiting for me in this house I renovated. It's filled with history, but more importantly, with people I love. Warmth and affection wait behind those doors. All the love in the world waits for me.

The next part of the history of Banover Place will be written by us.

"Hey, you coming?" Ani asks.

"She's having a moment." Ivy smiles my way.

I'm having the best moment, and it's time to share it.

I walk up the steps and join my family.

Discover the Park Avenue Promise Series

Three young women make a pact in high school—
to always be friends and to one day make it big in Manhattan.

Start Us Up

She's a high-tech boss who lost it all...

Ivy Jensen was the darling of the tech world, right up until her company fell apart completely after she trusted the wrong person. Her reputation in tatters, she finds herself back in the tiny apartment she grew up in, living with her mom. When a group of angel investors offer her a meeting, she knows she has to come up with the new big idea or her career is over.

He's an up and coming coder...

Heath Marino has always been fascinated with writing code. He's worked on a dozen games and apps and is considered one of the industry's more eccentric talents. But now he's back in New York to spend time with his grandmother. She was known as one of the city's greatest matchmakers, and he wants to know why. Surely there's some kind of code in his grandmother's methods, and he's going to find them.

When Ivy meets Heath it's instant attraction, but she's got a career to get back to and he just might be her on-ramp. It could be a perfect partnership or absolute heartbreak.

* * * *

My Royal Showmance

Anika Fox knows exactly where she wants to be, and it's not on the set of a reality TV dating show. She's working her way up at the production company she works for and she's close to achieving some of her dreams. The big boss just wants one thing from her. She's got a potential problem with the director of The King Takes a Bride and she wants Anika to pose as a production assistant and report back.

As the king of a tiny European country, Luca St. Marten knows the world views him as one of the pampered royalty of the world. It couldn't be further from the truth. His country is hurting and he's right there on the front lines with his citizens. When he's asked to do a dating show, his counselors point out that it could bring tourism back to Ralavia. It goes against his every desire, but he agrees.

When one of the contestants drops out at the last minute, Anika finds herself replacing the potential princess. She's sure she'll be asked to leave the first night, but Luca keeps picking her again and again. Suddenly she finds herself in the middle of a made-for-TV fantasy, and she's unsure what's real and what's simply reality TV.

Book Club Questions

1. Harper works in construction, a very male dominated field. What are a few ways she tries to deal with the realities of being the boss in a field where women are mostly in administrative positions? How has being in this position affected her and how she deals with Ross in the beginning?

2. The idea of family and family obligations hangs heavily over Built to Last. How do the characters deal with this? Specifically Harper and her family—including the business and Ross's dealings with his brother, Jeremiah. Do you think they choose to do the right thing by their families? At what point do the characters have to start thinking about themselves?

3. Harper's relationship with her mother is strained to say the least. How does this affect her view of herself in the beginning of the book? How do the events of the story change her perspective and why do you think they lead her to make the choice she makes at the end of the book?

4. Harper and Ross start the book as enemies. They're on opposite ends of what they want for Banover Place. Why do you think they end up compromising and how does it affect not only the project but their relationship in and out of the workplace?

5. There's a big discussion in Built to Last about renovation versus restoration when it comes to historical buildings. Harper takes the change nothing stance while Ross believes a home should reflect the times no matter the structure. What are your feelings on historic homes? Does the renovation versus reconstruction apply to Ross and Harper as characters as well? Do they also make a choice as to one or the other by the end of the book?

6. Park Avenue Promises is a series about found family. How do you feel about the idea of the family we make versus the one we are born in? Are the obligations the same? Is the bond stronger or weaker with blood relations? Or is it always, always about the choices we make?

Discover More Lexi Blake

The Bodyguard and the Bombshell: A Masters and Mercenaries: New Recruits Novella

The Bodyguard...

Nate Carter left Australia's elite SASR unit after a tragic accident. Shattered by the experience, he thought taking a job in the States might be a good way to start over. His father's former employer, McKay-Taggart, has a position for him in the bodyguard unit. He never imagined himself risking his life for celebrities and the wealthy, but it will do for now. It will also give him a chance to reconnect with old friends, including the girl who'd been like a little sis to him ten years before.

These days, however, his feelings for Daisy O'Donnell are anything but brotherly.

The Bombshell...

Daisy O'Donnell is a girl on a mission, and it does not include falling for one of her brother's best friends. She has plans, and while chaos always seems to follow her, she's determined to see this through. Daisy finds herself in need of a bodyguard when a job goes terribly wrong. She's sure her dad will find someone suitable, but she didn't expect a big, gloriously masculine Aussie to show up ready to take a bullet for her. Maybe spending some time with Nate Carter won't be so bad after all.

An explosive match...

Thrown together by danger, Nate and Daisy can't resist the insane chemistry between them. But when his past and her present collide, they must decide if they can hold it together or go their separate ways forever.

* * * *

Tempted: A Masters and Mercenaries Novella

When West Rycroft left his family's ranch to work in the big city, he never dreamed he would find himself surrounded by celebrities and politicians. Working at McKay-Taggart as a bodyguard and security expert quickly taught him how to navigate the sometimes shark-infested waters of the elite. While some would come to love that world, West has seen enough to know it's not for him, preferring to keep his distance from his clients—until the day he meets Ally Pearson.

Growing up in the entertainment world, Ally was always in the shadow of others, but now she has broken out from behind the scenes for her own day in the spotlight. The paparazzi isn't fun, but she knows all too well that it's part of the gig. She has a good life and lots of fans, but someone has been getting too close for comfort and making threats. To be safe, she hires her own personal knight in shining armor, a cowboy hottie by the name of West. They clash in the beginning, but the minute they fall into bed together something magical happens.

Just as everything seems too good to be true, they are both reminded that there was a reason Ally needed a bodyguard. Her problems have found her again, and this time West will have to put his life on the line or lose everything they've found.

* * * *

Delighted: A Masters and Mercenaries Novella

Brian "Boomer" Ward believes in sheltering strays. After all, the men and women of McKay-Taggart made him family when he had none. So when the kid next door needs help one night, he thinks nothing of protecting her until her mom gets home. But when he meets Daphne Carlton, the thoughts hit him hard. She's stunning and hardworking and obviously in need of someone to put her first. It doesn't hurt that she's as sweet as the cupcakes she bakes.

Daphne Carlton's life revolves around two things—her kid and her business. Daphne's Delights is her dream—to take the recipes of her childhood and share them with the world. Her daughter, Lula, is the best kid she could have hoped for. Lula's got a genius-level intelligence and a heart of gold. But she also has two grandparents who control her access to private school and the fortune her father left behind. They're impossible to please, and Daphne worries that one wrong move on her part could cost her daughter the life she deserves.

As Daphne and Boomer find themselves getting closer, outside forces put pressure on the new couple. But if they make it through the storm, love will just be the icing on the cake because family is the real prize.

* * * *

Treasured: A Masters and Mercenaries Novella

David Hawthorne has a great life. His job as a professor at a prestigious Dallas college is everything he hoped for. Now that his brother is back from the Navy, life seems to be settling down. All he needs to do is finish the book he's working on and his tenure will be assured. When he gets invited to interview a reclusive expert, he knows he's gotten lucky. But being the stepson of Sean Taggart comes with its drawbacks, including an overprotective mom who sends a security detail to keep him safe. He doesn't need a bodyguard, but when Tessa Santiago shows up on his doorstep, the idea of her giving him close cover doesn't seem so bad.

Tessa has always excelled at most anything she tried, except romance. The whole relationship thing just didn't work out for her. She's not looking for love, and she's certainly not looking for it with an academic who happens to be connected to her boss's family. The last thing she wants is to escort an overly pampered pretentious man-child around South America to ensure he doesn't get into trouble. Still, there's something about David that calls to her. In addition to watching his back, she will have to avoid falling into the trap of soulful eyes and a deep voice that gets her heart racing.

But when the seemingly simple mission turns into a treacherous race for a hidden artifact, David and Tess know this assignment could cost them far more than their jobs. If they can overcome the odds, the lost treasure might not be their most valuable reward.

* * * *

Charmed: A Masters and Mercenaries Novella

JT Malone is lucky, and he knows it. He is the heir to a billion-dollar petroleum empire, and he has a loving family. Between his good looks and his charm, he can have almost any woman he wants. The world is his oyster, and he really likes oysters. So why does it all feel so empty?

Nina Blunt is pretty sure she's cursed. She worked her way up through the ranks at Interpol, fighting for every step with hard work and discipline. Then she lost it all because she loved the wrong person. Rebuilding her career with McKay-Taggart, she can't help but feel lonely. It seems everyone around her is finding love and starting families. But she knows that isn't for her. She has vowed never to make the mistake of falling in love again.

JT comes to McKay-Taggart for assistance rooting out a corporate spy, and Nina signs on to the job. Their working relationship becomes tricky, however, as their personal chemistry flares like a wildfire. Completing the assignment without giving in to the attraction that threatens to overwhelm them seems like it might be the most difficult part of the job. When danger strikes, will they be able to count on each other when the bullets are flying? If not, JT's charmed life might just come to an end.

* * * *

Enchanted: A Masters and Mercenaries Novella

A snarky submissive princess
Sarah Steven's life is pretty sweet. By day, she's a dedicated trauma nurse and by night, a fun-loving club sub. She adores her job, has a group of friends who have her back, and is a member of the hottest club in Dallas. So why does it all feel hollow? Could it be because she fell for her dream man and can't forgive him for walking away from her? Nope. She's not going there again. No matter how much she wants to.

A prince of the silver screen
Jared Johns might be one of the most popular actors in Hollywood, but he lost more than a fan when he walked away from Sarah. He lost the only woman he's ever loved. He's been trying to get her back, but

she won't return his calls. A trip to Dallas to visit his brother might be exactly what he needs to jump-start his quest to claim the woman who holds his heart.

A masquerade to remember
For Charlotte Taggart's birthday, Sanctum becomes a fantasyland of kinky fun and games. Every unattached sub gets a new Dom for the festivities. The twist? The Doms must conceal their identities until the stroke of midnight at the end of the party. It's exactly what Sarah needs to forget the fact that Jared is pursuing her. She can't give in to him, and the mysterious Master D is making her rethink her position when it comes to signing a contract. Jared knows he was born to play this role, dashing suitor by day and dirty Dom at night.

When the masks come off, will she be able to forgive the man who loves her, or will she leave him forever?

* * * *

Protected: A Masters and Mercenaries Novella

A second chance at first love
Years before, Wade Rycroft fell in love with Geneva Harris, the smartest girl in his class. The rodeo star and the shy academic made for an odd pair but their chemistry was undeniable. They made plans to get married after high school but when Genny left him standing in the rain, he joined the Army and vowed to leave that life behind. Genny married the town's golden boy, and Wade knew that he couldn't go home again.

Could become the promise of a lifetime
Fifteen years later, Wade returns to his Texas hometown for his brother's wedding and walks into a storm of scandal. Genny's marriage has dissolved and the town has turned against her. But when someone tries to kill his old love, Wade can't refuse to help her. In his years after the Army, he's found his place in the world. His job at McKay-Taggart keeps him happy and busy but something is missing. When he takes the job watching over Genny, he realizes what it is.

As danger presses in, Wade must decide if he can forgive past sins or let the woman of his dreams walk into a nightmare...

Close Cover: A Masters and Mercenaries Novel

Remy Guidry doesn't do relationships. He tried the marriage thing once, back in Louisiana, and learned the hard way that all he really needs in life is a cold beer, some good friends, and the occasional hookup. His job as a bodyguard with McKay-Taggart gives him purpose and lovely perks, like access to Sanctum. The last thing he needs in his life is a woman with stars in her eyes and babies in her future.

Lisa Daley's life is going in the right direction. She has graduated from college after years of putting herself through school. She's got a new job at an accounting firm and she's finished her Sanctum training. Finally on her own and having fun, her life seems pretty perfect. Except she's lonely and the one man she wants won't give her a second look.

There is one other little glitch. Apparently, her new firm is really a front for the mob and now they want her dead. Assassins can really ruin a fun girls' night out. Suddenly strapped to the very same six-foot-five-inch hunk of a bodyguard who makes her heart pound, Lisa can't decide if this situation is a blessing or a curse.

As the mob closes in, Remy takes his tempting new charge back to the safest place he knows—his home in the bayou. Surrounded by his past, he can't help wondering if Lisa is his future. To answer that question, he just has to keep her alive.

* * * *

Arranged: A Masters and Mercenaries Novella

Kash Kamdar is the king of a peaceful but powerful island nation. As Loa Mali's sovereign, he is always in control, the final authority. Until his mother uses an ancient law to force her son into marriage. His prospective queen is a buttoned-up intellectual, nothing like Kash's usual party girl. Still, from the moment of their forced engagement, he can't stop thinking about her.

Dayita Samar comes from one of Loa Mali's most respected families. The Oxford-educated scientist has dedicated her life to her country's future. But under her staid and calm exterior, Day hides a few sexy secrets of her own. She is willing to marry her king, but also agrees that they can circumvent the law. Just because they're married doesn't mean they have to change their lives. It certainly doesn't mean they have to fall in love.

After one wild weekend in Dallas, Kash discovers his bride-to-be is more than she seems. Engulfed in a changing world, Kash finds exciting new possibilities for himself. Could Day help him find respite from the crushing responsibility he's carried all his life? This fairy tale could have a happy ending, if only they can escape Kash's past...

* * * *

Devoted: A Masters and Mercenaries Novella

A woman's work

Amy Slaten has devoted her life to Slaten Industries. After ousting her corrupt father and taking over the CEO role, she thought she could relax and enjoy taking her company to the next level. But an old business rivalry rears its ugly head. The only thing that can possibly take her mind off business is the training class at Sanctum...and her training partner, the gorgeous and funny Flynn Adler. If she can just manage to best her mysterious business rival, life might be perfect.

A man's commitment

Flynn Adler never thought he would fall for the enemy. Business is war, or so his father always claimed. He was raised to be ruthless when it came to the family company, and now he's raising his brother to one day work with him. The first order of business? The hostile takeover of Slaten Industries. It's a stressful job so when his brother offers him a spot in Sanctum's training program, Flynn jumps at the chance.

A lifetime of devotion....

When Flynn realizes the woman he's falling for is none other than the CEO of the firm he needs to take down, he has to make a choice. Does he take care of the woman he's falling in love with or the business he's worked a lifetime to build? And when Amy finally understands the man she's come to trust is none other than the enemy, will she walk away from him or fight for the love she's come to depend on?

* * * *

Adored: A Masters and Mercenaries Novella

A man who gave up on love

Mitch Bradford is an intimidating man. In his professional life, he has a reputation for demolishing his opponents in the courtroom. At the exclusive BDSM club Sanctum, he prefers disciplining pretty submissives with no strings attached. In his line of work, there's no time for a healthy relationship. After a few failed attempts, he knows he's not good for any woman—especially not his best friend's sister.

A woman who always gets what she wants

Laurel Daley knows what she wants, and her sights are set on Mitch. He's smart and sexy, and it doesn't matter that he's a few years older and has a couple of bitter ex-wives. Watching him in action at work and at play, she knows he just needs a little polish to make some woman the perfect lover. She intends to be that woman, but first she has to show him how good it could be.

A killer lurking in the shadows

When an unexpected turn of events throws the two together, Mitch and Laurel are confronted with the perfect opportunity to explore their mutual desire. Night after night of being close breaks down Mitch's defenses. The more he sees of Laurel, the more he knows he wants her. Unfortunately, someone else has their eyes on Laurel and they have murder in mind.

* * * *

Dungeon Games: A Masters and Mercenaries Novella

Obsessed

Derek Brighton has become one of Dallas's finest detectives through a combination of discipline and obsession. Once he has a target in his sights, nothing can stop him. When he isn't solving homicides, he applies the same intensity to his playtime at Sanctum, a secretive BDSM club. Unfortunately, no amount of beautiful submissives can fill the hole that one woman left in his heart.

Unhinged

Karina Mills has a reputation for being reckless, and her clients appreciate her results. As a private investigator, she pursues her cases with nothing holding her back. In her personal life, Karina yearns for something different. Playing at Sanctum has been a safe way to find peace, but the one Dom who could truly master her heart is out of reach.

Enflamed

On the hunt for a killer, Derek enters a shadowy underworld only to find the woman he aches for is working the same case. Karina is searching for a missing girl and won't stop until she finds her. To get close to their prime suspect, they need to pose as a couple. But as their operation goes under the covers, unlikely partners become passionate lovers while the killer prepares to strike.

Love the Way You Spy
Masters and Mercenaries: New Recruits, Book 1
By Lexi Blake

Tasha Taggart isn't a spy. That's her sisters' job. Tasha's support role is all about keeping them alive, playing referee when they fight amongst themselves, and soothing the toughest boss in the world. Working for the CIA isn't as glamorous as she imagined, and she's more than a little lonely. So when she meets a charming man in a bar the night before they start their latest op, she decides to give in to temptation. The night was perfect until she discovers she's just slept with the target of their new investigation. Her sisters will never let her hear the end of this. Even worse, she has to explain the situation to her overprotective father, who also happens to be their boss.

Dare Nash knew exactly how his week in Sydney was going to go—attending boring conferences to represent his family's business interests and eating hotel food alone. Until he falls under the spell of a stunning and mysterious American woman. Something in Tasha's eyes raises his body temperature every time she looks at him. She's captivating, and he's committed to spending every minute he can with her on this trip, even if her two friends seem awfully intense. He doesn't trust easily, but it's not long before he can imagine spending the rest of his life with her.

When Dare discovers Tash isn't who she seems, the dream turns into a nightmare. She isn't the only one who deceived him, and now he's in the crosshairs of adversaries way out of his league. He can't trust her, but it might take Tasha and her family to save his life and uncover the truth.

* * * *

"Okay, I am trying to fully grasp what happened here." Cooper sat back. "Someone piece this together for me because I do not understand."

Kala's lips curled up. "Tasha and the new target." She used her thumb and forefinger to make a circle which she pushed the forefinger of her other hand through back and forth while making squeaking sounds.

Such a bitch. "I didn't know he was the target."

"Hey, he wasn't the target then," Tristan pointed out.

Zach was staring at his cell, likely reading through the reports Drake had sent. Of all the people in the room, he looked the most grim.

"Tash couldn't have possibly known," Lou argued.

"Tasha slept with Darren Nash." Cooper seemed to need a moment to wrap his head around that reality. "When? I wasn't aware you were seeing anyone. When did you have the time to meet this guy? Did you know him back in the States? I thought he was Canadian."

Captain America was in the house, and she wasn't going to let him make her feel slutty. He didn't mean it. Coop had been raised like the rest of them to be open about all their needs, but he could also be overly protective. He reminded her so much of his father, Alex McKay. Uncle Alex, though there wasn't a drop of blood between them. Kenzie had stopped calling him anything but Mr. McKay by the time they were ten and she'd realized the ramifications of the relationship. Like Tash herself, Cooper had been adopted and didn't look anything like his father or mother, but the gestures were so familiar they didn't need things like hair color or eye color to make it clear they were related.

Tasha enjoyed being told how like her mother she was. Her mom was the best. Her mom would know how to handle this situation.

"I didn't know him before. It was a one-night stand," Tasha explained. "Like you've had one-night stands. And the twins have had one-night stands."

"Mine ended in me stabbing someone," Kala admitted. "I didn't know he was a Russian operative. I just thought he was hot. I didn't actually get to sex, so it was more like a one-night violence. Kenzie is a true-love girl. Zach has had his share, but he's discreet. Coop is the manwhore here."

A light pink stained Coop's cheeks. "I thought we weren't going to use hurtful words anymore."

"Well, I've never had a one-night stand." Tristan acted like he was adjusting his halo. "As the purest person here, I'm proud of Tash for getting some."

"I didn't say she shouldn't have a good sex life, but it might have been nice if it hadn't been with the freaking target," Coop shot back.

"Hey, it's not Tash's fault, and this conversation is doing none of us any favors," Zach proclaimed.

Kala's expression had lost its humor, and Kenzie had gone quiet.

"Well, I think I'm probably purer than Tris since I've never had a three way." Lou filled in the awkward silence. "And I'm proud of Tash, too. He seemed like a great guy. I spent a lot of time talking to him. What are these rumors?"

Tasha wasn't sure she wanted to know the answer to that question, but here she was. "Cooper, can you give us a report on what you know about the target?"

She'd called Dare the target. It made her stomach roll.

But the op was important. It wasn't terribly dangerous. Not compared to some of the stuff they'd been through, but there was a reason this op had been selected as their first solo mission. It was supposed to be fairly easy, with Kenzie and Kala tag teaming a man profiled for his harmlessness. They were to listen and evaluate relationships. If they had a chance to gather more intel in a safe fashion, they had the go ahead. Easy peasy. In and out.

If this op went well, they would be allowed more freedom.

She might have screwed that all up.

About Lexi Blake

New York Times bestselling author Lexi Blake lives in North Texas with her husband and three kids. Since starting her publishing journey in 2010, she's sold over three million copies of her books. She began writing at a young age, concentrating on plays and journalism. It wasn't until she started writing romance that she found success. She likes to find humor in the strangest places and believes in happy endings.

Connect with Lexi online:

Facebook: Lexi Blake
Website: www.LexiBlake.net
Instagram: AuthorLexiBlake

On Behalf of Blue Box Press,

Liz Berry and Jillian Stein would like to thank ~

Steve Berry
Benjamin Stein
Kim Guidroz
Chelle Olson
Tanaka Kangara
Stacey Tardif
Chris Graham
Jessica Saunders
Ann-Marie Nieves
Grace Wenk
Dylan Stockton
Kate Boggs
Richard Blake
and Simon Lipskar

www.ingramcontent.com/pod-product-compliance
Lightning Source LLC
LaVergne TN
LVHW032226280325
806890LV00001B/1